To Hazard Our Own Security

Maine's Role in the American Revolution

Michael Cecere

HERITAGE BOOKS
2010

HERITAGE BOOKS
AN IMPRINT OF HERITAGE BOOKS, INC.

Books, CDs, and more—Worldwide
For our listing of thousands of titles see our website at
www.HeritageBooks.com

Published 2010 by
HERITAGE BOOKS, INC.
Publishing Division
100 Railroad Ave. #104
Westminster, Maryland 21157

Copyright © 2010 Michael Cecere

Other books by the author:

Captain Thomas Posey and the 7th Virginia Regiment

An Officer of Very Extraordinary Merit: Charles Porterfield and the American War for Independence, 1775-1780

Great Things Are Expected from the Virginians: Virginia in the American Revolution

In This Time of Extreme Danger: Northern Virginia in the American Revolution

They Are Indeed a Very Useful Corps: American Riflemen in the Revolutionary War

They Behaved Like Soldiers: Captain John Chilton and the Third Virginia Regiment, 1775-1778

All rights reserved. No part of this book may be reproduced or transmitted in any form or by any means, electronic or mechanical, including photocopying, recording or by any information storage and retrieval system without written permission from the author, except for the inclusion of brief quotations in a review.

International Standard Book Numbers
Paperbound: 978-0-7884-5174-4
Clothbound: 978-0-7884-8366-0

Contents

Ch. 1   "The People...have become more attentive to their Liberties" : 1763-1773..............1

Ch. 2   "What can these things indicate but a civil war?" : 1774-75.....................21

Ch. 3   "A most obstinate engagement ensued": 1775........................37

Ch. 4   "Never perhaps was their a more forlorn set of human beings" : 1775 77

Ch. 5   "The only Alternative is Independence or Slavery" : 1776 99

Ch. 6   "The present is emphatically the crisis which will decide our destiny" : 1776....121

Ch. 7   "Everything shall be done... to frustrate the Enemy's Designs": 1777................161

Ch. 8   "Both armies seemed to be determined on death or victory" : 1777..................189

Ch. 9 "Never did men behave with so much Courage" : 1778-79..........................…..…219

Ch. 10 "Our publick affairs never looked in so Dubious and precarious a situation" : 1780-81……………………...281

Bibliography……………………………………………..313

Index…………………………………..……………………337

Maps

Map of Massachusetts..2

Battle of Lexington and Concord......................38

Map of Machias...48

Battle of Bunker Hill..55

Map of Falmouth...70

Arnold's March to Quebec.................................78

Map of Canada...105

Battle of Long Island..125

Battle of Long Island..131

New York Campaign.......................................136

Defense of Lake Champlain............................141

Washington's Position Along the
Delaware River..143

Battle of Trenton...150

March to Princeton..157

Fort Ticonderoga and Mount Independence......168

Battle of Hubbardton.......................................173

New York Campaign of 1777..........................178

Fort Stanwix and Oriskany..........................182

Battle of Bennington..........................186

Battle of Freeman Farm..........................191

Battle of Bemis Heights..........................206

Fall of Breymann's Redoubt..........................210

Machias 1777..........................216

Valley Forge..........................222

Battle of Monmouth..........................231

Battle of Rhode Island..........................240

New York Frontier..........................248

Penobscot Bay..........................258

Bagaduce..........................262

Destruction of Penobscot Fleet..........................268

Attack on Stony Point..........................271

Virginia Campaign of 1781..........................287

Siege of Yorktown..........................299

Acknowledgements

Once again, as with all of my books, I am immensely indebted to Marguerite Knickmeyer, my friend and teaching partner, for her invaluable editorial assistance and support. I'm also indebted to the Simpson Library at the University of Mary Washington. Their extensive collection of resources on the American Revolution was tremendously helpful in my research.

My interest and knowledge of the American Revolution has also been greatly enhanced by my decade long involvement with Revolutionary War reenacting. Many fellow reenactors and Rev War researchers and enthusiasts contributed to my understanding of the Revolution with countless comments and responses to my questions. I am truly grateful to all of them.

Thanks also go out to Carl Fuller at Hubbardton Battlefield State Historic Site, Mark Turdo at Fort Ticonderoga, Paul Perrine at Newtown Battlefield, Eric Schnitzer at Satatoga National Historical Park, and Stephen Clark, the president of the Arnold Expedition Historical Society. All of these individuals generously assisted me in my research. The Maine, Massachusetts, and Vermont Historical Societies, the Burnham Tavern Museum in Machias, the Lake Champlain Maritime Museum, and the Castine Historical Society were also very helpful and informative sites to visit.

As always, I want to thank my wife Susan, and my children, Jenny and Michael, for allowing me to devote as much time as I do to my research, writing, and reenacting.

Lastly, I want to thank my cousin, Kevin Witham, for all of his enthusiasm, support, and interest in my work. It's always rewarding when someone close to you appreciates your work and Kevin's enthusiasm for my earlier writings inspired me to write about Maine's role in the Revolution. Thanks Kev!

Introduction

Any examination of Maine's role in the American Revolution must begin with the realization that the territory that now constitutes the state of Maine was actually part of Massachusetts during the Revolution. This region, which was separated from the rest of Massachusetts by New Hampshire and was sometimes referred to as "downeast," was settled in the 17th and 18th centuries by hardy colonists who traded lumber, firewood, and fish to the merchants of Boston and New England in exchange for foodstuffs, clothing, and tools.

On the eve of the American Revolution the region that is now Maine was divided into three counties: York, Cumberland, and Lincoln. Although the inhabitants of these counties were physically separated from the rest of Massachusetts, they were still residents of the colony with close political and economic ties to Boston. As a result, the actions of the downeast settlers were intertwined with those of Boston and the rest of Massachusetts.

Maine communities sent representatives to Boston to participate in the legislative assemblies, conventions and extra-legal meetings of the 1760's and 1770's. Many of these same Maine communities actively enforced measures adopted by Massachusetts leaders to protest and resist Parliament's new colonial polices.

When the dispute between the colonists and Great Britain turned violent, thousands of men from the three downeast counties served in continental regiments alongside comrades from other Massachusetts counties. Although some regiments held more men from Maine than others, it is likely that all of the Massachusetts continental regiments included men from Maine in their ranks.

Thus, any study of Maine's role in the Revolution must invariably include the role of Massachusetts, because the two regions struggled as one against the British. Both regions experienced significant conflict with the British in 1775, but both were largely spared bloodshed and destruction in the following years. The shift of combat operations out of Massachusetts in 1776 did not diminish the important role that Maine and Massachusetts troops played in the war, however. These troops were crucial in the defense of Lake Champlain in 1776 and the Saratoga campaign of 1777. Troops from Maine and Massachusetts helped defend New York City (unsuccessfully) in 1776 and participated in Washington's dramatic victories at Trenton and Princeton in late 1776-77. Hundreds of Maine troops endured the difficult winter encampment of Valley Forge with their comrades from the rest of Massachusetts, and together Maine and Massachusetts troops fought at Monmouth, Rhode Island, Stony Point, Penobscot Bay, and on the New York frontier in 1778-79.

When the war shifted south, hundreds of Massachusetts troops, including scores from Maine, marched to Virginia under General LaFayette. Although their efforts to stop British activities in Virginia met with limited success, LaFayette's troops played an important role in Washington's decisive victory at Yorktown in 1781.

Given their long and distinguished service in the war, it was only fitting that Massachusetts (and Maine) troops were present at the last major battle of the war. Massachusetts could proudly boast that it not only had a leading role in the political actions of America, but its troops, including thousands of men from "downeast" Maine, also significantly contributed to America's war effort and played a crucial role in America's victory over the British.

Chapter One

"The People...have become more attentive to their Liberties" 1763-73

The Treaty of Paris made it official; the long, bloody French and Indian War was over. What started in 1754 as a struggle between Britain and France for control of the Ohio River Valley ended in 1763 with France relinquishing possession of Canada, and Great Britain emerging as the uncontested power in North America.

Like all of the American colonies, Massachusetts warmly embraced the news. Thousands of the colony's men had served in the war alongside British redcoats and militia from neighboring colonies, and the treaty provided all of them with greater security. The colonists' ancient adversary, France, was leaving the continent, abandoning 70,000 French settlers in Canada to British rule.

Like all of British America, the colonists of Massachusetts, especially those living in the eastern counties of York, Cumberland, and Lincoln (present day Maine) were thankful that the French threat was eliminated. The isolated settlements of the three "downeast" counties of Massachusetts had been particularly vulnerable to French and Indian raids, so the end of French rule in Canada was especially good news for them. Not only did it mean an end to French raids upon the settlers of Maine, but also a dramatic reduction in conflict with the Indians, for without the support of their French allies, the Indian tribes of Maine were much weaker.

Map of Massachusetts

One result of this new arrangement in North America was a flood of downeast settlement. The population of the three easternmost counties of Massachusetts doubled to almost 50,000 people in the decade following the Treaty of Paris, and new settlements were established all along Maine's coast and rivers.[1] Many of these settlers were eager to exploit the region's abundant resources of timber and fish, two commodities that Boston and the British Empire clamored for. Although many Maine settlers lived austere lives along the coast, most believed that the future held great promise for them. Yet, within months of the happy news of the Treaty of Paris, troubling reports began to circulate in the colonies about a shift in British policy towards British America.

The British policy changes were triggered by two factors: the enormous debt Britain incurred during the war and the British Ministry's decision to maintain a large peacetime army. Britain's national debt nearly doubled during the French and Indian War and reached an amount that was barely manageable by the war's conclusion in 1763.[2] British taxpayers groaned under the increased tax burden yet, despite the financial pressures and the fact that France was no longer a threat in North America, the British Ministry decided to keep 10,000 troops in the American colonies and the Caribbean. The decision to maintain such a large military presence in North America was largely the result of the Ministry's desire to avoid downsizing the officer corps too greatly.

Many American colonists questioned the need to garrison so many troops in North America. The freeholders of Boston asked at a town meeting in May 1764,

---

[1] James S. Leamon, *Revolution Downeast: The War for American Independence in Maine*, (Amherst: University of Massachusetts Press, 1993), 6
[2] Edmund S. Morgan, *Prologue to Revolution: Sources and Documents on the Stamp Act Crisis, 1764-1766*, (Chapel Hill, NC: University of North Carolina Press, 1959), 1

> *Whether any expence can now be necessary to maintain the garrison service on our eastern frontier, considering that we are now in a state of profound peace ; our French enemies being totally subdued and there being hardly any remains of the Indian tribes left, ever again to annoy us.*[3]

The colonists were particularly disturbed to learn that they were to bear most of the expense of these troops through new trade regulations and stricter enforcement of existing laws such as the Sugar Act. Bostonians reminded their representatives to the Massachusetts General Court (the colony's legislature) that Massachusetts had its own financial problems to deal with:

> *This province hath been at a very great expence in carrying on the war and...lies under a very grievous burden of* [its own] *debt.*[4]

The Bostonians also charged that the proposed trade regulations would reduce colonial commerce and hamper the colonists' ability to buy goods manufactured in Britain. In other words, the Sugar Act would actually harm British merchants and the economy. The members of the town meeting declared that,

> *Our trade, as it is now, and always has been conducted, centers in Great Britain, and in return for manufactured* [goods] *affords* [Britain] *more ready cash, beyond any comparison, than can possibly be expected by* [the proposed Sugar Acts]. *We are ultimately yielding large supplies to the revenues of*

---

[3] "Instructions to Representatives in the General Assembly at a Town Meeting in Boston, 28 May, 1764," *The Massachusetts Gazette & Boston News-Letter*, 31 May, 1764, 2

[4] Ibid.

> *the mother country, while we are labouring for a very moderate subsistence for ourselves. But if our trade is to be curtail'd in its most profitable branches, and burthens...laid upon that which...remain, we shall be so far from being able to take off the manufactures of Great Britain, that it will be scarce possible for us to earn our bread.*[5]

A decline in Boston's economic fortunes would also impact thousands of colonists in Maine who depended on Boston as their primary market for fish, lumber, and firewood and their primary supplier of food, clothing, and other necessities. If Bostonians were forced to reduce their level of trade because of the Sugar Act, it could mean economic hardship for many settlers in Maine.

As concerned as the Bostonians were about the new trade regulations under the Sugar Act, they were even more disturbed by reports of an entirely new tax under consideration by Parliament. The freeholders of Boston asserted that

> *What still heightens our apprehensions is, that these unexpected proceedings may be preparatory to new taxations upon us: For if our trade may be taxed, why not our lands? Why not the produce of our lands, and every thing we possess or make use of? This we apprehend annihilates our charter right to govern and tax ourselves – It strikes at our British privileges, which as we have never forfeited them, we hold in common with our fellow subjects who are natives of Britain : If taxes are laid upon us in any shape without our having a legal representation where they are made, are we not reduc'd from the character of*

---

[5] Ibid.

> *free Subjects to the miserable state of tributary slaves.*[6]

The colonists' long tradition of local autonomy was jeopardized by the rumored parliamentary plan of taxation on the colonists. The right to govern and tax themselves, a principle the colonists had long held and something every Englishman held dear, was threatened. The colonists had no vote or voice in Parliament, therefore they had no way to influence Parliament short of pleas and appeals. To allow Parliament to levy new, direct taxes on the colonists was tantamount to surrendering their rights as Englishmen and becoming slaves to Parliament.

The Stamp Act : 1765

Parliament did not agree with such claims and passed the Stamp Act on March 22, 1765. The tax was designed to generate revenue from the American colonies to help offset the cost of British troops stationed in North America. It required colonists to use stamped paper for legal and business documents, newspapers, and even playing cards. Heavy fines would be levied on anyone caught violating the act.

Opposition to the Stamp Act developed swiftly among the colonists; they argued that the tax was unlike any previous measure imposed on them. The colonists were used to paying taxes to Britain in the form of tariffs on imported goods; it was one way that Britain regulated colonial trade. Such taxes were viewed by most colonists as optional in nature because they only applied to those who purchased the imported goods.

The Stamp Act, however, had a far greater reach and taxed items that the colonists were often required to possess such as business and legal documents, licenses, and commissions. Such an unavoidable tax could have but one purpose in the

---

[6] Ibid.

minds of many colonists, to raise revenue for the British treasury, and that was completely unacceptable. If the stamp tax was allowed to stand, it would establish a dangerous precedent: taxation without representation. It would also signal a significant expansion of parliamentary power over the colonies, an expansion that many colonists feared would turn them into virtual slaves of Britain.

Six months before the passage of the Stamp Act, James Otis, a member of the Massachusetts House of Representatives from Boston, published a political pamphlet that opposed this sort of parliamentary taxation as a violation of the colonists' natural rights:

> *I can see no reason to doubt but the imposition of [British] taxes...in the colonies is absolutely irreconcilable with the rights of the colonists as British subjects and as men. I say men, for in a state of nature no man can take my property from me without my consent: if he does, he deprives me of my liberty and makes me a slave. If such a proceeding is a breach of the law of nature, no law of society can make it just. The very act of taxing exercised over those who are not represented appears to me to be depriving them of one of their most essential rights as freemen....*[7]

Despite the contentious tone of his words, Otis ended his pamphlet with a reassurance that the colonists held Great Britain in the highest regard:

> *We all think ourselves happy under Great Britain. We love, esteem, and reverence our mother country, and adore our King. And could the choice of independency be offered the colonies or subjection to*

---

[7] James Otis, *The Rights of the British Colonies Asserted and Proved*, 1764

Great Britain upon any terms above absolute slavery, I am convinced they would accept the latter. The ministry in all future generations may rely on it that British America will never prove undutiful till driven to it as the last fatal resort against ministerial oppression.[8]

Six months after Otis wrote those words, it appeared to many colonists that ministerial oppression had arrived in the form of the stamp tax, and the response in Massachusetts was decisive.

The Massachusetts House of Representatives called for a meeting of delegates from all the colonies in the summer of 1765 to discuss a unified response to Parliament's Stamp Act. Nine colonies sent delegates to New York in October to attend the Stamp Act Congress. The Congress met for nearly three weeks and closed with a statement to Parliament proclaiming that the American colonists were English citizens, entitled to the same rights as native-born Englishmen. They also complained that the new duties under the Sugar Act placed a large burden on colonial trade and that the stamp tax violated the principle of no taxation without representation.[9] Although the result of the meeting was largely symbolic, the degree of unity between the delegates of the Stamp Act Congress established a foundation for future cooperation in their dealings with Parliament.

Stronger opposition to the Stamp Act was displayed in Boston two months prior to the Stamp Act Congress when a mob ransacked the office and home of Andrew Oliver, the appointed stamp tax distributor for Massachusetts. Oliver barely escaped with his life and resigned his commission the

---

[8] Ibid.
[9] Edmund S. Morgan, *Prologue to Revolution: Sources and Documents on the Stamp Act Crisis, 1764-1766*, 62-63

next day.[10] Two weeks later, on August 24th, a similar assault occurred on the residence of Lieutenant Governor Thomas Hutchinson. The unrest that erupted in Boston spread to Cumberland County in September when a Falmouth mob attacked William Bennet and looted his house. Reverend Thomas Smith of Falmouth (present day Portland, Maine) noted in his journal on September 12th, 1765, that

> *We hear of mobs continually at Newport, Connecticut, &ct. as well as in this Province. Affairs seem to be ripening to a universal mob; all relative to the Stamp officers, who are obliged to give up their commissions.*[11]

Such attacks, or in some cases the threat of attack, convinced most of the appointed stamp distributors in the colonies to resign their commissions over the fall. As a result, when the Stamp Act went into effect on November 1st, Georgia was the only colony prepared to enforce it.

Business and legal affairs temporarily came to a halt in most of British America as the absence of stamp tax distributors made it impossible to legally transact business. A backlog of court cases soon created pressure on the courts to ignore the law and resume hearings without the stamps. On January 1st, 1766, the court in Falmouth reacted to public pressure and illegally resumed operations without the stamps. A week later, a crowd assembled at the customs house in Falmouth to pressure customs officials to disregard the law and open the port without stamp clearances. When a shipment of stamped paper arrived in Falmouth at the end of January, the townspeople seized the stamps and burned them.[12]

---

[10] Edmund Morgan and Helen Morgan, *The Stamp Act Crisis: Prologue to Revolution*, (Chapel Hill, NC: Univ. of NC Press, 1953), 123-126
[11] William Willis, *Journals of the Reverend Thomas Smith and the Reverend Samuel Deane*, (Portland: Joseph S. Bailey, 1849), 206
[12] Leamon, 41-42

Merchants in Boston, New York, and Philadelphia employed a different approach to protest the stamp tax; they launched a boycott of British goods. By the close of 1765 hundreds of colonial merchants were withholding business orders with their counterparts in Britain. John Adams, of Massachusetts, was inspired by all of the protests and recorded in his journal that,

> *The Year 1765 has been the most remarkable Year of my Life. That enormous Engine, fabricated by the british Parliament, for battering down all the Rights and Liberties of America, I mean the Stamp Act, has raised and spread, thro the whole Continent, a Spirit that will be recorded to our Honour, with all future Generations. In every Colony, from Georgia to New Hampshire inclusively, the Stamp Distributors and Inspectors have been compelled, by the unconquerable Rage of the People, to renounce their offices. Such and so universal has been the Resentment of the People, that every Man who has dared to speak in favour of the Stamps, or to soften the detestation in which they are held...has been seen to sink into universal Contempt and Ignominy. The People, even to the lowest Ranks, have become more attentive to their Liberties, more inquisitive about them, and more determined to defend them, than they were ever before known or had occasion to be.... Our Presses have groaned, our Pulpits have thundered, our Legislatures have resolved, our Towns have voted, The Crown Officers have every where trembled, and all their little Tools and Creatures, been afraid to Speak and ashamed to be seen.*[13]

---

[13] John Adams, Diary 11, entry for 18 December 1765
From Adams Family Papers, Massachusetts Historical Society

Repeal of the Stamp Act

It was clear to Parliament by the spring of 1766 that the stamp tax was more trouble than it was worth. The act was repealed in March to the great satisfaction of the colonies. The inhabitants of Falmouth greeted the news with church bells, cannon fire, and numerous toasts. Reverend Smith recorded in his journal that,

> *Our people are mad with drink and joy; bells ringing, drums beating, colors flying and the court house illuminated and some others, and a bonfire, and a deluge of drunkenness.*[14]

British supporters of the colonists also expressed their satisfaction with the repeal, but their joy, which was published in colonial newspapers, was tempered with caution:

> *Blessed to God the act is repealed, after a terrible struggle. O that Boston, that America may be truly thankful and humble, and frugal, and not insult the parliament in their rejoicings....*[15]

> *Prevail upon* [the colonists] *to mix discretion with this great joy, that you do not exult as conquerors, but receive the blessing (now confirmed to you) with thankfulness and gratitude.*[16]

George Mason, one of the landed gentry of Virginia, resented the idea that the colonists should be grateful to Parliament for reversing something that was wrong in the first

---

[14] Willis, "Journal of Reverend Thomas Smith, 16 May, 1776, 209
[15] "Extract of a letter from a Rev. Divine in London dated March 3, 1766," Purdie & Dixon, *Virginia Gazette*, 23 May, 1766, 2
[16] "Extract of a letter from a Gentleman in London to his friend in New York, February 27," Purdie & Dixon, *Virginia Gazette*, 23 May, 1766, 2

place. Mason noted that, as Englishmen, the colonists possessed the same rights and privileges as native Britons, rights that they expected to pass on to their children:

> *We claim nothing but the liberty and privileges of Englishmen, in the same degree, as if we still* [lived] *among our brethren in Great Britain; these rights have not been forfeited by any act of ours; we cannot be deprived of them, without our consent, but by violence and injustice; we have received them from our ancestors, and, with God's leave, we will transmit them, unimpaired, to our posterity.*[17]

Parliament was disinterested in such views. Stung by colonial opposition to the Stamp Act -- which most members of Parliament still believed was a legal tax -- Parliament reaffirmed its authority over the colonies with the Declaratory Act. The act proclaimed that

> *The said colonies...in America have been, are, and of right ought to be, subordinate unto, and dependent upon the imperial crown and Parliament of Great Britain; and that the king...with the advice and consent of...Parliament...hath...full power and authority to make laws...to bind the colonies and people of America, subjects of the crown of Great Britain, in all cases whatsoever.*[18]

---

[17] Robert A. Rutland, ed., "To the Committee of Merchants in London 6 June, 1766," *The Papers of George Mason, Vol. 1*, (University of North Carolina Press, 1970), 68

[18] Henry Steele Commager, "The Declaratory Act, 18 March, 1766," *Documents of American History*, (New York: Appleton-Century-Crofts, 1963), 60-61

Most colonists dismissed the Declaratory Act as empty rhetoric because Parliament initially did little to enforce its newly asserted authority. This changed in 1767 when Parliament passed the Townshend Duties.

Townshend Duties : 1767

In the four years since the end of the French and Indian War little had been done to effectively address Britain's overwhelming debt. The Stamp Act only increased the financial crisis by disrupting trade and commerce with the colonies, and the Sugar Act earned little revenue. Desperate for a way to shift some of the financial burden of the empire to the colonies and determined to re-assert Parliament's authority over the colonists, Parliament adopted the Townshend Duties in 1767. This act placed tariffs on a long list of imported goods from Britain. The newly taxed items included tea, glass, paint, and paper. The British Ministry argued that since the colonists had long accepted Parliament's right to tax imports, they could not legally oppose the new duties.

The colonists replied that past duties (tariffs) were designed to regulate trade by discouraging the purchase of foreign goods, but the Townshend Duties were placed on many goods that the colonists could only purchase from England. In other words, since there was no foreign competition for many of the newly taxed items, there was no need to levy a duty on them.

Boston merchants led the opposition to the Townshend Duties in October 1767 with a pledge to boycott a list of taxed goods.[19] The Massachusetts legislature followed this with a letter to the other colonies in February 1768 stating that

---

[19] Boston Merchants Broadside, 31 October, 1767, Massachusetts Historical Society

Duties on the People of this province with the sole & express purpose of raising a Revenue, are Infringements of [the colonists'] Natural & Constitutional Rights because [they] are not represented in the British Parliament....[20]

The British Secretary of State for the colonies objected to the letter and demanded that it be rescinded, but the Massachusetts legislature refused. When Governor Francis Bernard postponed the autumn meeting of the legislature for fear that such a gathering might provoke increased unrest (which had become a common occurrence and an effective tool to intimidate British customs agents), Boston's leaders called for a convention. Over one hundred Massachusetts towns, including some from Maine, sent representatives to Boston in September 1768. This marked the first substantial participation in the dispute for many of the Maine towns and an important step towards unity for Massachusetts as a whole.

The convention was held in a very tense setting for news had spread through Boston that British troops were on their way. Governor Bernard had had enough of the harassment and intimidation of government officials by Boston's mobs and asked the British government to send troops to Boston to re-establish order. On September 22nd, the Massachusetts convention published its proceedings which were very moderate in tone and substance. The delegates unanimously asserted their loyalty to the King and British constitution and repeatedly discouraged violent acts of opposition to the Townshend Duties. At the same time, the delegates questioned the need for a standing army in the colonies and expressed the view that the presence of such troops was

---

[20] Harry A. Cushing, ed., "The House of Representatives of Massachusetts to the Other House of Representatives, 11 February, 1768," *The Writings of Samuel Adams, Vol. 1*, (NY:G.P. Putnam's Sons, 1904), 185-186

"*dangerous to their civil Liberty.*"[21] They also maintained that the Townshend Duties threatened their freedom as Englishmen:

> *If these Acts of Parliament should remain in force, and* [Parliament] *shall continue to exercise the Power of* [taxing] *their Fellow-Subjects in this Province, his Majesty's People here must then regret their unhappy Fate in having only the Name left of free Subjects.*[22]

The convention's concern went unheeded by Parliament, and within days of its adjournment two British regiments arrived in Boston. The British troops were greeted by the townsfolk on October 1st with fierce resentment. Two more regiments squeezed into Boston in November. Despite frequent verbal altercations and fistfights between the soldiers and townsfolk, a tense calm descended over the town and continued into 1769. In the summer of that year, General Thomas Gage, the overall British commander in North America, decided to transfer two of the regiments to Halifax, Nova Scotia. He hoped that this would mollify the public a bit and reduce the hardship his troops experienced in the overcrowded town. His hopes were not met.

Non-Importation Association : 1769

Colonial resistance to the Townshend Duties involved more than the harassment of British soldiers. The boycott, adopted by many of Boston's merchants in 1767, slowly gained support throughout the colonies as Parliament steadfastly upheld the Townshend Duties. George Washington expressed the view of many colonists in early 1769 in a letter to his friend George Mason:

---

[21] Massachusetts Convention, 22 September, 1768, Massachusetts Historical Society
[22] Ibid.

> *At a time when our lordly Masters in Great Britain will be satisfied with nothing less than the deprivation of American freedom, it seems highly necessary that some thing shou'd be done to avert the stroke and maintain the liberty which we have derived from our Ancestors....*[23]

A colonial boycott of items taxed by the Townshend Act gradually gained support throughout the colonies. It was moderately effective in the northern colonies where imported goods from Britain were channeled through local merchants. A significant amount of public pressure was exerted on reluctant merchants to abide by the boycott. The boycott was harder to enforce in the southern colonies where individual planters often traded directly with British merchants and felt less pressure to observe it.

Back in Boston, tension between the townsfolk and British troops was on the rise again, in part because the rules under which the British army operated severely limited their conduct and invited insult and injury from the public. A frustrated General Gage noted that

> *The People were as Lawless and Licentious after the Troops arrived, as they were before. The Troops could not act by Military Authority, and no Person in Civil Authority would ask their aid. They were there contrary to the wishes of the Council, Assembly, Magistrates and People, and seemed only offered to abuse and Ruin. And the Soldiers were either to suffer ill usage and even assaults upon their Persons till their Lives were in Danger, or by resisting and*

---

[23] Rutland, "George Washington to George Mason, 5 April, 1769," *The Papers of George Mason, Vol. 1*, 96-98

defending themselves, to run almost a Certainty of suffering by the Law.[24]

The tension between the colonists and troops finally erupted into bloodshed on March 5, 1770, when a detachment of British troops fired into a large crowd that was taunting and pelting them with ice, snowballs, and clubs. The incident, dubbed the Boston Massacre by the colonists, resulted in five dead colonists and an outraged public. The next day, thousands of Bostonians gathered to demand the removal of the British soldiers from Boston. Within days, the 14th and 29th British Regiments relocated to Castle Island in Boston Harbor. Months later, a Boston jury cleared all but two of the soldiers of any wrongdoing. The two convicted soldiers were found guilty of manslaughter and branded on their thumbs as a punishment.

Not all of the news of 1770 was bad for the colonists; on the very same day of the Boston Massacre, the British Parliament repealed nearly all of the Townshend Duties. The disruption of trade caused by the colonial boycott and the added expense of the troops in Boston cost Britain significantly more than the revenue collected from the duties. The Townshend Duties had become another drain on the treasury and Parliament abandoned them in frustration. This was an economic decision, not a political one, and Parliament stressed that it still had the authority to tax the colonists by keeping the duty on tea in place. Although some of the colonists called for a continuation of the boycott until the duty on tea was also repealed, merchants in New York and Philadelphia ceased to participate, and the boycott dissolved. British goods, including small quantities of taxed tea, once again flowed into the colonies.

---

[24] Hiller B. Zobel, *The Boston Massacre*, (New York: W.W. Norton, 1970), 180-81.

Parliament's repeal of the Townshend Duties helped ease tensions between the colonies and Great Britain. The brief respite ended in 1772 when the colonists learned that Britain had assumed responsibility for paying the salaries of the Massachusetts governor and other royal appointees. This gave these officials more independence from the Massachusetts legislature (which used to control their pay). By itself, this change may not have troubled the legislators, but in the climate of 1772, where distrust between the colonists and Britain remained high, the change triggered alarms. Some feared that it was another step toward the British Ministry's goal of destroying popular government in Massachusetts by removing the legislature's ability to influence these appointed officials. A town meeting in Boston in November 1772 asserted that,

> *There is abundant Reasons to be alarmed that the plan of Despotism which the Enemies of our invaluable Rights have concerted, is rapidly hastening to a completion and* [we] *can no longer conceal our impatience under a constant, unremitted, uniform Aim to inslave us.... Making* [executive officials] *not only intirely independent of the People...but absolutely dependent on the crown (which may hereafter be worn by a Tyrant) both for their Appointment and Support, we cannot but be extremely alarm'd at the mischievous Tendency of this Innovation.*[25]

Boston's leaders responded to this policy change by forming a committee of correspondence, which was designed to keep the populace outside of Boston informed of the latest news and generate more support from them. A number of

---

[25] Circular Letter from the Freeholders of Boston, 20 November, 1772, Massachusetts Historical Society

towns in Maine followed Boston's example and formed their own committees. One town in particular, Old Georgetown, stressed their willingness to fight to protect their freedom and rights:

> *It is but a few years since we have felt the effects of the most inhumane cruelty from the savage natives of this country. We have had many of our friends and relatives cruelly slain by them.* The idea [of fighting against British troops] *is shocking, but our losing our freedom and becoming slaves is much more so. We are situated on the banks of the river Sagadahock, where some of our forefathers who left their native country for the sake of their liberty first landed, many of whom fell a sacrifice to savage barbarity rather than endure oppression; their graves are with us and we would by no means affront their relics by a tame submission to oppression and slavery....*[26]

Parliament was bothered by the formation of these committees but did nothing to stop them. Their attention was focused on a plan to save the financially troubled East India Company, which was burdened with a huge surplus of tea due in large part to a significant decrease in British tea consumption among the American colonists. To help the East India Company unload its surplus tea and remain solvent, Parliament passed the Tea Act in early 1773. On the surface the Tea Act appeared to benefit the American colonists. The East India Company was allowed to sell its taxed tea directly to the colonists at an equivalent, and in some cases lower price than smuggled Dutch tea.

---

[26] Parker McCobb Read, "Committee of Correspondence of Old Georgetown to the Boston Committee of Correspondence, 16 March, 1773," *History of Bath and Environs, Sagadahoc County, Maine 1677-1894*, (Portland, ME: Lakeside Press, 1894), 45

The potential financial savings of this new arrangement for the colonists created a dilemma for colonial leaders. Although some colonists had resumed drinking taxed English tea when the boycott collapsed in 1770, many others, at the urging of local leaders, had continued to boycott the tea. As a result, colonial leaders could argue in 1773 that most colonists still viewed the tea tax as unconstitutional.

This argument would unravel, however, if the colonists purchased a large amount of the surplus East India tea at its bargain prices. Colonial leaders feared that Parliament would interpret a surge in British tea sales as tacit acceptance of the tea tax. This would be the precedent Parliament needed to re-impose all of the Townshend Duties and reaffirm the Declaratory Act.

Colonial leaders were determined to prevent this from happening and undertook efforts to block the delivery of the surplus tea in Charleston, Philadelphia, New York, and Boston. They succeeded without mishap in all the ports except Boston. On December 16th, 1773, scores of Bostonians took the extreme measure of dumping the controversial tea into Boston Harbor. This action won applause among many towns in Maine, but outraged Parliament and the King; they interpreted the act as a blatant challenge to their authority and responded forcefully.

Chapter Two

"What can these things indicate but a civil war?"

1774-75

The American colonists anxiously waited all spring for Parliament's response to the Boston Tea Party. When the news finally arrived in May, it shocked nearly everyone. Parliament and the King, determined to severely punish Massachusetts (particularly Boston), closed Boston Harbor, abolished the Massachusetts Assembly, and placed the colony under martial law. Additional British troops were sent to Boston to enforce the crackdown and Massachusetts fell under the rule of General Thomas Gage.

The colonists were stunned by the harsh measures and dubbed Parliament's actions the Intolerable Acts. Edmund Pendleton, a moderate burgess in Virginia's House of Burgesses, expressed the view of many colonists:

> *Tho' it should be granted that the Bostonians did wrong in destroying the tea, yet the Parliament giving Judgement and sending ships and troops to* [punish all of Massachusetts] *in a case of Private property is* [an] *Attack upon constitutional Rights, of which we could not remain Idle Spectators.....*[1]

---

[1] David John Mays, ed., "Edmund Pendleton to Joseph Chew, 20 June, 1774," *The Letters and Papers of Edmund Pendleton, Vol. 1* (Charlottesville: University Press of Virginia, 1967), 93

Prior to the Intolerable Acts, most of the inhabitants of York, Cumberland, and Lincoln Counties (downeast Maine), were only moderately engaged in the dispute with Parliament. They dutifully opposed the Stamp Act and Townshend Duties, and were outraged at the Boston Massacre, but they essentially followed the lead of Boston in opposing British policies. The Intolerable Acts changed this because the closure of Boston Harbor directly threatened the livelihood of many Mainers who relied heavily on trade with Boston for food and clothing.

Maine towns took a defiant stand against the Intolerable Acts and expressed anger at Parliament through public statements of support for Boston. On June 13th, 1774, the freeholders of North Yarmouth, in Cumberland County, announced that,

> *We are ready to unite with our brethren of the town of Boston, and of the other towns in this province in any constitutional plan that may be formed, and generally agreed upon, as the most likely to procure a repeal of the aforesaid unrighteous oppressive and cruel act.*[2]

The North Yarmouth freeholders also stressed their support for a non-importation and non-exportation policy towards Britain. The freeholders of Buxton, in York County, proclaimed their opposition to the Intolerable Acts on June 20th, 1774:

> *We deem* [the closure of Boston Harbor] *as an Attack upon Us which tends to utterly destroy our civil Liberties – For the same Power may at Pleasure destroy the Trade And Shut up the Harbors of any*

---

[2] L. Kinvin Wroth, ed., "North Yarmouth to Boston Committee, 13 June, 1774," *Province in Rebellion: A Documentary History of the Founding of the Commonwealth of Massachusetts, 1774-75,* (Cambridge, MA: Harvard University Press, 1975), 482-483

other colonies in their Turn and thus bring on a total End to our Liberties & Privileges...a Dread of being enslaved ourselves, & transporting the Chains to our Posterity is the principal Inducement to [our opposition to the Intolerable Acts].[3]

Buxton's freeholders pledged to support all constitutional means of opposing the crackdown and continue their opposition to taxation without representation. In Falmouth, participants at a town meeting reminded Parliament that,

A sacred compact [existed in the form of] *a Provincial charter, purchased by our forefathers, and sanctioned by the parent government; whereby, we have a Parliament of our own, or rather a Supreme Provincial Legislature, in which we are equally represented, and to whose laws, in obedience to the law of God alone, ought we to be subservient.*[4]

Falmouth's freeholders agreed with the resolves passed in Buxton and contended that subservience to the dictates of the British Parliament would expose them, *"to the worst kind of slavery."*[5]

Like most colonists in America, the freeholders of Falmouth saw a great distinction between Parliament and the King. They rejected the authority of Parliament to rule over them but asserted that *"there can be found no subjects more loyal to their prince than we, in all his dominions."*[6] This desire to remain faithful to the King placed the colonists in a dilemma. The freeholders of Falmouth proclaimed:

---

[3] James Phinney Baxter, ed., *Documentary History of the State of Maine, Vol. 14*, (Portland: LaFavor-Tower Co., 1910), 235-36
[4] William Williamson, *The History of the State of Maine, Vol. 2*, (Hallowell: Glazer, Masters & Smith, 1839), 410
[5] Ibid.
[6] Ibid.

> *We have no desire to be released from the restraints of good government and reasonable laws; while to obey such as are oppressive or to resist them is a most unhappy and trying alternative. If we yield, we [accept] the power that oppresses us, and must forever submit to its despotic sway; we detach ourselves from the great body of our fellow countrymen, and must endure their just and severe reproaches; nay, we must endure all the evils which a servile submission will bring upon us and our posterity in succeeding generations. If we resist, we help to sever a mighty empire; we arouse against ourselves, a most powerful nation; and in the midst of our greatest exertions, we put to hazard our own security, and all that is dear.*[7]

Realizing that the crisis demanded action, Falmouth's freeholders announced:

> *We have weighed the subject fully and fairly; and we feel constrained by the scared obligations of patriotism and self preservation, and the tender ties of filial affections, to join our brethren of the several towns on the continent, in opposing the operation of despotic measures. The dictates of nature, of reason and of conscience admonish and urge us to the support of our freedom; for upon this all our political happiness must depend. Our cause is just, and we trust in God, if we do our duty, he will enable us to transmit to our children that Sacred Freedom, which we have inherited from our fathers.*[8]

The freeholders agreed in July to support a non-importation policy with Britain, the implementation of which would be

---

[7] Ibid.
[8] Ibid.

determined by the Continental Congress in Philadelphia in the fall.[9]

As Boston began to suffer from the Intolerable Acts, communities throughout America responded with aid. Despite suffering from their own shortages, residents of the three "downeast" counties of York, Cumberland, and Lincoln sent firewood, fish, and potatoes to their brethren in Boston.[10] Some also supported Boston's call for a suspension of trade with Britain.[11] This proposal, which would entail significant economic sacrifice for many colonists, garnered a mixed reaction in Maine. Inland settlements like Gorham and Brunswick supported a cessation of trade, but coastal communities like Falmouth and Scarborough had more to lose and were hesitant. These coastal towns were vulnerable to harassment from the British navy, and their economies were heavily dependent on shipping and trade. For many Maine towns, the loss of their primary trading partner, Boston, was already a great economic shock, the cessation of all trade with Britain would be disastrous.

Disagreement over the extent of the boycott led to confrontations in Cumberland County between armed parties who supported a full boycott and merchants who opposed it. One of the most outspoken proponents of a general boycott was Samuel Thompson of Brunswick. Thompson was a prominent resident of Brunswick who served as a town selectman and an officer in the local militia. In the late summer and fall of 1774, Thompson led armed bands of boycott supporters to neighboring towns to "encourage" support for a boycott. They harassed and intimidated Tories and suspected Tories and left the general impression that royal government was powerless in Cumberland County.[12]

---

[9] Wroth, ed., "Falmouth Proceedings, 21 July, 1774," 749-750
[10] Leamon, 56
[11] Ibid., 60
[12] Ibid., 63

Although many people disapproved of Thompson's strong arm tactics, Tory sentiment in Cumberland County was significantly suppressed.

Most moderate leaders in Maine preferred a less violent way to express their opposition to Britain. Cumberland and York Counties held special conventions in September and November to discuss the crisis. Both declared their loyalty to the King but condemned Parliament for the Intolerable Acts.[13] On September 22nd, 1774, the Cumberland County Convention declared:

> *It is too apparent that the British Ministry have long been hatching monstrous Acts to break our Constitution...We are* [his Majesty's] *loyal subjects and...cannot help thinking that if he would...lay aside the selfish council of wicked and designing men, he and his subjects would be mutually happy, and provocations on both sides cease.*[14]

The convention delegates recommended a "*manly opposition*" to the Intolerable Acts and predicted that firm action would be difficult, but necessary:

> *We believe our enemies supposed we must submit, and tamely give up all our rights. It is true a vigorous opposition will subject us to many inconveniences; but how much greater will our misery be if we relinquish all we now enjoy, and lay our future earnings at the mercy of despotick men? We cannot bear the thought; distant posterity would have cause to curse our folly, and the rising generation would justly execrate our memory. We*

---

[13] Ibid., 59

[14] Peter Force, ed., "Proceedings of Cumberland County Convention, 22 September, 1774," *American Archives, 4th Series, Volume 1*, (Washington D.C.: M St. Clair Clarke and Peter Force, 1837), 800

> *therefore recommend a manly opposition to those cruel Acts....* [15]

York County held its convention two months later in November and resolved to "*put the Militia on a reputable and formidable footing.*"[16]

A month earlier, a much bigger political gathering of Massachusetts leaders occurred in Cambridge. Over ninety representatives from scores of towns met and formed themselves into a Provincial Congress to replace the suspended colonial assembly (General Court). A number of Maine towns sent delegates to this extralegal assembly. General Gage ignored its proceedings, but soon discovered that the Provincial Congress held far more weight over Massachusetts than he and his troops did. While the Provincial Congress met in Cambridge to address the concerns of Massachusetts, another body of men met in Philadelphia. Their goal was to agree upon a united response to the Intolerable Acts.

The First Continental Congress

Calls for a Continental Congress followed on the heels of the Intolerable Acts and resulted in a gathering of representatives from all thirteen colonies in Philadelphia in early September 1774. Although Massachusetts was at the center of the dispute with Britain, the delegates chose Peyton Randolph, Virginia's Speaker of the House of Burgesses, to preside over the Congress. Randolph was a political moderate from Williamsburg and universally esteemed by Virginians.

Once the necessary procedural matters were settled, the delegates tackled the main issue, a unified response to the

---

[15] Ibid.
[16] Force, "Proceedings of York County Congress, 16 November, 1774," 985

Intolerable Acts. Patrick Henry set the benchmark for colonial unity when he boldly proclaimed:

> *The Distinctions between Virginians, Pennsylvanians, New Yorkers, and New Englanders, are no more. I am not a Virginian, but an American!*[17]

The Massachusetts delegates were undoubtedly pleased by Henry's display of unity. It remained to be seen whether the rest of the congress shared his view.

A week of deliberations provided John Adams with the answer. He informed his wife in mid-September that

> *Congress will, to all present Appearance, be well united...A Tory here is the most despicable Animal...The Spirit, the Firmness, the Prudence of* [Massachusetts] *are vastly applauded and We are universally acknowledged the Saviours and Defenders of American Liberty.*[18]

Adams was decidedly less enthusiastic about the congress after three more weeks of deliberation:

> *I am wearied to Death with the Life I lead. The Business of the Congress is tedious, beyond Expression. This Assembly is like no other that ever existed. Every Man in it is a great Man – an orator, a Critick, a statesman, and therefore every Man upon every Question must shew his oratory, his criticism and his Political Abilities. The Consequence of this is, that Business is drawn and spun out to an immeasurable Length. I believe if it was moved and seconded that We should come to a Resolution that Three and two make five, We should be entertained*

---

[17] Paul H. Smith, "James Duane's Notes on the Debates, 6 September, 1774," *Letters of Delegates to Congress: 1774-1789*, 28

[18] Smith, "John Adams to Abigail Adams, 14 September, 1774," 69-70

with Logick and Rhetorick, Law, History, Politicks and Mathematicks, concerning the Subject for two whole Days, and then We should pass a Resolution unanimously in the Affirmative.[19]

Two more weeks passed before the delegates finally agreed on a course of action. They called for a boycott of British goods and the discontinuation of the slave trade, effective December 1st, 1774. If Parliament persisted with the Intolerable Acts, a ban on all colonial exports to Britain would follow on September 1st, 1775. Congress also called on the colonists to be more frugal and industrious and to avoid extravagant activities like horse-racing, gambling, and dancing.[20]

Massachusetts Stands Firm

While the Continental Congress wrapped up its work in Philadelphia, the Massachusetts Provincial Congress met in Cambridge and pledged to protect Massachusetts from any person or persons who "*attempt...the destruction, invasion, detriment or annoyance of this province.*"[21] A committee of safety was formed to act as the governing body of the province when the Provincial Congress was not in session. The Massachusetts Congress also took measures to strengthen the militia and urged communities to form minute companies out of their most active troops. These companies were to be ready at a moment's notice and were the colony's first line of defense.

Six weeks later, on December 10th, the Provincial Congress passed a resolution urging the inhabitants of Massachusetts to

---

[19] Smith, "John Adams to Abigail Adams, 9 October, 1774," 164
[20] Journal of Continental Congress, 20 October, 1774, 75-80
   (Accessed via the Library of Congress website at www.loc.gov)
[21] Massachusetts Provincial Laws, 2nd Session – 1774, (Livermore & Knight Co., 1931), 28

be firm but measured in their opposition to the Intolerable Acts:

> *At a time when the good people of this colony were deprived of their laws, and the administration of justice, civil and criminal; when the cruel oppressions brought on their capital had stagnated almost all their commerce; when a standing army was illegally posted among us for the express purpose of enforcing submission to a system of tyranny; and when the general court was, with the same design, prohibited to sit; we were chosen and empowered by you to assemble and consult upon measures necessary for our common safety and defense....*
>
> *The general tenor of our intelligence from Great Britain, with the frequent reinforcements of the army and navy at Boston, excites the strongest jealousy that the system of colonial administration, so unfriendly to the protestant religion, and destructive of American liberty, is still to be pursued and attempted with force to be carried into execution.*
>
> *You are placed by Providence in the post of honor, because it is the post of danger; and while struggling for the noblest objectives, the liberties of your country, the happiness of posterity, and the rights of human nature, the eyes not only of North America and the whole British empire, but of all Europe, are upon you. Let us therefore altogether solicitous, that no disorderly behavior, nothing unbecoming our character as Americans, as citizens, be justly chargeable to us.*[22]

---

[22] Massachusetts Provincial Laws, 69-70

The Provincial Congress then assured the colonists that

> [The boycott] *will soon produce in Great Britain such dangerous effects, as cannot fail to convince the ministry, the parliament, and people, that it is in their best interest and duty to grant us relief.*[23]

But just in case the boycott failed to change British policy, the representatives urged every town to enhance their military preparedness:

> *Care should be taken by the towns and districts in this colony, that each of the minute men, not already provided therewith, should be immediately equipped with an effective fire arm, bayonet, pouch, knapsack, thirty rounds of cartridges and balls, and that they be disciplined three times a week, and oftener, as opportunity may offer.*[24]

Securing an adequate supply of gunpowder was essential for the colonists, especially after General Gage seized 250 half barrels of powder from the Provincial Powder House in early September. This successful British raid had infuriated the colonists and nearly led to armed conflict as militia companies throughout Massachusetts mustered and marched to Boston. Large crowds harassed suspected Tories in Cambridge but did not challenge the British troops at Boston Neck. Nevertheless, General Gage was surprised by the colonists' strong reaction and suspended further raids.

By early December, however, reports circulated throughout New England of a new directive from London instructing the colonial governors to secure "*any Gunpowder, or any Sort of Arms or Ammunition which may be...imported into the*

---

[23] Ibid., 70
[24] Ibid., 71

Colonies."[25] These reports triggered incidents in Rhode Island and New Hampshire where colonists seized gunpowder and weapons from British posts. The tiny British garrison at Fort William and Mary in Portsmouth, New Hampshire actually fired at hundreds of colonists who approached the fort. Luckily, they missed their mark. Governor John Wentworth described the incident in a letter to General Gage:

> *On* [December 14th] *after 12 o' clock, an insurrection suddenly took place in town and immediately proceeded to his Majesty's castle, attacked, overpowered, wounded and confined the Captain, and thence took away all of King's powder. Yesterday numbers more assembled, and last night brought off many cannon, and about sixty muskets. This day the town is full of armed men, who refuse to disperse, but appear determined to complete the dismantling of the fortress entirely.*[26]

The arrival of two British warships, *H.M.S. Canceaux* (8 guns and 45 men) and *H.M.S. Scarborough* (20 guns and 130 men) prevented any further destruction of the fort. Nevertheless, such bold action signaled the determination of many colonists to risk bloodshed to defend their rights. To loyalists in America, such action signaled open rebellion. One loyalist, responding to similar unrest in Rhode Island, observed in the *New York Gazetteer* that

> *The people here have, I think openly declared themselves against government, and in such a manner, as surely must be pronounced rebellion. Is it possible that a people without arms, ammunition,*

---

[25] William Bell Clark, ed., *Naval Documents of the American Revolution, Vol. 1*, (Washington, 1964), 9

[26] Clark, ed., "Governor John Wentworth to Governor Thomas Gage, 16 December, 1774," *Naval Documents of the American Revolution, Vol. 1*, 27

money, or navy, should dare to brave a nation, dreaded and respected by all the powers on earth. What black ingratitude to the parent state, who has nourished, protected and supported them from their infancy. What can these things indicate but a civil war?[27]

The threat of civil war did not deter General Gage from resuming his efforts to secure gunpowder and weapons in Massachusetts. On February 26th, 1775, a detachment of British troops under Colonel Alexander Leslie landed in Marblehead and rapidly marched towards Salem to seize cannon and military stores. The raid caught the inhabitants by surprise, but Colonel Leslie was forced to stop at a drawbridge before he reached his objective. An account of the incident appeared in the Essex Gazette:

Last Sabbath the Peace of the Town was disturbed by the coming of a Regiment of the King's Troops...A Transport arrived at Marblehead...covered with Soldiers, who having loaded and fixed their Bayonets, landed with great Dispatch; and instantly marched off. Some of the Inhabitants suspecting they were bound to Salem, to seize some Materials there preparing for an Artillery, dispatched several Messengers to inform us of it. These Materials were on the North Side of the North River, and to come at them it was necessary to cross a Bridge, one Part of which was made to draw up...the Regiment marched off with a quick Pace, in a direct Course for the North Bridge; just before their Entrance upon which, the Draw-Bridge was pulled up...The Colonel who led them expressed some Surprize; and then turning

---

[27] Clark, ed., "Extract of a Letter from Newport, 14 December, 1774," *Naval Documents of the American Revolution, Vol. 1,* 20

> *about, ordered an Officer to face his Company to a Body of Men standing on a Wharf on the other Side of the Draw-Bridge, and fire. One of our Townsmen (who had kept along Side the Colonel)...instantly told him he had better not fire, that he had no Right to fire without further Orders, "and if you do fire (said he) you will be all dead Men." The company neither fired or faced....* [28]

Colonel Leslie consulted with his officers and informed the colonists that *"he would maintain his Ground, and go over the Bridge before he returned, if it was a Month first."* [29] The townspeople replied that they could stay as long as they liked, but the bridge would not be lowered. They then asked Colonel Leslie what his purpose was for crossing the bridge. Leslie replied that he had orders to cross it and that he must comply with those orders. After a ninety minute standoff, a compromise was reached:

> *Finally the Colonel said he must go over; and if the Draw-Bridge were let down so that he might pass, he pledged his Honour he would march not above thirty Rods beyond it, and then immediately return. The Regiment had now been on the Bridge about an Hour and an Half; and every Thing being secured, the Inhabitants directed the Draw-Bridge to be let down. The Regiment immediately passed over, marched a few Rods, returned, and with great Expedition went back to Marblehead, where they embarked on board the Transport without Delay.* [30]

---

[28] Clark, ed., "Essex Gazette, Tuesday, February 21 to 28, 1775," *Naval Documents of the American Revolution, Vol. 1*, 114-16
[29] Ibid.
[30] Ibid.

Other American accounts of the incident tell a similar story, one of local militia facing British regulars in a tense and explosive confrontation that was defused only through creative diplomacy. The British version of the incident was a bit different. Major John Pitcairn reported that

> *The Colonel landed, and marched with great expedition to Salem: the people beat their drums, rung their alarm bells: but the Colonel saw none in arms but five, and those took care to get out of the way as fast as they could. The people behaved as I suppose they will ever do, made a great noise when there is nobody to oppose them, but the moment they see us in arms and in earnest they will talk very differently. The Colonel found no guns – it is supposed a false information. He marched back to Marblehead and embarked for this place. The moment he left Salem, I am told the people got arms and paraded about....*[31]

Such confrontations, along with the constant abuse leveled at British soldiers by an angry Massachusetts populace, increased the animosity British troops felt towards the colonists. Major Pitcairn expressed the view of many British officers in early March 1775:

> *Orders are anxiously expected from England to chastise those very bad people. The General had some of the Great Wigs, as they are called here, with him two days ago, when he took that opportunity of telling them, and swore to it by the living God, that if there was a single man of the King's troops killed in any of their towns he would burn it to the ground. What fools you are, said he, to pretend to resist the*

---

[31] Clark, ed., "Major John Pitcairn to Lord Sandwich, 4 March, 1775," *Naval Documents of the American Revolution, Vol. 1*, 124-126

> *power of Great Britain; she maintained last war three hundred thousand men, and will do the same now rather than suffer the ungrateful people of this country to continue in their rebellion. This behavior of the General's gives great satisfaction to the friends of Government* [Tories]. *I am satisfied that one active campaign, a smart action, and burning of two or three of their towns, will set everything to rights. Nothing now, I am afraid, but this will ever convince those foolish bad people that England is in earnest. What a sad misfortune it was to this country, the repealing of the Stamp Act; every friend to Government here asserts in the strongest terms that this has been the cause of all their misfortunes.*[32]

Major Pitcairn would get his wish to chastise the colonists just six weeks later.

---

[32] Ibid.

Chapter Three

"A most obstinate engagement ensued"
1775

Indications that General Gage was about to launch another raid into the Massachusetts countryside were numerous in April 1775, and colonial leaders expected that Concord would be his target. The town, which was about twenty miles from Boston, was both a depot for military supplies and the meeting place of the Provincial Congress. A warning from Paul Revere on April 8th (which proved to be ten days early), prompted the inhabitants of Concord to relocate most of the military supplies to outlying farms where it would be harder to discover. A week later, on April 15th, the Provincial Congress heeded new warnings of an impending raid and adjourned.[1]

In Boston, General Gage continued with his preparations. His plan called for Lieutenant Colonel Francis Smith to march a force of approximately 800 men into the Massachusetts countryside under cover of darkness and arrive at Concord at dawn to catch the town by surprise. The expedition stepped off on the evening of April 18th using longboats to cross the Back Bay. By midnight they were on the road to Concord via Cambridge, Menotomy, and Lexington. Ahead of them rode a handful of colonists determined to spread the alarm about the approaching troops.

---

[1] David Hackett Fischer, *Paul Revere's Ride*, (New York: Oxford University Press, 1994), 87

Battle of Lexington and Concord

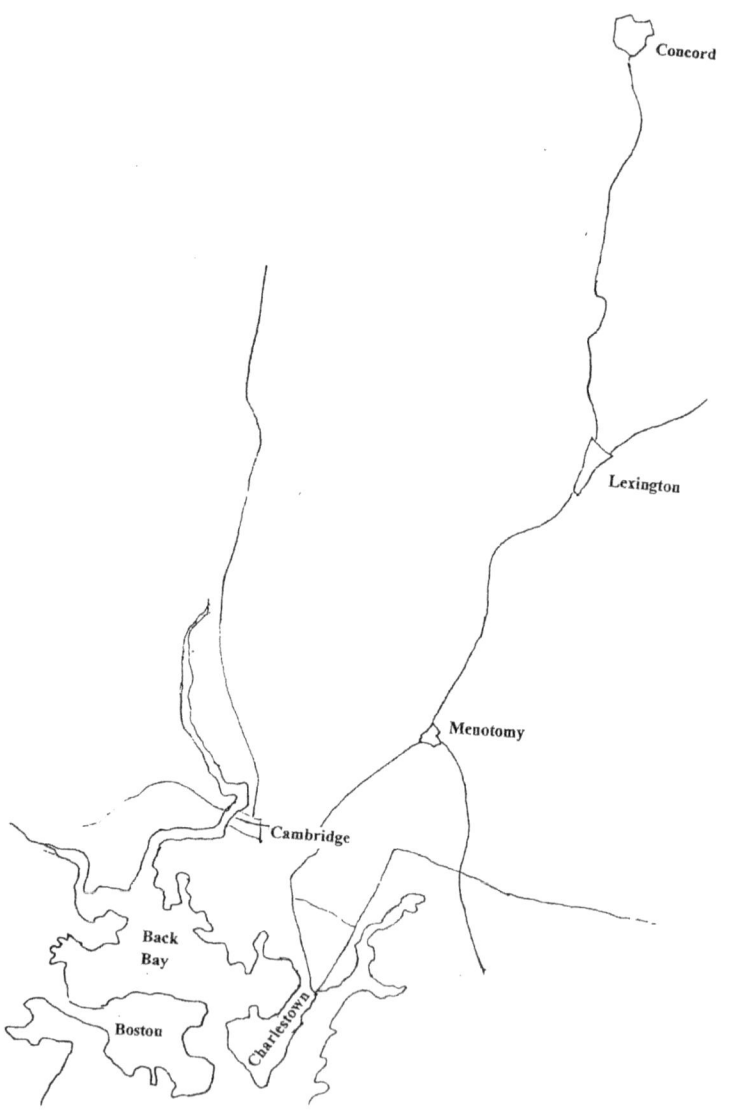

The news reached Lexington around midnight with the arrival of Paul Revere and William Dawes. Captain John Parker mustered the village militia on the green while Samuel Adams and John Hancock, who were in Lexington on their way to the Continental Congress in Philadelphia, prepared to flee.

Approximately 75 men waited on Lexington Green when the British column arrived at dawn. They were under orders to hold their fire. Similar orders were issued to the British troops, some of who formed on the green facing the militia. While two companies of British light infantry faced the militia on the green, Major John Pitcairn of the Royal Marines rode ahead and ordered the militia to lay down their arms and disperse. Captain Parker wisely ordered his men to leave the green and most were doing so when a shot rang out. Although the origin of the shot will never be known, each side believed the other fired it. The British troops on the green responded with musket fire and bayonets, all without orders. Months of pent up anger at the colonists was unleashed on the green, and for a few moments the British officers lost control of their men. Seventeen colonists were killed or wounded in the incident before the officers restored order and continued on to Concord.[2]

When the British arrived at Concord, they found little of military value there. The military supplies and militia were gone. While Colonel Smith's main body searched the town, detachments were sent beyond Concord to inspect a few sites. One of these detachments secured a bridge about half a mile from the town. They soon faced hundreds of militia who were determined to cross the bridge. Musket fire erupted from both

---

[2] Ibid., 188-200

sides and each suffered casualties.[3] The outnumbered British regulars fled back to Concord where they found Colonel Smith preparing to return to Boston. The British retraced their route, but this time they encountered hundreds of militiamen from the surrounding area who fired at them from behind stone walls, trees, and buildings. Casualties among the British officers were extreme, and by the time Colonel Smith's men reached Lexington, nearly all order had broken down.

The expedition was saved by the timely arrival of reinforcements under Lord Hugh Percy. The ever cautious General Gage had ordered Percy's 1,000 man force to follow Smith's expedition just in case trouble erupted.[4] They left Boston later than planned and arrived in Lexington just in time to save Smith's detachment.

Percy's men joined the fight, and the combined British force continued on towards Boston. The militia continued their attacks on the British and caused Lord Percy to redirect his march to Charlestown Neck, a peninsula located across the Charles River from Boston. British cannon covered the narrow crossing point of Charlestown Neck and prevented the militia from continuing their pursuit. Hundreds gathered at Cambridge and other areas outside of Boston ready to resume the fight if the British ventured out of Boston again. There was little chance of that happening. Many of Smith's and Percy's exhausted troops collapsed where they halted, desperate to rest after their long ordeal. Nearly 275 of their number were casualties of the day's fight. Less than half that number fell among the militia.[5]

---

[3] Ibid., 212-214
[4] Ibid., note 36, 412-13
[5] Ibid., 321

News of the fighting at Lexington and Concord reached southern Maine on the evening of April 19th. A company of sixty men from the town of York was the first to march to Boston, but they were stopped in New Hampshire and ordered back.[6] There was no need for short term troops to travel such a distance when thousands of troops were already outside of Boston. With the British army contained in Boston and Charlestown, the Massachusetts Provincial Congress directed its efforts towards creating a stable and long term military force to confront them. On April 23rd, the Congress authorized the recruitment of 13,600 men to serve for the remainder of the year in regiments of 600 men.[7]

Colonel James Scamman of Saco commanded one of these regiments. It was raised in York County and included men from York, Kittery, Berwick, Wells, Sanford, Biddeford, Saco, Buxton, and Arundel.[8] The regiment, designated the 30th Massachusetts Regiment by the Committee of Safety, arrived in Cambridge on May 23rd and was assigned to General William Heath's brigade.[9]

Cumberland County also raised a regiment and chose Colonel Edmund Phinney of Gorham to command it. Men from Falmouth, Gorham, Windham, North Yarmouth,

---

[6] Nathan Goold, "Capt. Johnson Moulton's Company: The First to Leave the District of Maine in the Revolution," *Collections and Proceedings of the Maine Historical Society,* 2nd ser. 10, (1899), 301

[7] Nathan Goold, "History of Col. Edmund Phinney's 31st Regiment of Foot: The First Regiment Raised in the County of Cumberland in the Revolutionary War," *Collections and Proceedings of the Maine Historical Society,* 2nd Ser. 7, (1895), 85

[8] Nathan Goold, "Col. James Scamman's 30th Regiment of Foot, 1775," *Collections and Proceedings of the Maine Historical Society,* 2nd ser. 10, (1899), 362-364

[9] Ibid., 345, 360

Scarborough, New Gloucester, and Cape Elizabeth enlisted in Phinney's 31st Massachusetts Regiment.[10] The unit's arrival at Cambridge was delayed until July by confusion over recruitment instructions and command. Some of Phinney's men also participated in an incident in Falmouth in May that reflected poorly on the town's leaders.

Thompson's War

A dispute in Falmouth that had been brewing since March erupted into a significant crisis in May when Colonel Samuel Thompson of Brunswick seized Lieutenant Henry Mowat, the commander of the H.M.S. *Canceaux*, while Mowat was ashore in Falmouth. The *Canceaux* had arrived in Falmouth in April to protect loyalist Thomas Coulson as he unloaded a shipment of rigging, sails, and ship stores from Britain that had arrived in March. The Falmouth Committee of Inspection had ruled that this shipment violated the continental boycott and refused to allow it to be unloaded, but Coulson rejected the committee's decision and turned to the British navy for protection. A stand off ensued until the *Canceaux* arrived in April, at which point Coulson, protected by the guns of the *Canceaux*, transferred the disputed goods to the ship under construction.[11] Falmouth's leaders, fearful of both mob unrest and the British navy, refused to use force against the *Canceaux* to halt the transfer and it was completed without incident.

Colonel Samuel Thompson was not so hesitant to act, however. When an opportunity arose a month later to seize

---

[10] Nathan Goold, "History of Col. Edmund Phinney's 31st Regiment of Foot," *Maine Historical Society*, 100-102
[11] Leamon, 65

the commander of the *Canceaux* while he was ashore in Falmouth, Thompson grabbed it and captured Lieutenant Mowat with a small party of armed men. Thompson hoped to use Mowat to gain control of the *Canceaux*.

Falmouth's leaders were horrified by Thompson's actions. They feared retribution from the British navy and demanded that Mowat be released. The *Canceaux* threatened to bombard Falmouth unless Mowat was immediately released, and many of Falmouth's inhabitants fled the town in panic.[12] They passed hundreds of armed men marching towards Falmouth from the surrounding communities. By nightfall, six hundred men, including some from Colonel Phinney's 31st Massachusetts Regiment, were in Falmouth ready for a fight.[13] They were outraged to learn that Falmouth's leaders had arranged for Mowat's release (on the promise that he would return the following day).

When Mowat failed to return, the militia turned their anger on Falmouth's leaders, whom they saw as weak and cowardly, and threatened to burn the town as a den of Tories. It did not help Falmouth's standing with the militia when the troops learned that town leaders had profusely apologized to Lieutenant Mowat for his treatment. The disgruntled militia ultimately spared Falmouth, but unleashed some of their wrath on suspected Tories like Samuel Coulson and William Tyng, the county sheriff.[14] Both suffered the destruction of property. The departure of Mowat and the *Canceaux* from Falmouth prompted a rapid reduction of militia in town. Most of the troops had returned to their homes by the middle of May.

---

[12] Williamson, 423
[13] Ibid.
[14] Ibid., 424 and Leamon, 66

The Margaretta Affair

Less than a month after the crisis in Falmouth, a similar incident occurred in the distant settlement of Machias. Approximately a hundred families lived in Machias in 1775, and they were all dependent on trade to supplement their food stocks.[15] As the colonial boycott continued into the summer of 1775, the inhabitants of Machias, and much of Maine, found themselves desperately low on provisions and supplies. Petitions were sent to the Massachusetts Provincial Congress in May and June pleading for relief.[16] The residents of Machias acknowledged the Provincial Congress as the guardian of the province and confidently predicted, under their guidance, "*a happy deliverance from the iron chains of tyranny.*"[17] The petition continued:

> *We, the distressed inhabitants of Machias, beg leave to approach your presence, and to spread our grievances at your feet. We dare not say we are the foremost in supporting the glorious cause of American liberty; but this we can truly affirm, that we have done our utmost to encourage and strengthen the hands of all the advocates for America with whom we have been connected; that we have not even purchased any goods of those persons, whom we*

---

[15] John Howard Ahlin, "Petition from the Residents of Machias to the Massachusetts Provincial Congress, 25 May, 1775," *Maine Rubicon: Downeast Settlers during the American Revolution*, (Camden, ME: Picton Press, 1966), 15-16

[16] Ahlin, 15-16 and Clark, "Committee of Penobscot to the Massachusetts Provincial Congress, 7 June, 1775," *Naval Documents of the American Revolution, Vol. 1,* 620

[17] Ahlin, 15-16

suspected to be [hostile] *to our country, except when constrained by necessity....*

We must now inform your honors that the inhabitants of this place exceed one hundred families, some of which are very numerous, and that divine Providence has cut off all our usual resources. A very severe drought last fall prevented our laying in sufficient stores; and had no vessels visited us in the winter, we must have suffered; nor have we this spring been able to procure provisions sufficient for carrying on our business..... We must add, we have no country behind us to lean upon, nor can we make an escape by flight; the wilderness is impervious, and vessels we have none.

To you, therefore, honored gentlemen, we humbly apply for relief. You are our last, our only resource... We cannot take a denial, for, under God, you are all our dependence, and if you neglect us, we are ruined.[18]

The Provincial Congress barely had time to consider Machias's plea when stunning news of a naval engagement between a British warship and the settlers of Machias arrived. The incident stemmed from a commercial arrangement between a Machias merchant, Ichabod Jones, and the British in Boston. Firewood and lumber were the primary commodities of Machias, and the British garrison in Boston needed both. Jones embraced this business opportunity and reached an agreement with General Gage (in violation of the boycott) to ship firewood and lumber to Boston in exchange

---
[18] Ibid.

for much needed food and supplies that he planned to sell to the inhabitants of Machias.

On June 2nd, 1775, two sloops loaded with provisions from Boston arrived at Machias escorted by the *H.M.S. Margaretta* (a lightly armed British tender). The town's freeholders were split on whether they should allow the exchange and debated the issue for days. The Reverend James Lyons, the chairman of the Machias Committee, recounted what happened:

> *On the 2d instant Capt Ichabod Jones arrived in this River with two sloops, accompanied with one of the Kings Tenders: On the 3d instant, a paper was handed about for the people to sign, as a prerequisite to their obtaining any provisions, of which we were in great want. The contents of this paper, required the signers to indulge Capt Jones in carrying Lumber to Boston, & to protect him and his property, at all events...On the 6th the people generally assembled at the place appointed, and seemed so averse to the measures proposed, that Capt. Jones privately went down to the Tender & caused her to move up so near the Town that her Guns would reach the Houses.... The people...considering themselves nearly as prisoners of war...passed a Vote, that Capt Jones might proceed in his Business as usual without molestation, that they would purchase the provisions he brought into the place and pay him according to Contract.*
>
> *After obtaining this Vote, Capt. Jones immediately ordered his Vessels to the Wharf & distributed his provisions among those only, who voted in favour of*

> *his carrying Lumber to Boston. This gave such offence to the aggrieved party, that they determined to take Capt. Jones, if possible, & put a final stop to his supplying the Kings troops with any thing.*[19]

Colonel Benjamin Foster was one of those determined to prevent this violation of the boycott. He hatched a plan to seize Jones and the British officers of the *Margaretta* while they attended church. The attempt failed when Foster's armed party was spotted approaching the Meeting House.[20] The British officers escaped to the *Margaretta,* while Captain Jones scurried off into the woods where he was eventually apprehended.

The commander of the British warship, Midshipman James Moore, vowed to protect Captain Jones and his vessels and threatened to burn the town if necessary.[21] This threat was ignored and both of Captain Jones's sloops were seized. James Lyons described what happened next:

---

[19] Clark, ed., "James Lyons, Chairman of the Machias Committee, to the Massachusetts Provincial Congress, 14 June, 1775," *Naval Documents of the American Revolution, Vol. 1,* 676-77
[20] Clark, ed., "Pilot Nathaniel Godfrey's Report on the Action Between the Schooner Margueritta and the Rebels at Machias, 11 June," 1775, *Naval Documents of the American Revolution, Vol. 1,* 655
[21] Ibid.

Map of Machias

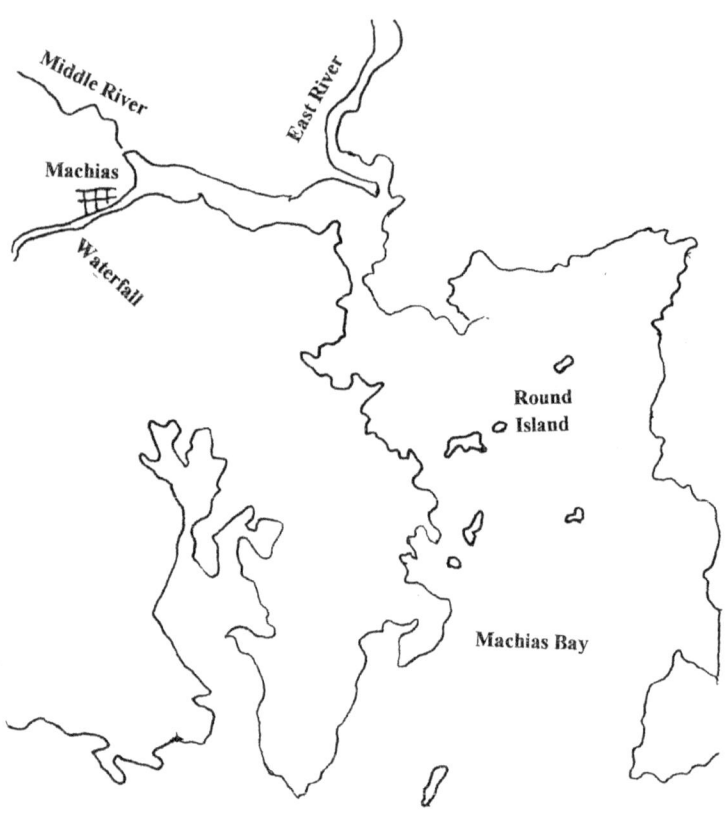

> *Upon this, a party of our men went directly to stripping the sloop that lay at the wharf, and another party went off to take possession of the other sloop which lay below & brought her up nigh a Wharf, and anchored her in the stream. The tender did not fire but weighed her anchors as privately as possible, and in the dusk of the evening fell down & came...within Musket shott of the [second] sloop, which obliged our people to slip their Cable, & run the sloop aground. In the mean time, a considerable number of our people went down in boats and canoes, lined the shore directly opposite to the Tender, and having demanded her to surrender to America, received for answer, 'fire and be damn'd': they immediately fired in upon her, which she returned, and a smart engagement ensued.*[22]

Nathaniel Godfrey, a pilot aboard the *Margaretta* who was pressed into service by the British, described the exchange:

> *Mr. Moore...was hailed on Shore by the Rebels, once more desiring him to strike to the Sons of Liberty, threatening him with Death if he resisted, upon Mr. Moore's replying he was not yet ready, they fired a Volley of small Arms, which was returned from the Schooner with Swivels and Small Arms. The Firing continued about an hour and a half, Mr. Moore then cut the Cable, drop't down Half a Mile lower, & anchored near a Sloop laden with Boards. In the*

---

[22] Clark, ed., "James Lyons, Chairman of the Machias Committee, to the Massachusetts Provincial Congress, 14 June, 1775," *Naval Documents of the American Revolution, Vol. 1*, 676-77

Night they [the Americans] *endeavoured to Board us with a Number of Boats & Canoes, but were beat off by a brisk fire from the Swivels & obliged to quit their Boats, four of which in the Morning were left upon the Flats full of holes.*[23]

By daybreak, the British commander, having re-assessed his situation, abandoned Machias (and Captain Jones) and set sail for the open sea. The *Margaretta* was peppered by musket fire from the shore, but gradually made its way towards Machias Bay.[24] The incident may have ended there, but the determination of Jeremiah O'Brien and Benjamin Foster to capture the *Margaretta* led the Americans to pursue the British in two ships. James Lyons described what happened:

Our people, seeing [the Margaretta] *go off in the morning, determined to follow her. About forty men, armed with guns, swords, axes & pick forks, went in Capt Jones's sloop, under the command of Capt Jeremiah O Brien: about Twenty, armed in the same manner, & under the command of Capt Benjamin Foster, went in a small Schooner. During the Chase, our people built them breast works of pine boards, and any thing they could find in the Vessels, that would screen them from the enemy's fire. The* [Margaretta], *upon the first appearance of our people, cut her boats from the stern, & made all the*

---

[23] Clark, ed., "Pilot Nathaniel Godfrey's Report on the Action Between the Schooner Margueritta and the Rebels at Machias, 11 June, 1775," *Naval Documents of the American Revolution, Vol. 1,* 655
[24] Ibid.

sail she could – but being a very dull sailor, they soon came up with her, and a most obstinate engagement ensued, both sides being determined to conquer or die: but the [Margaretta] *was obliged to yield, her Captain was wounded in the breast with two balls, of which wounds he died next morning.... The Battle was fought at the entrance of our harbour, & lasted for over the space of one hour.*[25]

Nathaniel Godfrey, aboard the *Margaretta*, also described the engagement:

A Sloop & Schooner appeared, we immediately weighed Anchor & stood out for the Sea, they coming up with us very fast, we began to fire our Stern Swivels, & small Arms as soon as within reach. When within hail, they again desired us to strike to the Sons of Liberty, promising to treat us well, but if we made any resistance they [would] *put us to Death. Mr. Moore seeing there was no possibility of getting clear,* [swung] *the Vessel too and gave them a Broadside with Swivels & Small Arms in the best manner he was able, and likewise threw some Hand Grenadoes into them; they immediately laid us Onboard,* [mortally wounded Mr. Moore and] *took possession of the Schooner* [carrying] *her up to Mechias, in great triumph....*[26]

---

[25] Clark, ed., "James Lyons, Chairman of the Machias Committee, to the Massachusetts Provincial Congress, 14 June, 1775," *Naval Documents of the American Revolution, Vol. 1*, 676-77

[26] Clark, ed., "Pilot Nathaniel Godfrey's Report...11 June, 1775," *Naval Documents of the American Revolution, Vol. 1*, 655-56

The bold actions of the people of Machias, which resulted in the loss of a handful of men on both sides and the capture of a British warship and two other vessels, garnered the thanks of the Massachusetts Provincial Congress in late June.[27] Appreciation was also extended to the efforts of two young ladies from Jonesborough, sixteen year old Hannah Weston and her sister-in-law Rebecca, who gathered lead, pewter, and powder from the surrounding communities and travelled sixteen miles over rough terrain to deliver their much needed military supplies to Machias.[28]

In July, more good news reached Cambridge when it was reported that Captain O' Brien, aboard the same vessel that captured the *Margaretta*, surprised the British schooner *Diligent* and captured it without loss.[29] The British commanders in Boston undoubtedly wished to retaliate against Machias, but they had their hands full with the situation in Boston.

By the time word reached Boston of the capture of the *Margaretta*, the siege of Boston was two months old. Thousands of New England troops, including hundreds from the counties of York, Cumberland, and Lincoln, encircled the British troops in Boston. Many of the Massachusetts men had enlisted in eight month regiments authorized by the Provincial Congress a few days after Lexington. They were encamped at Cambridge, Roxbury, and on the many hills outside of Boston. Their large number compensated for their lack of organization and helped persuade General Gage to remain in Boston.

---

[27] Williamson, 431
[28] Ahlin, 22
[29] Ibid.

Not everyone was impressed by the Americans, however. One British surgeon who visited the American lines observed that

> *This army...is truly nothing but a drunken, canting, lying, praying, hypocritical rabble, without order, subjugation, discipline, or cleanliness; and must fall to pieces of itself in the course of three months.*[30]

Concern about the viability of the army caused the Massachusetts Provincial Congress to request that the Continental Congress take charge of the army in early June. Congress did so on June 14th, and expanded the army by adding ten rifle companies from Pennsylvania, Virginia, and Maryland.[31] These companies were ordered to join the newly designated Continental army in Massachusetts as soon as possible.

The army's new commander in chief, General George Washington of Virginia, was also ordered to Massachusetts. The surprising choice of a Virginian to command what was primarily a New England army was meant to encourage the southern colonies to take a more active role in the conflict. General Washington, who was a delegate to the Continental Congress, left Philadelphia on June 23rd and arrived in Cambridge on July 3rd, two weeks after the Battle of Bunker Hill.

---

[30] Henry Steele Commager and Richard B. Morris, ed. *The Spirit of Seventy-Six*, (New York: Harper Collins, 2002), 152 (Originally published in 1958)
[31] Journals of the Continental Congress, June 14, 1775 (accessed thru the Library of Congress website)

Bunker Hill

On the evening of June 16th, Colonel William Prescott of Massachusetts led hundreds of troops from their camp at Cambridge onto Charlestown peninsula. His objective was to fortify Bunker Hill and increase the pressure on the British in Boston. After consulting with his officers, Colonel Prescott decided to march past Bunker Hill and fortify Breed's Hill, which was closer to Boston. Prescott's men began work on an earthen redoubt and breastwork around midnight. At dawn, British sailors in the Charles River noticed the Americans and sounded the alarm with cannon fire. The tired Americans soon found themselves under a steady bombardment from the British navy. As noon approached, the exhausted Americans wondered where their relief and reinforcements were. One solder recalled:

> [At] *about eleven oClock...they began to fire as brisk as ever, which caus'd many of our young Country people to desert, apprehending the danger in a clearer manner than others who were more diligent in digging, & fortifying ourselves against them. We began to be almost beat out, being fatigued by our Labour, having no sleep the night before, very little to eat, no drink but rum, but what we hazarded our lives to get, we grew faint, Thirsty, hungry and weary.*[32]

---

[32] Letter from Peter Brown to his Mother, 25 June, 1775 Massachusetts Historical Society

Battle of Bunker Hill

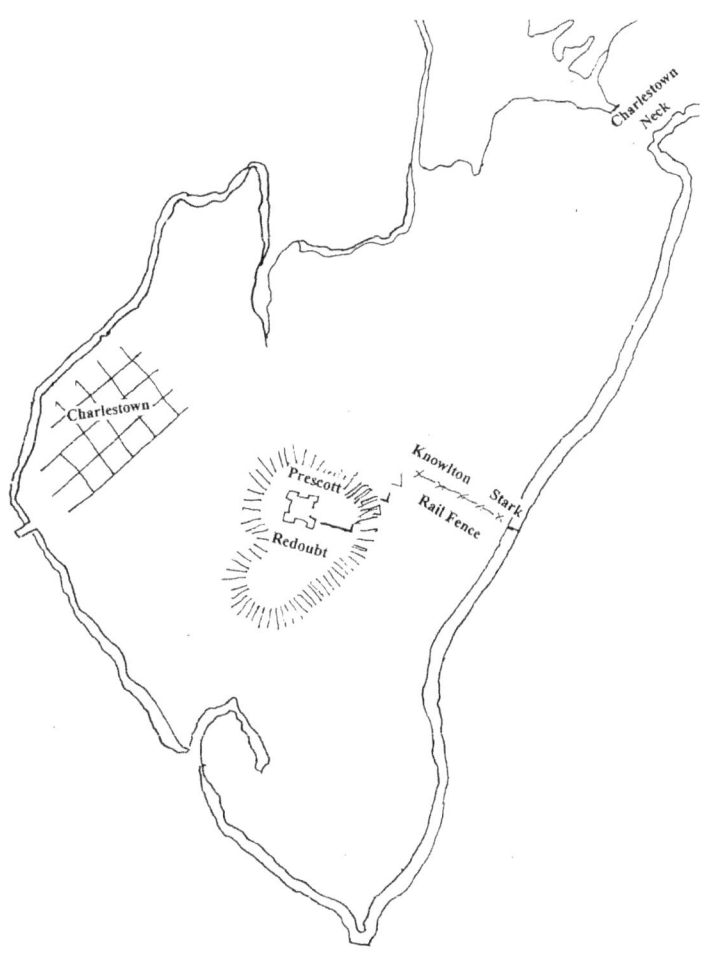

Many of Colonel Prescott's men were angered at the absence of American artillery to respond to the British:

> *Our Officers sent time after time for Cannon from Cambridge in the Morning & could get but four, the Captn of which fir'd a few times then swung his Hat three times round to the enemy and ceas'd to fire.*[33]

Although artillery support was a disappointment to the Americans, Prescott did receive infantry reinforcements. Colonel John Stark arrived in the early afternoon with hundreds of troops from New Hampshire. Stark reinforced a detachment of Connecticut militia under Captain Thomas Knowlton who were posted along a low stone wall and rail fence about 300 yards behind and to the left of Breed's Hill. The gap between the hill and rail fence was covered by three fleches (v-shaped breastworks) positioned at right angles to the redoubt and breastwork. Colonel Prescott also sent men into Charlestown, on the opposite side of Breed's Hill, to screen the American right flank. Lastly, Colonel Stark erected a breastwork along the narrow shore of the Mystic River to protect the extreme left flank of the American position. The total American force that stretched across Charlestown peninsula was around 1200 men.[34] They were tired, hungry, and low on ammunition, but determined to make a stand.

By early afternoon, it was apparent to everyone that the British army was going to attack. They crossed the Charles River in long boats and formed along the southern end of Charlestown peninsula. General Gage placed General

---

[33] Ibid.
[34] Richard Ketchum, *Decisive Day: The Battle for Bunker Hill*, (New York: Henry Holt and Co., 1962), 160, 245

William Howe, who had only recently arrived in Boston, in command of the assault. Howe hoped to break through the American left with an attack along the Mystic River shore and the rail fence line while General Robert Pigot attacked the Americans in the redoubt.

Colonel Stark had anticipated such a move and covered the shore with a large number of troops. When the British light infantry, marching only four across because of the narrow shoreline, came within fifty yards of Stark's New Hampshire troops, they unleashed a murderous fire on the British. The Redcoats were repulsed and suffered nearly 100 casualties.[35] Similar results occurred at the rail fence and at the redoubt. At both positions the Americans displayed outstanding fire discipline and waited until the British were within point blank range before they leveled devastating volleys into their ranks. The stunned British withdrew on all fronts.

They soon returned, bloodied but resolved to break the American line. The second British assault concentrated on the rail fence and redoubt. Once again the Americans displayed amazing fire discipline, holding their fire until the British came within a hundred feet. They then unleashed devastating volleys that decimated the British ranks. One British officer described the carnage inflicted on the British at the rail fence:

> *Most of our Grenadiers and Light-infantry, the moment of presenting themselves lost three-fourths, and many nine-tenths, of their men. Some had only eight or nine men a company left; some only three, four, and five....*"[36]

---

[35] Ketchum, 160
[36] Ibid., 161-62

While a pitched battle raged at the rail fence, Colonel Prescott's men repulsed another British attack on the redoubt. Prescott described this part of the battle to John Adams in a letter:

> *The Enemy advanced and fired very hotly on the Fort and meeting with a Warm Reception there was a very smart firing on both sides, after a considerable Time finding our Ammunition was almost spent I commanded a sessation till the Enemy advanced within 30 yards when we gave them such a hot fire, that they were obliged to retire nearly 150 yards before they could Rally and come again to the Attack.*[37]

Despite their enormous casualties, the British would not quit and General Howe called up his reserves for a third assault. Howe's third attack was an all out bayonet charge against Prescott's redoubt and breastwork. The British attacked the position from three directions and did not stop to fire. By this point many of the Americans were out of ammunition so resistance to the British advance was much reduced. Colonel Prescott described what happened:

> *Our Ammunition being nearly exhausted* [we] *could keep up only a scattering Fire. The Enemy being numerous surrounded our little Fort begun to mount our Lines and enter with their Bayonets, we were obliged to retreat through them while they kept up as hot a fire as it was possible for them to make. We*

---

[37] Letter from William Prescott to John Adams, 25 August, 1775 Massachusetts Historical Society

having very few Bayonets could make no resistance. We kept the fort about one hour and twenty Minutes after the Attack with small Arms.[38]

British Lieutenant John Waller participated in the third assault and described the scene within the redoubt once the British breached the American walls:

I cannot pretend to describe the Horror of the Scene within the Redoubt when we enter'd it, 'twas streaming with Blood & strew'd with dead & dying Men the Soldiers stabbing some and dashing out the Brains of others was a sight too dreadful for me to dwell any longer on.[39]

General Joseph Warren, president of the Massachusetts Provincial Congress but only a volunteer private in the battle, was killed in the assault as were scores of other Americans. Those that could fled to the rear, past Bunker Hill and across Charlestown Neck. Colonel Stark and his men at the rail fence realized that their position was untenable and joined the flight to the rear. The British were victorious at the Battle of Bunker Hill and controlled Charlestown peninsula, but the cost of their victory, approximately 1,150 casualties to 440 for the Americans, was enormous.[40] The combined British losses from Concord and Bunker Hill accounted for nearly a quarter of the army, and yet, the British remained firmly in Boston. Some in Congress hoped that the arrival of General George

---
[38] Ibid.
[39] Letter from Lt. J. Waller to a Friend, 21 June, 1775, Massachusetts Historical Society
[40] Mark M. Boatner, *Encyclopedia of the American Revolution*, (Stackpole Books, 1966), 129

Washington, the new commander in chief of the army, would change this.

Siege of Boston

General Washington arrived in Cambridge on July 3rd. He found an army of about 14,000 effective men spread out around Boston in haphazard camps.[41] One visitor to the American lines observed that the encampments

> *Are as different in their form as the owners are in their dress: and every tent is a portraiture of the temper and taste of the persons that incamp in it. Some are made of boards, some of sailcloth, and some partly of one and partly of the other. Others are made of stone and turf, and others again of birch and others brush. Some are thrown up in a hurry and look as if they could not help it, others are curiously wrought with doors and windows down with wreaths....*[42]

Hundreds of troops from Maine, primarily concentrated in the regiments of Colonel James Scamman (550 men) and Colonel Edmund Phinney (400 men), were part of this army.[43]

---

[41] Philander D. Chase, ed. "General Washington to Richard Henry Lee, 10 July, 1775," *The Papers of George Washington, Revolutionary War Series, Vol. 1* (Charlottesville: University Press of Virginia, 1985), 99
[42] Commager and Morris, ed. *The Spirit of Seventy-Six*, 152
[43] Nathan Goold, "Col. James Scamman's 30th Regiment of Foot, 1775," *Collections and Proceedings of the Maine Historical Society*, 2nd ser. 10, 345 and "History of Col. Edmund Phinney's 31st Regiment of Foot," *Collections and Proceedings of the Maine Historical Society*, 2nd Ser. 7, 93

Colonel Scamman endured the embarrassment of a court martial in July for his actions (or lack of) at Bunker Hill. He was charged with cowardice for not leading his regiment to Breed's Hill during the battle. The court acquitted him when it was revealed that the orders Scammon received were unclear. Nevertheless, his reputation was tarnished by the affair.

Colonel Phinney's regiment of Cumberland County troops arrived in Cambridge a month after Bunker Hill. A portion of the regiment remained in Maine to help defend Cumberland and Lincoln counties from possible British raids.[44] Both regiments were attached to General William Heath's brigade and took their place among the civilian army.

It did not take General Washington long to realize that he faced an enormous challenge in leading such a force. He expressed his disappoint with the New England army in mid-August in a letter home:

The People of this Government have obtained a Character they by no means deserved – their Officers generally speaking are the most indifferent kind of People I ever saw. I have already broken one Colo. And five Captains for Cowardice & for drawing more Pay & Provisions than they had men in their Companies...in short they are by no means such Troops, in any respect, as you are led to believe of them from the Accts which are published, but I need not make myself Enemies among them, by this declaration, although it is consistent with truth. I

---

[44] Nathan Goold, "History of Col. Edmund Phinney's 31st Regiment of Foot," *Collections and Proceedings of the Maine Historical Society*, 2nd Ser. 7, 93

> *daresay the Men would fight very well (if properly Officered) although they are an exceedingly dirty & nasty people....* [45]

General Washington's disappointment continued into September when a mutiny among a company of Pennsylvania riflemen erupted. The mutiny was suppressed without bloodshed, but added to Washington's many concerns. He revealed these concerns to John Hancock and Congress on September 21st:

> *My Situation is inexpressibly distressing, to see the Winter fast approaching upon a naked Army: The Time of their Service within a few Weeks of expiring, & no Provision, yet made of such important Events. Added to these, the Military Chest is totally exhausted. The Paymaster has not a single Dollar in Hand. The Commissary General assures me, he has strained his Credit for the Subsistence of the Army to the utmost. The Quarter Master General is precisely in the same situation: And the greater Part of the Troops are in a State not far from Mutiny, upon the Deduction from their stated Allowance. I know not to whom I am to impute this Failure, but I am of Opinion, if the Evil is not immediately remedied & more punctuality observed in future, the Army must absolutely break up.* [46]

---

[45] Chase, ed. "General Washington to Lund Washington, 20 August, 1775," *The Papers of George Washington, Revolutionary War Series, Vol. 1,* 335-36

[46] Chase, ed. "General Washington to John Hancock, 21 September 1775," *The Papers of George Washington, Revolutionary War Series, Vol. 2,* 29

The siege itself developed into a monotonous routine. Washington described it to his brother in late September:

> *So little hath happened of consequence since my last, that I should hardly have given you the trouble of a Letter at this time.... The Enemy keep themselves close shut up within their own Lines on Boston & Charles Town Necks, & are to all intents & purposes as much besieged as ever Troops were that had an opening to the Sea – They are constantly Cannonading & Bombarding us without any damage to our works & almost as little hurt to the Men; but take care never to advance beyond their own Works.*[47]

Destruction of Falmouth

Although the British army was relatively inactive in the second half of 1775, the British navy was not. Admiral Samuel Graves was determined to retaliate for a number of incidents including the embarrassing loss of the *Margaretta* at Machias in June. In October, a small British squadron sailed from Boston with orders to

> *Chastize Marblehead, Salem, Newbury Port, Cape Anne Harbour, Portsmouth, Ipsich, Saco, Falmouth in Casco Bay, and particularly Mechias where the Margaretta was taken, the Officer commanding her killed, and the People made Prisoners, and where the*

---

[47] Chase, ed. "General Washington to Samuel Washington, 30 September, 1775," *The Papers of George Washington, Revolutionary War Series*, Vol. 2, 72

> *Diligent Schooner was seized and the Officers and Crew carried up the Country, and where preparations I am informed are now making to invade the Province of Nova Scotia. You are to go to all or to as many of the above named Places as you can, and make the most vigorous Efforts to burn the Towns, and destroy the Shipping in the Harbours.*[48]

Admiral Graves gave Lieutenant Henry Mowat, the commander of the British squadron, the discretion as to how to execute his orders. As it turned out, only one town bore the brunt of Mowat's wrath, Falmouth.

Mowat's squadron arrived at Falmouth on October 16th, and immediately provoked the ire of the townspeople by firing on a small schooner in the harbor that refused to heave to. The Reverend Jacob Bailey witnessed the incident and recalled that

> *Notwithstanding the discharge of several muskets and two cannon* [from the British, the schooner] *escaped in safety to the town. The populace, which were gazing by hundreds, were immediately thrown into furious agitation by this incident, and vowed revenge with the utmost menace and caution. The Committee, composed of tradesmen and persons of no property, prompted only for a flaming zeal for the liberty of their country, were not less enraged at this hostile appearance and...ordered the company of*

---

[48] Clark, ed., "Vice Admiral Graves to Lieutenant Henry Mowat, H.M. Armed Vessel Canceaux, 6 October, 1775," *Naval Documents of the American Revolution, Vol. 2,* 324

> guards to...secure the cattle, intimidate the tories and observe the motions of the enemy.[49]

The townsfolk endured an anxious evening and grew more troubled the next day when they observed the squadron position itself as if to bombard the town. Reverend Bailey recalled,

> *The whole fleet stood directly up the river, and formed in line of battle before the town. We now plainly discovered one ship of twenty guns, one of sixteen, a large schooner of fourteen, a bomb sloop and two other armed vessels.*[50]

Many of Falmouth's residents were confused by the hostile movement of the flotilla because they believed that Lieutenant Mowat held Falmouth in high regard for its assistance in foiling Samuel Thompson's efforts to capture the *Canceaux* in May.[51] They soon learned otherwise when Mowat sent an officer ashore with a dire warning to the townspeople. Reverend Bailey recalled that

> [The officer] *landed at the lower end of King street, amid a prodigious assembly of people, which curiosity and expectation had drawn together from every quarter. Some of the multitude appeared in arms, who united with the rest to convey the officer with uncommon parade and ceremony along the*

---

[49] Clark, ed., "Letter from Rev. Jacob Bailey, 16 October, 1775," *Naval Documents of the American Revolution, Vol. 2*, 471
[50] Ibid., 487
[51] Clark, ed., "Narrative of Daniel Tucker of Falmouth, 17 October, 1775," *Naval Documents of the American Revolution, Vol. 2*, 488

street to the Town House. His entrance was immediately followed by a confused mixture, which filled the apartment with noise and tumult.[52]

The British officer stunned the gathering with a shocking proclamation from Lieutenant Mowat:

After so many premeditated Attacks on the legal Prerogatives of the best of Sovereigns; After the repeated Instances [of] *Britain's long forbearance of the Rod of Correction; and the Merciful and Paternal extension of her Hands to embrace you, again and again, have been regarded as vain and nugatory. And in place of a dutiful and grateful return to your King and Parent state; you have been guilty of the most unpardonable Rebellion.... Having it in orders to execute a just Punishment on the Town of Falmouth...I warn you to remove without delay the Human Species out of the said town; for which purpose I give you the time of two hours.*[53]

Lieutenant Mowat gave the residents of Falmouth just two hours to evacuate the town and avoid the imminent bombardment. Reverend Bailey described the reaction of the townspeople to Mowat's proclamation:

---

[52] Ibid.
[53] Clark, ed., "Lieutenant Henry Mowat to the People of Falmouth, 16 October, 1775," *Naval Documents of the American Revolution, Vol. 2,* 471

> *It is impossible to describe the amazement which prevailed upon reading this alarming declaration: a frightful consternation ran through the assembly, every heart was seized with terror, every countenance changed colour, and a profound silence ensured for several moments. During the astonishment which had seized the multitude, I quitted the apartment of justice and became a spectator on what passed in the street, where nothing occurred but scenes of tumult, confusion, and bustle.*[54]

A small committee was hastily formed to appeal to Lieutenant Mowat directly, and he agreed to delay the bombardment until the next morning if the townspeople delivered up their arms. A handful of weapons were delivered in the evening as a gesture of good will. This prompted Lieutenant Mowat to proclaim

> *If the town would surrender their cannon and musketry, and give hostages for their future good behaviour, he would delay the execution of his orders till he could represent their situation to the Admiral, and intercede for their final deliverance.*[55]

Panic swept through Falmouth on the evening of October 17th, as residents scrambled to save what possessions they could from the impending bombardment. At the same time, militia from surrounding communities arrived and added to

---

[54] Clark, ed., "Letter from Rev. Jacob Bailey, 17 October, 1775," *Naval Documents of the American Revolution, Vol. 2,* 487
[55] Ibid., 488

the confusion. It appears that in all the chaos little consideration was given to Lieutenant Mowat's demand that the town's cannon and muskets, along with a few hostages, be delivered to him by 9:00 a.m. As a result, the committee returned to Mowat at 8:30 a.m. the next morning to inform him that,

> *To their...astonishment, they found that no part of the Inhabitants* [had] *assembled in the morning,* [to hand over their muskets] *and that the whole town was then in the greatest confusion, with many women and children still remaining in it.*[56]

Mowat allowed the 9:00 a.m. deadline to pass to let stragglers in the town flee inland and commenced the bombardment at 9:40 a.m. Reverend Bailey described the destruction:

> *The cannon began to roar with incessant and tremendous fury.... In a few minutes the whole town was involved in smoak and combustion. About a thousand men in arms attended this scene of devastation, besides a prodigious number of both sexes, without attempting any repulsion. The bombardment continued from half after nine till sunset, during which all the lower end and middle of the town was reduced to a heap of rubbish. Several houses in the back street and in the upper part, together with the church shared the same fate. The front of the Meeting house was torn to pieces by the*

---

[56] Clark, ed., "Lieutenant Henry Mowat to Vice Admiral Samuel Graves, 19 October, 1775," *Naval Documents of the American Revolution, Vol. 2,* 515

bursting of a bomb, and the buildings which were left standing had their glass windows broken, and both walls and apartments terribly shattered. In a word about three quarters of the town was consumed and between two and three hundred families who twenty four hours before enjoyed in tranquility their commodious habitations, were now in many instances destitute of a hut for themselves and families, and as a tedious winter was approaching they had before them a most gloomy and distressing prospect.[57]

The bombardment lasted until nightfall, after which the British squadron, low on ammunition, sailed out of Falmouth harbor with two captured vessels. Eleven other boats were destroyed in the harbor.[58]

The once proud community of Falmouth, the largest town in Maine with nearly 4,000 inhabitants, was left a smoldering ruin.[59] British landing parties had added to the destruction by coming ashore with torches to set fires where the shells failed to do so. Despite the presence of hundreds of armed militia, no effective opposition was offered against Mowat's landing parties or the bombardment. This became a point of criticism for people who believed that Falmouth got what it deserved for its timid response to Mowat. Daniel Tucker, an inhabitant of Falmouth and a witness to the destruction, defended the town from such criticism:

---

[57] Clark, ed., "Letter from Rev. Jacob Bailey, 18 October, 1775," *Naval Documents of the American Revolution, Vol. 2,* 500
[58] Donald A. Yerxa, "The Burning of Falmouth, 1775: A Case Study in British Imperial Pacification," *Maine Historical Society Quarterly,* Vol. 14, 142
[59] Leamon, 9

Map of Falmouth

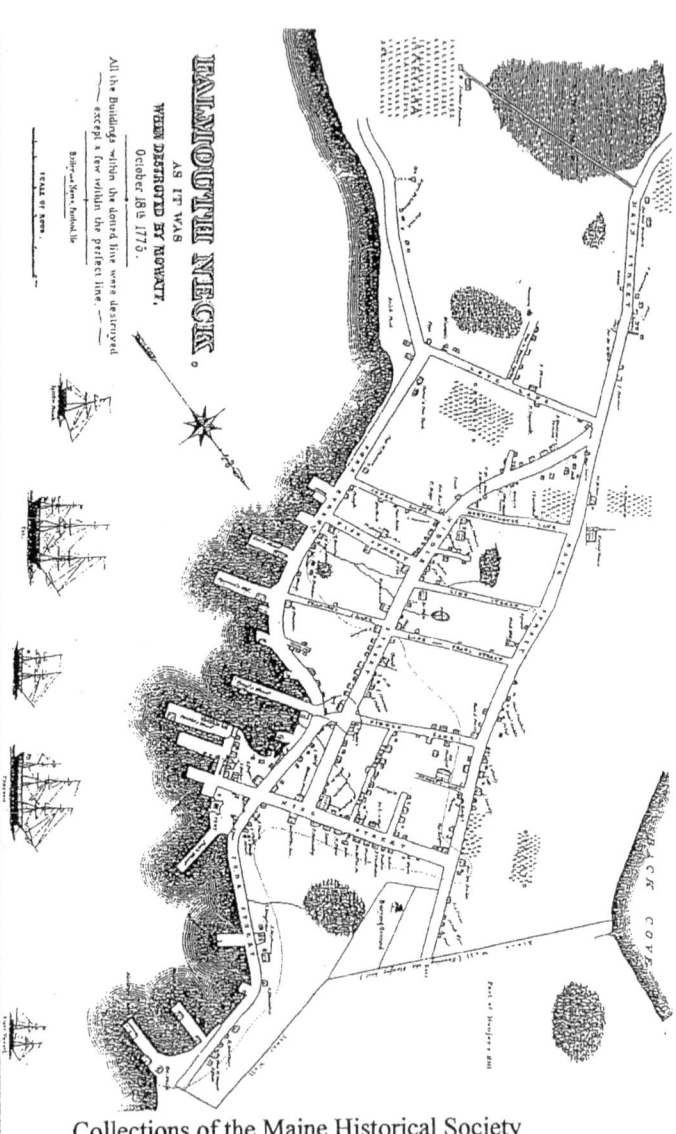

Collections of the Maine Historical Society
Map F 468 Item # 4176 on www.MaineMemory.net

> *Many people have blamed the inhabitants of Falmouth for not defending the town against so small a force: but the truth is it was not in their power, for there was not a cannon mounted in town at that time, and there was a great scarcity of powder.*[60]

A scarcity of gunpowder was something that General Washington knew all too much about. He had been concerned about the shortage of gunpowder in Cambridge for weeks and, despite the obvious need for gunpowder in Falmouth, was forced to decline a request from the Falmouth Committee of Safety for a supply of it on October 24th:

> *The Desolation and Misery which...has been so lately brought on the Town of Falmouth, I know not, how Sufficiently to detest. Nor can my Compassion for the general Suffering, be Conceived beyond the true Measure of my Feelings. But my Readiness to relieve you, by complying with your Request* [for assistance] *is Circumscribed by my Inability. The immediate necessities of the Army under my Command, require all the Powder & Ball, that can be collected with the utmost Industry & Trouble.*[61]

---

[60] Clark, ed., "Narrative of Daniel Tucker of Falmouth, 18 October, 1775," *Naval Documents of the American Revolution, Vol. 2,* 500-01
[61] Chase, ed. "General Washington to the Falmouth Committee of Safety, 24 October, 1775," *The Papers of George Washington, Revolutionary War Series, Vol. 2,* 225-26

The Falmouth Committee of Safety expressed its disappointment with Washington's decision in a letter announcing the arrival of yet another British ship, the *Cerberus* (20 guns), on November 2nd :

> *It gives us inexpressible Concern to find that it is out of your Power to afford us any Aid. And we are the more concerned, on the Arrival yesterday of the ship Cerberus* [with 400 men]...*How soon they will penetrate the Country, God only knows, for what can a People do without Arms & Ammunition to defend themselves. The Poor distress'd People drove from their Habitations by the late cruel destruction of the Town, can scarcely find sufficient Places for their accommodation, & the Country is so engaged for making provision for them, that we find it difficult to raise the Militia for our present defense. But we have only two half barrels of Powder in Stock, & we almost fear to make an Opposition...We are in great want of some Person of a martial Spirit to conduct the few Forces we already have.*[62]

The arrival of the *Cerberus* threw Falmouth into a new frenzy. It's commander, Captain John Symons, threatened to unleash "*the most vigorous efforts*" against Falmouth if troops were raised or military works erected in response to his

---

[62] Chase, ed. "The Falmouth Committee of Safety to General Washington, 2 November, 1775," *The Papers of George Washington, Revolutionary War Series, Vol. 2,* 286-87

arrival.[63] Reverend Samuel Deane described the response of the inhabitants:

> *The Militia is call'd in, and they with part of the soldiery, are gone to throw up some breast works this night, so that we expect a cannonade at least tomorrow morng. We have cannon that would be able to annoy the ship much if we had ammunition: But we have not half enough for our small arms. Symons has asked for a few cattle and offer'd pay for them and has been refused.*[64]

The unexpected resolve of the militia surprised Captain Symons. Jonathan Mitchell, Chairman of the Cumberland County Convention, explained what happened:

> *A number of the Militia and soldiers repaired to Falmouth...but, the weather being very stormy, nothing could be done till [November 4], when the ground was viewed, the men put under some regulation, and tools prepared to begin an intrenchment that night, (while Captain Symons, not thinking it proper to stay and see his orders put in execution, came to sail in the evening, and went out of the harbour.) The men accordingly broke ground, and worked most of the night, and have continued to do so ever since...while we have some who are fitting out the few cannon we have for use, with a small*

---

[63] Clark, ed., "Captain John Symons to the People of Falmouth, 1 November, 1775," *Naval Documents of the American Revolution, Vol. 2*, 831-32

[64] Clark, ed., "Rev. Samuel Deane to Benjamin Greenleaf, 4 November, 1775," *Naval Documents of the American Revolution, Vol. 2*, 877

> *matter of powder we have got, but our want of men, and want of powder, and other military stores, throw us into great anxiety.*[65]

General Washington tried to relieve some of this anxiety by sending Colonel Edmund Phinney to Falmouth to "*raise all the force you can and give the Town every assistance in* [your] *power.*"[66] Thankfully for the inhabitants of the town, the departure of the *Cerberus* marked an end to major British operations in Maine until 1777.

With the crisis in Falmouth over, General Washington turned his full attention to his own troops. The situation in Washington's army was grave due to the lack of supplies and a steady decline of troops. Benjamin Thompson noted the deplorable condition of the army in November:

> *The army in general is not very badly accoutered, but most wretchedly clothed, and as dirty a set of mortals as ever disgraced the name of a soldier...They have no women in the camp to do washing for the men, and they in general not being used to doing things of this sort, and thinking it rather a disparagement to them, choose rather to let their linen rot upon their backs than to be at the trouble of cleaning 'em themselves.*[67]

---

[65] Clark, ed., "Cumberland County Convention to the Massachusetts General Court, 8 November, 1775," *Naval Documents of the American Revolution, Vol. 2*, 926-27

[66] Chase, ed. "General Washington to Colonel Edmund Phinney, 6 November, 1775," *The Papers of George Washington, Revolutionary War Series, Vol. 2*, 314

[67] Commager and Morris, ed. *The Spirit of Seventy-Six*, 153-54

Thompson also noted that illness was widespread due to a diet based primarily on meat, and there was little discipline or subordination. He closed with the comment that "*The soldiers in general are most heartily sick of the service....*"[68] General Washington was well aware of the low morale of his men and lamented to Lieutenant Colonel Joseph Reed in late November about the difficulty of raising new recruits to replace the bulk of the steadily shrinking army:

> *Such a dirty, mercenary Spirit pervades the whole, that I should not be at all surprized at any disaster that may happen. In short, after the last of this Month, our lines will be so weakened that the Minute Men and Militia must be call'd in for their defence – these being under no kind of Government themselves, will destroy the little subordination I have been labouring to establish, and run me into one evil, whilst I am endeavouring to avoid another...Could I have forseen what I have & am like to experience, no consideration upon Earth should have induced me to accept this Command.*[69]

Washington was not completely crestfallen, however. He remained hopeful that an expeditionary force that he sent to Canada in September would meet with success and significantly alter the situation in North America.

---

[68] Ibid.
[69] Chase, ed. "General Washington to Lieutenant Colonel Joseph Reed, 28 November, 1775," *The Papers of George Washington, Revolutionary War Series, Vol. 2,* 449

Chapter Four

"Never perhaps was there a more forlorn set of human beings"
1775

On June 27th, 1775, three and a half months before the destruction of Falmouth, the Continental Congress took the bold measure of authorizing an invasion of Canada. With General Washington and the main American army tied down in Boston, Congress looked to General Philip Schuyler of New York to "*promote the peace and security of these Colonies*," by securing Canada.[1] Congress hoped that the expulsion of British troops from Canada would deny Britain a base of operation to attack the colonies and limit their ability to incite the Indians.[2] Two months passed before General Schuyler was ready to march. His 2,000 man force assembled at Fort Ticonderoga and started north up Lake Champlain in late August. Days before Schuyler's departure, General Washington revealed to Schuyler a daring plan to support Schuyler's attack on Canada. Washington would send an expedition of his own to Canada through the Maine wilderness to attack the British at Quebec.[3] General Guy Carleton, the British commander in Canada, would be trapped in an American pincer movement and his small force of British troops would be overwhelmed from two directions.

---

[1] Journals of the Continental Congress, June 27, 1775
[2] Chase, ed., "Richard Henry Lee to General Washington, 29 June, 1775," *The Papers of George Washington, Revolutionary Series, Vol. 1*, 45
[3] Chase, ed., "General Washington to Maj. General Philip Schuyler, 20 August, 1775," *The Papers of George Washington, Vol. 1*, 332

Arnold's March to Quebec

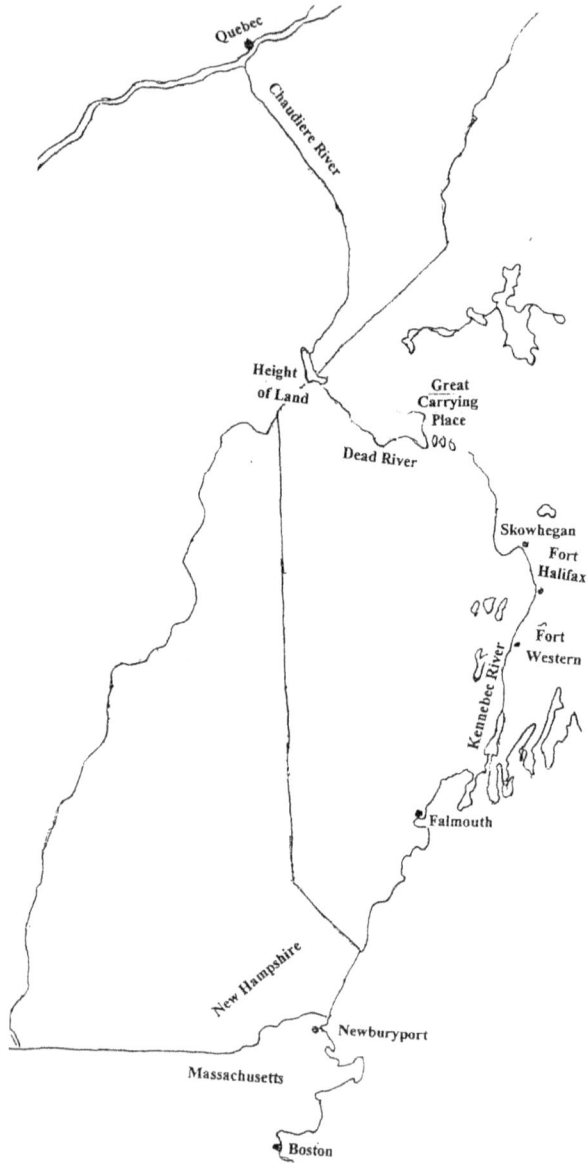

It is difficult to say with certainty where General Washington got the idea that a march through Maine to Quebec was feasible, but one person who may have influenced him was Reuben Colburn, a sawmill owner and boat builder from Gardiner, Maine. Colburn arrived in Cambridge in mid-August in the company of a small delegation of Abenaki Indians led by Chief Swashan. Unhappy with British rule in Canada, Chief Swashan and his entourage traveled through the Maine wilderness and down the Kennebec River where Colburn encountered them. Colburn accompanied them to Cambridge where Chief Swashan offered his services to General Washington. The arrival of Chief Swashan and his men from Canada confirmed reports that a passage to Quebec via Maine was possible.[4]

General Washington began plans for a second expedition to Canada and selected Colonel Benedict Arnold of Connecticut to command it. Washington instructed Colburn to return to Maine and construct 200 bateaux (heavy, canoe like boats used to haul supplies on rivers and lakes) at his sawmill and boatyard on the Kennebec River. Colburn was also instructed to gather provisions and intelligence about the route to Canada.[5]

Colburn rushed back to Maine to gather the necessary men and supplies to complete these tasks. By early September, Colburn's boatyard was humming with activity. Unfortunately, there was not enough seasoned wood or nails for such a large number of bateaux, so the boats were not built very well. Nevertheless, when Arnold's lead elements arrived on September 21st, 200 bateaux were waiting for them.

---

[4] Arthur S. Lefkowitz, *Benedict Arnold's Army: The 1775 American Invasion of Canada During the Revolutionary War*, (NY & CA: Savas Beatie, 2008), 26-27

[5] Chase, ed., "Instructions to Reuben Colburn, 3 September 1775," *The Papers of George Washington, Vol. 1,* 409-10

When Colonel Arnold's 1100 man expedition entered the mouth of the Kennebec River on September 20th, it had just passed its second week of existence. Formed from Washington's army at Boston, Arnold's detachment consisted of three rifle companies from Pennsylvania and Virginia and ten musket companies from New England. General Washington's orders specified that only *"active Woodsmen...well acquainted with bateaus"* should volunteer for this service and many of those selected would prove their worthiness along the march.[6]

One of the musket companies selected for the expedition hailed from the region around present day Bath, Maine. Captain Samuel McCobb and his men were eager to leave the stalemate at Boston and participate in an attack on Quebec. McCobb sailed ahead of the expedition to recruit more men from coastal Maine while his company gathered with the rest of Arnold's force at Newburyport for the one day voyage to the Kennebec River. Eleven ships crowded with men and supplies left Newburyport on September 19th, and arrived safely at the mouth of the Kennebec River the next day. The flotilla anchored near Arrowsic Island for the evening, where Captain McCobb rejoined the expedition with twenty new recruits.

Arnold's fleet, with the help of local pilots, slowly sailed upriver. It entered Merrymeeting Bay and continued on past the ruins of Fort Richmond. When they reached Pownalborough (Dresden) some of the men went ashore and *"Drank 7 or 8 bowls of egg rum"* at a Dutch tavern.[7]

The first of Arnold's ships reached Reuben Colburn's boatyard late on September 21st, and the others arrived over the next few days. Two hundred freshly built bateaux capable

---

[6] Chase, ed., "General Orders, 5 September, 1775," *The Papers of George Washington, Vol. 1,* 473

[7] Kenneth Roberts, *March to Quebec: Journals of the Members of Arnold's Expedition,* (New York: Country Life Press, 1938), 655 (John Pierce Journal)

of carrying hundreds of pounds of supplies and men awaited them. Although problems with the bateaux soon revealed themselves in the form of numerous leaks, the construction of so many craft in so short a time was a significant accomplishment and one that was crucial for the expedition.

Arnold originally planned to sail the transport ships further up the Kennebec to Fort Western (an abandoned French and Indian era fort in present day Augusta), but shallow water forced him to continue upriver by bateaux, instead. Fort Western had been converted into a trading post and residence by James Howard in 1769, and Howard generously provided shelter and provisions to as many of Arnold's men as he could. The site was soon teeming with men and supplies. Unfortunately there was not enough shelter for all of Arnold's men, so some spent a rainy and cold night on the ground.[8]

While Colonel Arnold and his detachment organized themselves for the long trek ahead, a small scouting party was sent forward. It was led by Lieutenant Archibald Steele of Pennsylvania and included five other Pennsylvania riflemen and three Virginian riflemen. Two local men from Vassalboro, John Getchell and Jeremiah Horne, accompanied the party as guides. Weeks earlier, at the request of Reuben Colburn, two of Getchell's brothers, Dennis and Nehemiah, accompanied by Samuel Berry, two other local men and an Indian guide, reconnoitered the expedition's route all the way to the Dead River. They reported meeting a Norridgewock Indian named Natanis who claimed that British troops were posted just across the border in Canada. This small party traveled approximately thirty miles along the Dead River before it became too shallow to continue by boat, so they turned around without verifying Natanis's claim. Their report was passed on to Colonel Arnold, via Reuben Colburn, but Arnold apparently paid it little heed.

---

[8] Roberts, 474 (Caleb Haskell Journal)

Lieutenant Steele's scouting party left Fort Western on September 24th, in two birch bark canoes. These lightweight craft were better suited for the shallow water of the Kennebec River than the heavy bateaux built for Arnold's main force. As a result, the scouts averaged twenty miles a day.[9] Steele's party was followed a few hours later by another small party with instructions to survey the route. The first detachment of Arnold's main body started upriver the next day.

To avoid bottlenecks at some of the narrow portage passages of the river (carrying paths around rapids and waterfalls), Colonel Arnold divided the main body of his force into four divisions with four different departure dates. The first division consisted of the three rifle companies and was commanded by Captain Daniel Morgan of Virginia. The second division was commanded by Lieutenant Colonel Christopher Greene of Rhode Island and consisted of three musket companies. Four musket companies under Major Return Meigs of Connecticut made up the third division, and the last division of three musket companies under Lieutenant Colonel Roger Enos of Connecticut brought up the rear. Enos's division, which included Captain Samuel McCobb's company from Maine, carried the most supplies because they had the advantage of following in the wake of the other divisions. Reuben Colburn and a party of boat builders accompanied the last division to repair the bateaux when necessary.

As each division left Fort Western, they struggled to move the heavy bateaux through the shallow water and rocky shoals of the river. Two days into the trip, Private Caleb Haskell of the third division noted

---

[9] Roberts, 303 (Joseph Henry Journal)

> We begin to see that we have a scene of trouble to go through in this river, the water is swift and the shoal full of rocks, ripples, and falls, which oblige us to wade a great part of the way.[10]

Pennsylvania rifleman George Morison shared a similar observation from the first division:

> The water in many places being so shallow, that we were often obliged to haul the boats after us through rock and shoals, frequently up to our middle and over our heads in the water; and some of us with difficulty escaped being drowned.[11]

While the men in the bateaux battled the swift current and rocky shoals, the rest of the expedition marched alongside the river. They were frequently called upon to assist with the boats, especially when difficult rapids were encountered.

It took each division two days to travel the eighteen miles to Fort Halifax (Winslow). This French and Indian era fort was connected to Fort Western by a rough road and was similar in design and condition. Within site of the fort was the Ticonic Falls. The expedition had to leave the river and carry their boats around the rapids and falls in order to continue upriver. Local settlers assisted with oxen and carts, but the work was still difficult and exhausting. The falls of Skowhegan were even worse, requiring Arnold's men to scale a steep precipice nearly thirty feet high in order to continue upriver. Abner Stocking noted

---

[10] Roberts, 303 (Caleb Haskell Journal)
[11] Roberts, 511 (George Morison Journal)

> "This day (September 29*th*) we arrived to the second carrying place...[present day Skowhegan, Maine] *it occasioned much delay and great fatigue. We had to ascend a ragged rock, near on 100 feet in height* [actually closer to 30 feet] *and almost perpendicular. Though it seemed as though we could hardly ascend it without any burden, we succeeded in dragging our bateaus and baggage up it.*"[12]

The difficult terrain was not the only challenge for the men; weather conditions also deteriorated and made the trek difficult. Captain Simeon Thayer noted on September 30th, that *"Last night, our clothes being wet, were frozen a pane of glass thick, which proved very disagreeable, being obliged to lie in them."*[13]

By early October, all of the divisions had passed Skowhegan Falls. They continued on, past Norridgewock Falls (Madison), and then Caratunk Falls. Numerous shoals slowed their progress, but Captain Morgan's lead division persevered and reached the Great Carrying Place on October 7th. This was the location of a twelve mile portage route that connected the Kennebec and Dead Rivers. Three ponds linked the path and provided brief respites along the difficult trek. Hauling the heavy boats and supplies over the rough terrain was a daunting task. Rifleman George Morison described the difficulties they endured:

> *This morning we hauled out our Batteaux from the river and carried thro' brush and mire, over hills and swamps...to a pond which we crossed, and encamped for the night. This transportation occupied us three whole days, during which time we advanced but five miles. This was by far the most fatiguing movement*

---

[12] Roberts, 548 (Abner Stocking Journal)
[13] Roberts, 250 (Simon Thayer Journal)

> *that had yet befell us. The rains had rendered the earth a complete bog; insomuch that we were often half leg deep in the mud, stumbling over all fallen logs...Our encampments these two last nights were almost insupportable; for the ground was so soaked with rain that the driest situation we could find was too wet to lay upon any length of time; so that we got but little rest. Leaves to bed us could not be obtained and we amused ourselves around our fires most all the night...The incessant toil we experienced in ascending the river, as well as the still more fatiguing method of carrying our boats, laden with the provisions, camp equipage etc., from place to place, might have subdued the resolution of men less patient and less persevering than we were...Our gallant officers, who partook of all our hardships left nothing unsaid or undone that might hearten us to the enterprise.*[14]

Transporting the boats and supplies across the twelve mile portage required several trips back and forth and days of backbreaking work. Dr. Isaac Senter recalled,

> *The army was now much fatigued, being obliged to carry all the bateaus, barrels of provisions, warlike stores, etc. over on their backs through a most terrible piece of woods conceivable. Sometimes in the mud knee deep, then over ledgy hills, etc.*[15]

Many men grew sick from the foul water of the ponds and the excessive fatigue. Dr. Senter noted,

---

[14] Roberts, 513-514 (George Morison Journal)
[15] Roberts, 205 (Isaac Senter Journal)

> *Many of us were now in a sad plight with the diarrhea. Our water was of the worst quality. The lake was low, surrounded with mountains, situated in a low morass. Water was quite yellow. With this we were obliged not only to do all our cooking, but use it as our constant drink. Nor would a little of it suffice, as we were obliged to eat our meat exceeding salted. This with our constant fatigue called for large quantities of drink. No sooner had it got down than it was puked up by many of the poor fellows.*[16]

So many men succumbed to illness and fatigue that a hut was built to serve as a hospital. The spirits of the men were further dampened at the return of Lieutenant Steele and his scouting party. Steele and his men had nearly perished further up the trail when they ran out of provisions and their abysmal condition troubled the troops (who realized that they might soon find themselves in the same condition).

Each division spent a week on the difficult portage. The last major obstacle they faced before they reached the Dead River was a mile wide cedar swamp. Arnold's exhausted troops waded through knee deep muck and finally reached a stream that led to the river.

When Arnold's men reached the Dead River, they quickened their pace. The river was deep and the current slow. Unfortunately, just as spirits lifted among the men, the weather deteriorated again, and the expedition was forced to halt and endure the remnants of a hurricane. Rifleman Joseph Henry described the storm's impact:

> *A most heavy torrent of rain fell upon us, which continued all night...towards morning we were awakened by the water that flowed in upon us from the river. We fled to high ground. When morning*

---
[16] Ibid.

> came, the river presented a most frightful aspect: it had risen at least eight feet, and flowed with terrifying rapidity. None but the most strong and active boatmen entered the boats. The army marched on the south side of the river, making large circuits to avoid the overflowing (river)...This was one of the most fatiguing marches we had as yet performed, though the distance was not great in a direct line. But having no path, and being necessitated to climb the steepest hills and without food, for we took none with us, thinking the boats would be near us all day.[17]

To make matters worse, much of the food was spoiled by the wet weather. Dr. Isaac Senter noted,

> The bread casks not being water-proof, admitted the water in plenty, swelled the bread, burst the casks, as well as soured the whole bread. The same fate attended a number of fine casks of peas. These with the others were condemned. We were now curtailed of a very valuable and large part of our provisions...Our fare was now reduced to salt pork and flour. Beef we had now and then, when we could purchase a fat creature, but that was seldom. A few barrels of salt beef remained on hand, but of so indifferent quality, as scarce to be eaten, being killed in the heat of summer, took much damage after salting, that rendered it not only very unwholesome, but very unpalatable.[18]

The expedition had reached a critical phase. The original plan called for the 4th division under Lieutenant Colonel Enos to carry a reserve supply of provisions, but Enos reported that

---

[17] Roberts, 330 (Joseph Henry Journal)
[18] Roberts, 203 (Isaac Senter Journal)

he barely had enough for his men. Colonel Arnold was near the front of the column and out of contact when Enos reached Greene's 3rd division. An officers' council was called between the two division commanders and their company captains to discuss whether to continue forward or withdraw. Greene and his officers voted to continue, but the officers under Enos, including Captain Samuel McCobb, voted to return southward. Enos voted to continue, but informed Greene that since his officers were determined to leave, he was obligated to return with his division. Hard feelings passed between the two sides as Enos and his officers departed. They handed over two barrels of flour to Greene's starving division, all that they claimed they could spare, and commenced their retreat southward. Reuben Colburn's volunteer boat builders, who had struggled throughout the journey to repair the leaky and oft damaged boats, left with Enos.

News of the 4th division's desertion (as most saw it) quickly spread through the expedition and fostered much anger towards their former comrades. Captain Henry Dearborn recalled,

> *The unhappy News of Colo. Enos, and the three Company's in his Division, being so Imprudent as to return back...disheartened and discouraged our men very much as they Carri'd Back more than their part, or quota of Provision, and Ammunition, and our Detachment, before being but Small, and now losing these three Companies, We were Small, indeed, to think of entering such a place as Quebec, But being now almost out of Provisions we were Sure to die if we attempted to Return Back – and We Could be in no Worse Situation if we proceeded on our rout – Our men made a General Prayer, that Colo: Enos and all his men, might die by the way, or meet with some disaster, Equal to the Cowardly dastardly and*

unfriendly Spirit they discover'd in returning Back without orders, in such a manner as they had done.[19]

Despite the devastating news and difficult conditions, the expedition continued onward. On October 25th, a heavy snowfall hit the men, adding to their misery. Dr. Isaac Senter reported,

Every prospect of distress now came thundering on with a two fold rapidity. A storm of snow had covered the ground nigh six inches deep, attended with very severe weather.[20]

Private Morison of Morgan's division recorded a similar observation in his journal. *"Last night there fell a heavy snow, and this morning it blew up cold; we suffered considerably this day."*[21]

When Morgan's division reached the area known as the Height of Land (the highest point of the march) the two Pennsylvania rifle companies abandoned all but one of their bateaux. The Virginians, however, carried their remaining seven boats over the difficult portage. Joseph Henry described how the Virginians struggled to haul the boats overland:

It would have made your heart ache to view the intolerable labors of these fine fellows. Some of them, it was said, had the flesh worn from their shoulders, even to the bone.[22]

---

[19] Roberts, 137 (Henry Dearborn Journal)
[20] Roberts, 210 (Isaac Senter Journal)
[21] Roberts, 517-518 (George Morison Journal)
[22] Roberts, 335-336 (Joseph Henry Journal)

The Virginians were not alone in their suffering. The constant physical exertion and lack of provisions took its toll on all the men. George Morison reported,

> *The time had now arrived when our suffering began to assume a different shape. Famine stared us in the face. Our provisions began to grow scarce, many of our men too sick, and the whole of us much reduced by our fatigues; and this too in the midst of a horrid wilderness, far distant from any inhabitation.*[23]

A week later, Morison recorded in his journal that,

> *Never perhaps was there a more forlorn set of human beings...Every one of us shivering from head to foot, as hungry as wolves, and nothing to eat save a little flour we had left, which we made dough of and baked in the fires....*[24]

The expedition's ordeal peaked in early November. Dr. Senter recalled,

> *We had now arrived...to almost the zenith of distress. Several had been entirely destitute of either meat or bread for many days...The voracious disposition many of us had now arrived at, rendered almost anything admissible...In company was a poor dog, [who had] hitherto lived through all the tribulations...This poor animal was instantly devoured, without leaving any vestige of the sacrifice. Nor did the shaving soap, pomatum, and even the lip salve, leather of their shoes, cartridge boxes, &c., share any better fate....*[25]

---

[23] Roberts, 515-516 (George Morison Journal)
[24] Roberts, 524 (George Morison Journal)
[25] Roberts, 218-219 (Isaac Senter Journal)

Private Morison had a similar meal on November 2nd:

> *This morning when we arose to resume our march, many of us were so weak as to be unable to stand without the support of our guns. I myself...staggered about like a drunken man...This day I roasted my shot-pouch and eat it. It was now four days since I had eat anything save the skin of a squirrel...A number resorted to the same expedient; and in a short time there was not a shot-pouch to be seen among all those within my view...This was the last resort...Hope was now partly extinguished; and its place was supplied with deep insensibility.[26]*

The expedition had degenerated into a disorganized band of starving men, scattered along a twenty mile stretch of land. Many fell out of the march, resigned to die in the wilderness. Private Henry noted that the situation was so desperate that,

> *The men were told by the officers that order would not be required in the march – each one must put their best foot foremost.[27]*

In other words, it was every man for himself. Those that still had the strength pressed on. Their perseverance was rewarded on November 3rd, when the expedition sighted cattle being driven towards them by an American advance party. The cattle were immediately butchered, and the famished men gorged themselves on fresh beef and other provisions. Many of the rejuvenated men returned to the wilderness to assist their exhausted comrades and most made it out of the woods. Arnold's march through the Maine wilderness was mercifully over, but more challenges lay ahead.

---

[26] Roberts, 524 (George Morison Journal)
[27] Roberts, 336 (Joseph Henry Journal)

On November 14th, Arnold's detachment arrived outside of Quebec. His force, which was reduced to approximately 600 men, was too small to storm the fortified city, but strong enough to commence a siege. The siege was short lived, however, because Arnold was low on ammunition. On November 19th, Arnold withdrew southward to unite with General Richard Montgomery's force from New York. Montgomery had assumed command of General Schuyler's troops when Schuyler grew too ill to continue. The two American forces linked up on December 2nd, at Point aux Tremble, twenty miles south of Quebec. The need to leave detachments of men behind to secure Montreal and other captured sites meant that less than 400 of Schuyler's original 2,000 men arrived with General Montgomery. Nonetheless, Montgomery, who assumed command of the combined forces, was determined to capture Quebec. He promptly led the Americans back to Quebec and demanded the surrender of the town.

Governor Carleton, with only a small number of British troops, relied on the loyalty of the Canadian militia to defend the town and rejected Montgomery's demand. Both sides settled down for a siege, but with the Americans lacking sufficient artillery, equipment, or time for such an operation, Montgomery decided in late December to assault Quebec. General Montgomery's plan called for a small detachment of men to feign an attack on the western approach to town, while two columns of troops converged from opposite directions on the lower town, which sat just below the city's walls on the east end of town along the St. Lawrence River. General Montgomery would lead 300 New York troops along the St. Lawrence River toward the lower town while Colonel Arnold, with 600 men, circled around Quebec and attacked the lower town from the north.[28] Once this section of the town was

---

[28] Brendan Morrissey, *Quebec 1775: The American invasion of Canada*, (Osprey Publishing Ltd., 2003), 54

captured, Arnold's and Montgomery's united force would storm the upper town.

Early in the morning of December 31st, with a winter storm raging, the Americans began their attack. Disaster struck almost immediately when General Montgomery was killed in the early stage of the assault. His detachment withdrew leaving Colonel Arnold to storm Quebec alone. Arnold's column, unaware of Montgomery's withdrawal, approached the gates of Quebec through the northern suburbs. Charles Porterfield, a Virginian rifleman with Captain Morgan's company, recounted the attack in his diary:

> *We paraded at 4 o' clock, A.M....The signal given, with shouts we set out. In passing by the Palace gate, they fired, and the bells rung an alarm. We marched with as much precipitancy as possible, sustaining a heavy fire for some distance, without the opportunity to return it, being close under the wall.*[29]

Rifleman Joseph Henry gave a similar account of the approach:

> *Covering the locks of our guns with the lappets of our coats, and holding down our heads, (for it was impossible to bear up our faces against the imperious storm of wind and snow,) we ran along the foot of the hill in single file...we received a tremendous fire of musketry from the ramparts above us. Here we lost some brave men, when powerless to return the salutes we received, as the enemy was covered by his impregnable defences. They were even sightless to us – we could see nothing but the blaze from the muzzles of their muskets.*[30]

---

[29] "Diary of Colonel Charles Porterfield," *Magazine of American History*, Vol. 21, (April 1889), 318-319
[30] Roberts, 375-376 (Joseph Heth Journal)

As Arnold's detachment continued forward, the advance guard, led by Arnold, became separated from most of the main body. Captain Morgan's rifle company was one of the only units from Arnold's main body that kept up with Arnold. Rifleman Charles Porterfield described what happened:

> *Coming to the barrier of the entrance of the lower town, guarded by a captain and 50 men, with two pieces of cannon, one of which they discharged and killed two men, we forced them from the cannon, firing in at the port-holes, all the time exposed to the fire of the musketry from the bank above us in the upper town. Here, Colonel Arnold was wounded in the leg and had to retire. The scaling ladders being brought up, if there was any honor in being first over the barrier, I had it. I was immediately followed by Captain Morgan. Upon our approach the guards fled, and we followed close to the guard-house, when, making a halt till some more men should come up, we sallied through into the street. We took thirty men and a captain....*[31]

Daniel Morgan gave a similar account of the attack. With Colonel Arnold wounded and command falling upon him, Morgan recounted,

> *I had to attack a two-gun battery, supported by Captain M'Leod and 50 regular troops. The first gun that was fired missed us, the second flashed, when I ordered the ladder, which was on two men's shoulders, to be placed...I mounted myself, and was the first man who leaped into the town, among M'Leod's guard, who were panic struck, and, after a faint resistance, ran into a house that joined the*

---

[31] Porterfield Diary, 319

> *battery and platform...Charles Porterfield, who was then a Cadet in my company, was the first man who followed me; the rest lost not a moment, but spring in as fast as they could find room; all this was performed in a few seconds. I ordered the men to fire into the house, and follow up their fire with their pikes (for besides our rifles we were furnished with long espontoons) this was done, and the guard was driven into the street. I went through a sally-port at the end of the platform; met them in the street; and ordered them to lay down their arms, if they expected quarter; they took me at my word and every man threw down his gun.*[32]

The Americans had broken through the first barricade (blocked street) but in doing so, they were scattered about the lower town. A long delay ensued as Morgan waited for the rest of Arnold's detachment and General Montgomery's force to arrive. Charles Porterfield recalled, *"We paraded for some time in the street. Here we continued for near an hour, before two hundred men got into the barrier, some without officers, and some officers without men, all in confusion...."*[33]

At the beginning of this delay, Captain Morgan advanced forward to reconnoiter the second barricade. If this barrier was breeched, the Americans would have access to the upper town. Morgan observed, *"The sally-port through the barrier was standing open; the guard left it...I found no person in arms at all."* [34] Morgan returned to the first barricade and proposed to the other officers that had arrived that they continue forward. Morgan recalled,

---

[32] Henry B. Dawson, "General Daniel Morgan: An Autobiography," *The Historical Magazine and Notes and Queries Concerning the Antiquities, History and Biography of America*, 2nd Series, *Vol. 9* (Morrisania, NY, 1871), 379-380

[33] Porterfield Diary, 319

[34] Dawson, 380 (Morgan Autobiography)

> *I was overruled by hard reasoning; it was stated that, if I went on, I would break an order, in the first place; in the next place, I had more prisoners than I had men; that if I left them, they might break out, retake the battery, and cut off our retreat; that General Montgomery was certainly coming down the River St. Lawrence, and would join us in a few minutes, so that we were sure of conquest if we acted with caution. To these arguments I sacrificed my own opinion and lost the town.*[35]

Nearly an hour passed before the attack was resumed. During this delay, the British rushed men to the second barricade. Morgan's patience finally expired at daybreak, and he ordered his men forward to the second barrier. Charles Porterfield noted,

> *On approaching the second barrier, [the enemy] hailed us. We immediately fired; they returned it with a shower of shot. Being planted in houses on the opposite side of the barrier, a continual fire ensued for some time, while we rushed up to the barrier, set up our ladder, and, at the same instant, Captain Morgan mounted one, I the other, to force our way, spear in hand, but we were obliged to draw back. Here we were at a disadvantage. Our guns being wet, could not return the fire we were subject to; [we] were obliged to retreat into the street.*[36]

Rifleman George Morison also described the assault on the second barricade:

---

[35] Ibid.
[36] Porterfield Diary, 319

> *The ladders are laid to the wall – our gallant officers are mounting followed by several men when a furious discharge of musketry is let loose upon us from behind houses; in an instant we are assailed from different quarters with a deadly fire. We now find it impossible to force the battery or guard the port-holes any longer. –We rush on to every part, rouse the enemy from their coverts, and force a body of them to an open fight, some of our riflemen take to houses and do considerable execution. We are now attacked by thrice our number; the battle becomes hot, and is much scattered; but we distinguish each other by hemlock springs previously placed in our hats. All our officers act most gallantly. Betwixt every peal the awful voice of Morgan is heard, whose gigantic stature and terrible appearance carries dismay among the foe wherever he comes.*[37]

Despite Morgan's bold leadership, the American situation was critical. *"We are now attacked in our rear,"* wrote Morison, *"the enemy increase momentarily –they call out to us to surrender but we surrender them our bullets..."*[38] Charles Porterfield found cover inside a house where he, fellow Virginian Peter Bruin, and seven or eight other men continued the fight:

> *We fired...from the windows* [wrote Porterfield] *determined to stand it out or die...Upon seeing Colonel Green and others give up their arms, we held a council what to do, Bruin declaring to the men that, if they thought proper to risk it, he was willing to fight our way out – that he should stand or fall with them.*[39]

---

[37] Roberts, 537 (Morison Journal)
[38] Ibid. 538
[39] Porterfield Diary, 319

While the fight raged at the second barrier, a large British force moved to retake the first one. They encountered Captain Henry Dearborn's New Hampshire musket company who, because of their wet weapons, were unable to offer much resistance. Dearborn's company was overwhelmed and surrendered. With the first barricade back in British hands, Morgan and his men were cut off.

Nevertheless they fought on, hoping that General Montgomery's force would arrive to relieve them. By mid-morning, however, it was evident that Montgomery was not coming and that Morgan's men were trapped. Promised good treatment from their captors, they surrendered in small groups. Daniel Morgan was one of the last to do so, reportedly weeping with anger as he handed his sword, not to the enemy, but to a local clergyman.[40] The American effort to capture Quebec had failed and for hundreds of Americans, both the captives in Quebec with Captain Morgan and the soldiers encamped outside Quebec with Colonel Arnold, a long, miserable winter lay ahead.

---

[40] James Graham, *Life of General Daniel Morgan*, (Bloomingham, NY: Zebrowski: Historical Services Publishing Co., 1993), 103

Chapter Five

"The Only Alternative is Independence or Slavery" 1776

The year 1776 was greeted by General Washington with a great deal of anxiety, not because of the situation in Canada (which Washington did not learn about until mid-January), but because of his own precarious situation outside of Boston. Washington's once formidable army of 20,000 men had dissolved into a force less than half that size, and they were dangerously low on gunpowder.[1] In an effort to place his remaining troops on a more orderly footing, General Washington re-organized the army. The process, which took effect on January 1st, was a dangerous undertaking in the face of the enemy. Washington noted the challenge in a letter to Congress:

> *It is not in the pages of History perhaps, to furnish a case like ours; to maintain a post within Musket Shot of the Enemy for Six months... without [powder] and at the same time to disband one Army and recruit another, within the distance of Twenty odd British regiments, is more probably than ever was attempted.*[2]

---

[1] Charles Lesser, ed., *The Sinews of Independence: Monthly Strength Reports of the Continental Army*, (University of Chicago Press, 1976), Troop Returns for 26 August, 1775, 5
                23 September, 1775, 7
                28 January, 1776, 15

[2] Chase, ed. "General Washington to John Hancock," 4 January, 1776," *The Papers of George Washington, Revolutionary War Series, Vol. 3,* 19

General Washington was particularly frustrated by the low number of new recruits trickling into camp. He complained to Congress, that

> *We are now left with a good deal less than half rais'd Regiments, and about 5,000 Militia who only stand Ingaged to the middle of this Month.*[3]

The disappointing number of new recruits impacted General Washington's efforts to reorganize the army. Only twenty-seven continental regiments were formed out of the various New England units in camp.[4] Each continental regiment was comprised of hundreds of men from the same colony who agreed to serve in the army for a year. Troops from Maine likely served in all 16 Massachusetts continental regiments. Three of these regiments, however, the 7th, 15th, and 18th Continental Regiments, held a particularly large number of Maine troops. The 7th Continentals were commanded by Colonel William Prescott, one of the heroes of Bunker Hill. Two of Prescott's eight companies consisted of Maine men from Colonel Scamman's disbanded 30th Massachusetts Regiment under Captains Samuel Darby and Jonathan Nowell of York.[5] The 15th Continentals, under Colonel John Paterson, also consisted of two Maine companies from Scamman's old regiment under Captain Ebenezer Sullivan of Berwick (the brother of General John Sullivan) and Captain Samuel Sayer of Wells.[6] The 18th Continental Regiment, under Colonel Edmund Phinney of Gorham, was almost entirely composed of Maine men from

---

[3] Chase, ed. "General Washington to Lieutenant Colonel Joseph Reed," 4 January, 1776," *The Papers of George Washington, Revolutionary War Series, Vol. 3*, 24

[4] Lesser, 15

[5] Goold, "Col. James Scamman's 30th Regiment of Foot, 1775," *Maine Historical Society*, 2nd ser. 10, 375, 397

[6] Ibid., 380, 385

Phinney's old 31st Massachusetts Regiment and the remnants of Scamman's 30th Massachusetts Regiment.[7]

While the continental troops from Maine besieged Boston with the rest of General Washington's army, hundreds of other Maine men served on the high seas as privateers. American privateers sailed as far as the West Indies and Europe to attack British merchant ships and many profited considerably from the prize money they earned from captured vessels. Other privateers were not so lucky and spent years imprisoned in England.

Although thousands of men from the counties of York, Cumberland, and Lincoln served outside the border of Maine, a large number of men remained home. Massachusetts law required that all able bodied males between sixteen and sixty (except Quakers, ministers, blacks, and Indians), serve in the county militia.[8] In December 1775, the Massachusetts General Court strengthened the colony's defenses by appointing brigadier-generals to command the militia in each county. General John Frost of Kittery was appointed to command the militia in York County, General Samuel Thompson of Brunswick was placed in charge of the Cumberland County militia, and General Charles Cushing of Pownalborough commanded the militia in Lincoln County.

In Falmouth, the pleas for more protection from further British raids were partially answered in the spring of 1776 with the arrival of desperately needed gunpowder and a few cannon. A garrison of militia was posted in Falmouth to man the cannon.[9] A small garrison of thirty men (ten of whom were Indians), was also posted at Fort Pownal near the mouth of the Penobscot River to defend the settlements there.[10]

---

[7] Goold, "Col. Edmund Phinney's 18th Continental Regiment: One Year's Service Commencing January 1, 1776," *Collections and Proceedings of the Maine Historical Society,* 2nd Ser. 9, (1898), 71-105
[8] Williamson, 445
[9] Ibid., 446
[10] Ibid.

The British Evacuate Boston

Thanks to the efforts of Colonel Henry Knox, Washington's siege of Boston ended successfully in March 1776. Colonel Knox had travelled to New York that winter to retrieve something the Americans sorely lacked, heavy siege guns. Such cannon were in American hands at Fort Ticonderoga, the British fortress on Lake Champlain that was captured in May 1775 by Benedict Arnold and Ethan Allen. Knox led a detachment to the fort in December and began the laborious task of dragging the heavy cannon across the Berkshire Mountains to Boston. The cannon arrived at Boston in late February and were quickly employed in the siege. Washington's troops constructed earthworks and gun emplacements on the heights of Dorchester within range of Boston Harbor and the town itself. The British commander, General William Howe (who replaced General Thomas Gage in October 1775), initially issued orders to attack Dorchester Heights. Upon further consideration, however, Howe decided to end the ten month standoff with Washington and abandon Boston. In exchange for General Washington's pledge to suspend siege operations for three days, Howe's troops and their Tory supporters evacuated the city without incident.

The last British troops left Boston on March 17th; on their heels entered a portion of the American army. Great satisfaction was expressed throughout the colonies at the liberation of Boston, but this joy was tempered by the expectation that the British army would soon return to the colonies. Rumors of a large invasion force of British and Hessian (German) soldiers in Halifax, Nova Scotia greatly troubled the colonists. General Washington wasted no time in marching the bulk of his army, which had grown to over 10,000 continentals, to New York to reinforce the defenders of that important city.[11]

---

[11] Lesser, 20

While Colonel Edmund Phinney's 18th Continental Regiment remained in Boston as part of a garrison to defend the town if the British decided to return, Colonel William Prescott's 7th Continental Regiment and Colonel John Paterson's 15th Continentals marched to New York with the rest of Washington's army. Prescott's regiment was posted on an island at the mouth of the East River (Governor's Island). This placed them between the town of New York, on the tip of Manhattan Island, and Brooklyn Heights, on the western shore of Long Island. Prescott's men spent the spring and summer fortifying their position and keeping watch for the British, who landed in force on Staten Island in early summer.

Colonel Paterson's regiment was given a different assignment. It was sent north in mid-April to reinforce the beleaguered American forces in Canada. Among the men in Paterson's regiment were approximately 100 soldiers in two companies from Maine.

The Canadian Campaign of 1776

Following the failed American attack on Quebec in December 1775, the conflict in Canada settled into a siege that was similar to the one at Boston. The forlorn American force outside of Quebec was too weak to storm the fortress city, yet too stubborn to withdraw. Although hundreds of men left the army when their enlistments expired and others simply deserted, a hardy corps of Americans remained outside of Quebec for five miserable months. They endured the brutal Canadian winter, supply shortages, constant enemy harassment, and widespread illness, the worst of which was a smallpox epidemic. Despite all of these hardships, the Americans only withdrew when British reinforcements arrived in the spring to drive them away. Dr. Isaac Senter, a survivor of Arnold's march and assault on Quebec, described the hasty American retreat:

> *In the most irregular helter skelter manner we raised the siege, leaving everything. All the camp equipage, ammunition, and even our clothing, except what little we happened to have on us*.... [The British chased] *us up the river both by land and water, and in the most disorderly manner we were obliged to escape as we could.*[12]

Although the Americans had abandoned their quest to capture Quebec, they did not fully abandon Canada. They retreated southwestward up the St. Lawrence River to Sorel, (where the Richeleau River flowed into the St. Lawrence River from Lake Champlain.) General John Thomas, who had recently arrived from New York, took command of the American forces in Canada, but, like many of his men, he was struck down by smallpox in mid-May and died on June 2nd.

Fortunately for the exhausted and demoralized Americans, troops from Pennsylvania, New York, and New England, including Colonel John Paterson's 15th Continental Regiment, arrived to reinforce the battered American army at Sorel. Paterson's regiment was immediately sent to Montreal, forty miles up the St. Lawrence River, to bolster the small American garrison there.[13] Within days, many of Paterson's men contracted smallpox. Those who were still fit for duty braced themselves for an attack from the west.

---

[12] Roberts, 238-39 (Isaac Senter Journal)
[13] Chase, ed. "General William Thompson to General Washington, 14 May, 1776," *The Papers of George Washington, Revolutionary War Series, Vol. 4,* 303

Map of Canada

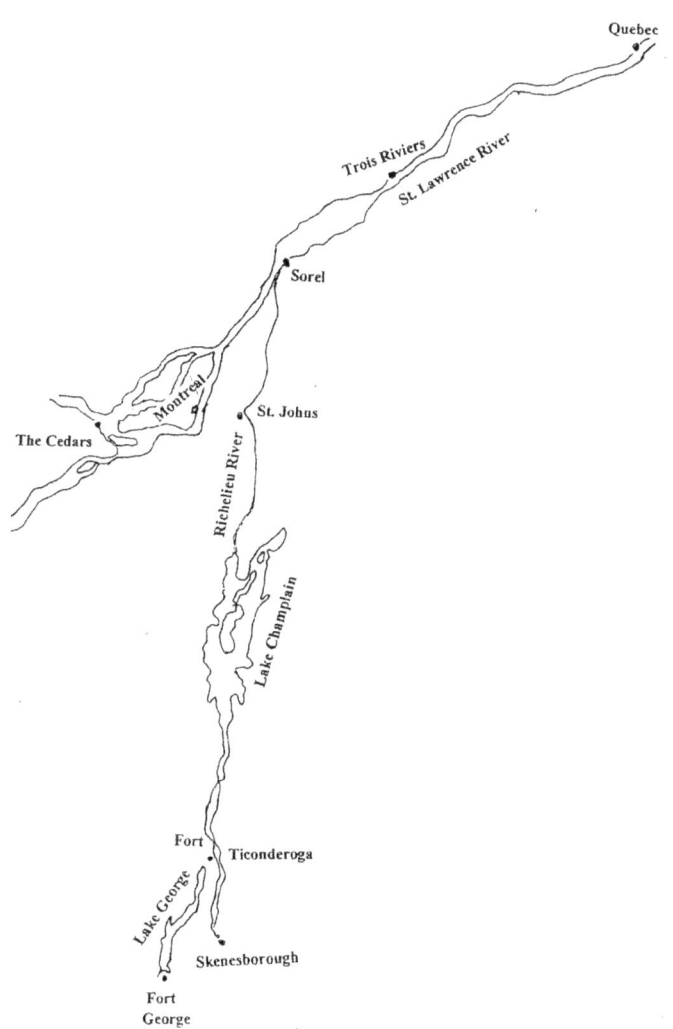

Battle of the Cedars

In April, a month before the arrival of Paterson's regiment, an American detachment of 400 men marched 40 miles west of Montreal to establish a fort at a location called the Cedars.[14] The American force was led by Colonel Timothy Bedel. In mid-May Colonel Bedel (reportedly suffering from smallpox) returned to Montreal to report that his garrison was short on supplies and in need of reinforcement. Major Isaac Butterfield was left in command of the American detachment at the Cedars.

On May 18th, Butterfield's 400 man force was confronted by approximately 40 British regulars and 200 Indians under the command of Captain George Forster.[15] Forster's smaller force surrounded the American fort and peppered it with musket fire into the evening. Major Butterfield responded with artillery fire from his two cannon and musket fire from his men. The raw American cannon crews were ineffective, but Butterfield's infantry maintained a steady fire of musketry and held the enemy at bay. Unfortunately, by the next morning, Major Butterfield had lost his nerve and, despite the protests of his subordinates, agreed to surrender the fort.[16]

Unbeknownst to Butterfield, reinforcements from the 15th Continental Regiment, including a company of Maine men under Captain Ebenezer Sullivan, were on the march from Montreal.[17] This small relief detachment of approximately 100 men was commanded by Major Henry Sherburne who, when he learned of Butterfield's surrender, marched on to confront Forster. As Sherburne's force approached the Cedars they fell into an ambush. John Greenwood, a fifer in the 15th

---

[14] Robert M. Hatch, *Thrust for Canada: The American Attempt on Quebec in 1775-76*, (Boston: Houghton Mifflin Co., 1979), 195, 197
[15] Ibid., 198
[16] Ibid., 199
[17] Ibid., 199-200

Regiment who had remained in Montreal, relayed details of the battle that participants shared with him:

> *As soon as the Americans came opposite to the place where the Indians were concealed, the latter rose up and poured upon them a tremendous fire, making at the same time a most hideous noise called the war-whoop.... Our men fought the...devils for upwards of two hours and killed a number of them, including several chiefs....*[18]

Despite being caught in the open by a superior force, Major Sherburne's men stubbornly resisted, losing a quarter of their strength in less than an hour.[19] For a time, they succeeded in waging a fighting withdrawal, but eventually the enemy cut off their retreat and completely surrounded them. With no hope of escape or relief, Major Sherburne surrendered. Sherburne and many of his men endured the humiliation of being stripped naked by the Indians. Accusations of physical abuse and torture were also leveled at the Indians by some of the American survivors.[20] Fortunately for Sherburne and his men, their captivity was short lived.

The British commander pushed on towards Montreal, but reports of a large American force bearing down of him from that direction, combined with the challenge of controlling nearly 500 prisoners, convinced Captain Forster to retreat. The approaching American force was led by General Benedict Arnold; he was determined to confront Forster and free the prisoners.

---

[18] John Greenwood, *The Wartime Services of John Greenwood: A Young Patriot in the American Revolution, 1775-1783*, (Westvaco, 1981), 66-67
[19] Hatch, 200
[20] Ibid., 200-201

Captain Forster, however, agreed to a prisoner exchange with the captured American officers before Arnold was able to attack. The agreement resulted in the release of the American prisoners on the promise that an equal number of British soldiers be released in the future. A few American hostages, including Captain Ebenezer Sullivan, were kept by Forster and, despite the American Congress's refusal to honor the terms of the agreement, were also eventually released. Unencumbered by the American prisoners, Captain Forster retreated westward. The chastised Americans returned to Montreal with General Arnold.

Although the American defeat at the Cedars was a humiliating military setback, a far bigger setback struck the Americans a few weeks later at Trois Rivieres (Three Rivers).

Battle of Three Rivers

The bulk of the American presence in Canada, nearly 5,000 men, was posted about 40 miles northwest of Montreal along the St. Lawrence River at Sorel.[21] They included veterans of the siege of Quebec and reinforcements from New England, New York, New Jersey, and Pennsylvania. General John Sullivan of New Hampshire, who arrived at the head of some of the reinforcements in June, assumed command of the American forces at Sorel upon General Thomas's death from smallpox.

When reports reached Sorel that only 800 British soldiers were posted at Trois Riviers, a village 45 miles down the St. Lawrence River, Sullivan saw an opportunity to attack. He ordered General William Thompson, a veteran of the siege of Boston, to advance on the British garrison with 1,500 men. They would join a force of about 700 men under Colonel Arthur St. Clair that was sent to Trois Riviers a few days

---

[21] Lesser, 25

earlier to reconnoiter and, if possible, attack Trois Riviers.[22] Thompson's force travelled most of the way by boat and rendezvoused with St. Clair's detachment on the south side of the St. Lawrence about ten miles from Trois Riviers. They were startled to learn that a much larger enemy force, consisting of ten ships and up to 1,500 troops, was present there.[23] Nevertheless, General Thompson hoped that the element of surprise might still win the day and proceeded with an attack.

The Americans, approximately 2,000 strong, crossed the river and advanced towards Trois Riviers in the early morning hours of June 8th. Two hundred and fifty men stayed behind to guard the boats, and the rest proceeded towards the enemy on foot.[24] Colonel Anthony Wayne of Pennsylvania commanded one of the four American columns and described what happened:

> *About 2 in the morning we landed nine Miles above the town, and after an Hour's march day began to appear. Our Guides had mistook the road, the Enemy Discovered and Cannonaded us from their ships, a Surprise was out of the Question – we therefore put our best face on it and Continued our line of march thro' a thick deep swamp three miles wide, and after four Hours Arrived at a more open piece of Ground – amidst the thickest firing of the shipping when all of a sudden a large Body of*

---

[22] Chase, ed. "General John Sullivan to General Washington, 5-6 June, 1776," *The Papers of George Washington, Revolutionary War Series*, Vol. 4, 440-444
[23] Hatch, 213
[24] Ibid., 212, 215

[British] *regulars marched down in good Order Immediately in front of me to prevent our forming.*[25]

Colonel Wayne ordered his light infantry and a company of riflemen to "*advance and amuse*" the British while the rest of his detachment positioned themselves to attack the British flanks. According to Colonel Wayne, his light troops

> *Continued the attack with great spirit until I advanced to support them* [on both flanks]... *I ordered* [the detachment's left and right wings] *to wheel to the Right & left and flank the Enemy at the same time* [the light troops] *poured in a well Aimed and heavy fire in front...*[The British] *attempted to Retreat in good Order at first but in a few minutes broke and ran in the utmost Confusion.*[26]

The American success was impressive but short-lived because British cannon and musket fire from the ships and entrenchments halted the American advance. Colonel Wayne noted,

> *We advanced in Column up to their breastworks...Gen'l Thompson with Cols St. Clair, Irvine, & Hartly were marching in full view to our support. Col. Maxwell now began to Engage on the left of me, the fire was so hot he could not maintain his post – the other* [American] *troops had also filed off to the left – my small Battalion...amounting in the whole to about 200 were left exposed to the whole fire of the shipping in flank and full three thousand men in front with all their Artillery.... Our people*

---

[25] Charles J. Stille, "Colonel Wayne to Dr. Franklin and Others," *Major-General Anthony Wayne and the Pennsylvania Line in the Continental Army*, (Kennikat Press: Port Washington, NY, 1968), 29 (Originally published in 1893)
[26] Ibid.

taking example by others gave way – Indeed it was Impossible for them to stand it longer.[27]

The American troops fled back into the woods and swamp. General Thompson and his officers attempted to rally the troops, but they were largely ineffective. Thompson's men had one thought now, to return to the boats nine miles upriver. The British pursued and attempted to cut off the Americans, but their effort to capture the American boats failed when the detachment guarding them rowed upriver to Sorel. Hundreds of Americans, including General Thompson, surrendered while the rest of his routed force staggered back to Sorel on foot. After a three day trek Colonel Wayne arrived *"almost worn out with fatigue, Hunger, & Difficulties, scarcely to be paralleld."*[28]

The situation in Canada looked bleak for the Americans. The despair felt by the survivors of Trois Riviers quickly spread throughout the American army at Sorel. Morale, which was already low due to the constant supply shortage and a seemingly endless outbreak of smallpox, sunk to new lows. General Sullivan reported to General Washington that only 2,533 were men fit for duty, and that both the officers and men were disheartened.[29]

In Montreal, the majority of Colonel Paterson's 15th Continentals, including scores of Maine men, continued to recover from smallpox. Many contracted the disease naturally while others inoculated themselves. It typically took a month to recover from the illness, so most were still ill when General Sullivan ordered all American forces to withdraw to St. John's on June 10th. Fifer John Greenwood recounted the 15th Continentals' hasty retreat from Montreal:

---

[27] Ibid., 30
[28] Ibid., 31
[29] Chase, ed. "General John Sullivan to General Washington, 12 June, 1776," *The Papers of George Washington, Revolutionary War Series, Vol. 4,* 466

> *Late one afternoon the order came, 'Retreat! Retreat! The British are upon us!' Down we scampered to the boats, those of the sick who were not led from the hospital crawling after us. Camp equipage, kettles, and everything were abandoned in the utmost confusion – even the bread that was baking in the ovens – for we were glad to get away with whole skins. When halfway across the river it began to grow very dark, and down came the rain in drops the size of large peas, wetting our smallpox fellows, huddled together like cord-wood in the boats, and causing the death of many.*[30]

Once across the river, Greenwood found shelter in a barn. His stay was brief, however, as angry officers chased everyone out and ordered them to rejoin the column marching eastward. The Americans struggled along muddy roads and finally halted at nightfall. Greenwood slipped away and bedded down in a windmill, but many of his ill comrades spent the evening in the open, exposed to the elements. Greenwood was shocked by what he saw the next day:

> *As we now marched along, the sad sight of many a companion who had died from exposure met our gaze.*[31]

Greenwood's severely depleted regiment joined the rest of the army at St. John's but remained just a few days. The British were in pursuit, and General Sullivan had no wish to engage the enemy with his sick and demoralized troops, so he pushed on to Lake Champlain. The Americans abandoned more equipment and supplies and were forced to make due with

---
[30] Greenwood, 75
[31] Ibid. 77

what little they had. Fifer Greenwood recalled that he received a pint of flour and a quarter pound of pork as a daily provision, but had nothing to cook with:

> *We were without camp-kettles or any utensils whatever to make bread in...* [so the flour was] *mixed up with water from the lake by fellows as lousy, itchy and nasty as hogs...and baked upon a piece of bark so black with dirt and smoke I do not think a dog could eat it. But with us it went down, lice, itch, and all, without any grumbling, while the pork was broiled on a wooden fork and the drippings caught by the beautiful flour cakes. Such was the life of our Continental soldiers who went to Canada.*[32]

The Americans continued their retreat southward and finally halted days later at Fort Ticonderoga. A small force was also posted twelve miles north at Crown Point. Work parties immediately began to strengthen the defenses of both forts. Other men, skilled in woodwork and boatbuilding, were sent down the lake to Skenesborough to build ships for the defense of the lake. The British focused much of their effort on the same task and hurried to construct a strong fleet of gunboats and ships at St. Johns (on the northern end of Lake Champlain). Control of the 110 mile long lake hung in the balance. With so much attention devoted to these activities, a three month lull in the fighting ensued.

---

[32] Ibid., 78

Independence

While American soldiers in 1776 prepared to meet impending British attacks on Lake Champlain and New York City, representatives from the colonies debated whether or not to sever all political connection with Great Britain. Calls for independence, which were virtually non-existent prior to 1775, gradually gained colonial support over the winter of 1775-76. The bloodshed at Lexington and Concord, Bunker Hill and Quebec, along with numerous other engagements from Machias to Moore's Creek Bridge, and the burning of Falmouth, (Portland) Maine and Norfolk, Virginia, undoubtedly contributed to the shift in colonial opinion. John Adams hinted at the possibility of independence as early as October 1775:

> *The situation of Things is so alarming, that it is our Duty to prepare our Minds and Hearts for every Event, even the Worst....The Thought that we might be driven to the sad Necessity of breaking our Connection with Great Britain...always gave me a great deal of Grief.*[33]

Two months later, with Falmouth in ruins and Virginia's royal governor, Lord Dunmore, inciting slaves to take up arms against their rebellious masters, Edward Rutledge of South Carolina asked a pointed question to a friend in Britain:

> *Are the people of* [England] *determined to force us, into Independence?...Do they expect that after our Towns have been destroyed – our Liberties repeatedly invaded – our women and children, driven from their Habitations – our nearest Relatives*

---

[33] Smith, "John Adams to Abigail Adams, 7 October, 1775," *Letters of Delegates to Congress, 1774-1789*, Vol. 2 (Washington: Library of Congress, 1977), 134-35

> *sacrificed at the Alter of Tyranny, our Slaves emancipated for the express purpose of massacreing their Masters – can they, I say, after all their injuries, expect that we shall return to our former connection with a forgiving, and cordial Disposition...Unless the Parliament improve the opportunity now offered them, they may loose forever their American Colonies.*[34]

By early 1776, additional factors increased colonial support for independence. King George III's proclamation declaring all of the colonies in rebellion significantly eroded colonial support for the king. Samuel Adams exclaimed that the king's proclamation

> *Breathes the most malevolent Spirit, wantonly proposed Measures calculated to distress Mankind, and determines my opinion of the Author of it as a Man of a wicked Heart....What have we to expect from Great Britain, but Chains and Slavery?*[35]

The influence of Thomas Paine's pamphlet *Common Sense* was also strongly felt in the colonies in early 1776. Josiah Bartlett, a delegate to Congress from New Hampshire, noted in mid-January that the pamphlet was "*greedily bought up and read by all ranks of people.*"[36] He sent a copy home from Philadelphia and urged that it be passed around. Nicholas Cresswell, a loyal Englishman stranded in Virginia, glumly recorded in his diary in January 1776 that "*Nothing But*

---

[34] Smith, "Edward Rutledge to Ralph Izard, 8 December, 1775," *Letters of Delegates to Congress, 1774-1789*, Vol. 2, 463
[35] Smith, "Samuel Adams to John Sullivan, 12 January, 1776," *Letters of Delegates to Congress, 1774-1789*, Vol. 3, 84-84
[36] Smith, "Josiah Bartlett to John Langdon, 13 January, 1776," *Letters of Delegates to Congress, 1774-1789*, Vol. 3, 87-88

Independence [is] *talked off...The Devil is in the people."*[37] Cresswell blamed Paine's pamphlet for much of the talk of independence:

> *A pamphlet called Commonsense makes a great noise. One of the vilest things that ever was published to the world. Full of false representations, lies, calumny, and treason, whose principles are to subvert all Kingly Governments and erect an Independent Republic...The sentiments are adopted by a great number of people who are indebted to Great Britain.*[38]

George Washington's brother-in-law, Fielding Lewis of Fredericksburg, Virginia, also acknowledged the influence of Paine's pamphlet:

> *The opinion for independence seems to be gaining ground, indeed most of those who have read the Pamphlet Common Sense say it's unanswerable.*[39]

By the end of winter, colonial leaders were openly discussing independence. In mid-February Pennsylvanian Robert Morris noted with a little irony,

> *America has long been charged by her Enemys in England with aiming at Independency. The charge was unjust, but we now plainly see, that the burning of Towns, seizing our ships, with numerous acts of wanton barbarity & Cruelty perpetrated by the British Forces has prepared Men's minds for an Independency, that were shock'd at the idea a few weeks ago. This you may depend on, and should this*

---

[37] Cresswell Journal, "26 January, 1776," 136
[38] Ibid.
[39] Chase, ed., "Fielding Lewis to George Washington, 6 March, 1776," *The Papers of George Washington, Vol. 3*, 418-419

> *Campaign open with furious Acts of Parliament, you may bid adieu to the American Colonies. They will then assuredly declare for Independency....*[40]

Joseph Hews, a delegate to Congress from North Carolina, noted in March,

> *Some among us* [in Congress] *urge strongly for Independency and eternal separation, others wish to wait a little longer and have the opinion of their Constituents on the subject.*[41]

Samuel Adams was one of the delegates who strongly urged independence. He believed that Britain had no intention to reconcile the dispute and that it was foolish to continue to hope for such a thing:

> *It is Folly for us to suffer our selves any longer to be amusd. Reconciliation upon reasonable Terms is no Part of their Plan. The only Alternative is Independence or Slavery. Their Designs still are as they ever have been to subjugate us. Our unalterable Resolution should be to be free.*[42]

The movement towards independence quickened in late spring. North Carolina authorized its delegates in Congress to support independence in April, and Virginia's leaders voted unanimously for independence in mid-May. The issue was finally considered in Congress on June 7th, when Richard Henry Lee of Virginia introduced a resolution on independence. Congress postponed debate on the resolution

---

[40] Smith, "Robert Morris to Robert Herries, 15 February, 1776," *Letters of Delegates to Congress, 1774-1789*, Vol. 3, 258-59
[41] Smith, "Joseph Hewes to Samuel Johnson, 20 March, 1776," *Letters of Delegates to Congress, 1774-1789*, Vol. 3, 416-17
[42] Smith, "Samuel Adams to James Warren, 16 April, 1776," *Letters of Delegates to Congress, 1774-1789*, Vol. 3, 540

for three weeks to allow some of the delegations to consult with their colonial governments. During the interlude, Thomas Jefferson, with the editorial assistance of Benjamin Franklin and John Adams, drafted a document that declared to the world the reasons behind American independence. The Continental Congress approved Lee's resolution on American independence on July 2nd, and adopted Jefferson's Declaration of Independence two days later on July 4th.

Fort Cumberland

In Machias, Colonel Jonathan Eddy hoped to extend independence to his compatriots in Nova Scotia. Eddy strongly supported the American cause and travelled to Massachusetts in the spring of 1776 to announce that the majority of Nova Scotia's inhabitants supported the Americans. He approached the Massachusetts government, General Washington, and ultimately, the Continental Congress with a plan to capture Fort Cumberland at the head of the Bay of Fundy and expel the British from Nova Scotia. All showed interest in the scheme but expressed an inability to assist.[43] Undeterred, Eddy sailed to Machias and put his plan into action. He recruited a small party of volunteers and sailed for the Bay of Fundy in mid-August with 28 men in a small schooner.[44] The intrepid lot attracted new recruits along the way, including a handful of Indians, and as their numbers approached 75, they were forced to use open whaling boats and canoes to transport the additional men and supplies.[45]

In late October 1776, the expedition captured a small party of the enemy about thirty miles south of Fort Cumberland, and a few days later, they captured a British sloop outside the fort

---

[43] Ahlin, 50-51
[44] Ibid., 52
[45] Ahlin, 53

loaded with provisions.[46] This alerted the one hundred man garrison within Fort Cumberland, and they braced themselves for an attack.[47] Eddy's success sparked a wave of volunteers from among the local inhabitants and soon his numbers approached 200 men.[48] Josiah Throop was part of Eddy's force and reported,

> *On the news Spreading* [of Colonel Eddy's arrival and success] *the Inhabitants...repaired to Eddy and his party to the number of about two hundred – and on* [November 10th] *a Summons was sent to Col* [Joseph] *Goreham to Surrender the fort – on the Eleventh they received his answer refusing to Surrender...*[49]

Colonel Gorham suggested that it was more appropriate for Eddy's force to surrender to him, and the colonel threatened the disloyal residents of Nova Scotia with harsh retribution if they continued to support the rebels. According to Josiah Throop, the locals replied that they would rather "*die like men than be hanged like dogs.*"[50]

The confrontation reached a climax the next night when Colonel Eddy led an assault on the fort. Josiah Throop described what happened:

> *On the twelfth they prepared for Scaling the walls and made an attempt that night but found it Impracticable as they had nothing but Small arms – and the Fort was Piquetted in and the walls and Ramparts lately repaired.* [The enemy] *have six*

---

[46] Clark, "Memorial of Josiah Throop to the Massachusetts General Court," *Naval Documents of the American Revolution, Vol. 7*, 562-63
[47] Ibid.
[48] Ibid., 563
[49] Ibid.
[50] Ibid.

Cannon about a Hundred men and Six hundred Small arms.[51]

Although Colonel Eddy was discouraged by the setback and wrote to the Massachusetts government for reinforcements and supplies, he was determined to maintain a siege of the fort.[52] Unfortunately, British reinforcements arrived in late November and launched a night attack that routed Eddy's force. Captain Sir George Collier, the commander of one of the vessels who conveyed the reinforcements, succinctly summarized the attack:

> *A Sally from the Fort struck such a Panic into the Rebels, that they fled with the greatest Precipitation, (& have thereby left this Province without further Apprehensions of being invaded again, for the Winter.)*[53]

Although Eddy's force suffered only slight casualties, it dissolved in the face of the British, and over 200 men surrendered when they were offered a pardon for their actions.[54] Colonel Eddy had no choice but to retreat to Machias with his few remaining men.

---

[51] Ibid.
[52] Clark, Colonel Jonathan Eddy to the Massachusetts General Court," 12 November, 1776, *Naval Documents of the American Revolution, Vol. 7*, 110
[53] Clark, "Captain Sir George Collier to Philip Stephens, 8 January, 1777," *Naval Documents of the American Revolution, Vol. 7*, 883
[54] Ahlin, 57

Chapter Six

"The Present is Emphatically the Crisis which is to Decide our Destiny" 1776

Retreating was something that General Washington and the American army understood well in the second half of 1776. In the days following the Declaration of Independence, American enthusiasm for independence soared and confidence was high that Washington's army could repel an impending British attack on New York City. The city was located on the southern end of Manhattan Island, a fourteen mile long island surrounded by the Hudson, Harlem, and East Rivers and Upper New York Bay. However, Washington's task to defend the town was daunting because the British and Hessian invasion force significantly outnumbered Washington's 20,000 man army, and the British navy dominated the waters off of New York. This meant that General William Howe could land his troops almost anywhere in the area and potentially trap the Americans.

To discourage the British navy from sailing up the East River, General Washington placed artillery batteries on Brooklyn Heights and on the tip of Manhattan. He also fortified Governor's Island, which was located at the mouth of the East River just south of Manhattan and Brooklyn Heights. Colonel William Prescott's 7th Continental Regiment manned the earthworks on the island and kept a close watch on the enemy fleet and troops on Staten Island.[1] Prescott's troops were Massachusetts men, about a quarter of them from coastal Maine under Captains Samuel Darby and Jonathan Nowell,

---

[1] W.W. Abbot and Dorothy Twohig, eds., "General Orders, 16 April 1776," *The Papers of George Washington, Vol. 4*, 76-77

and they labored all summer to strengthen the island's fortifications.[2]

General Howe, who experienced the carnage of Bunker Hill a year earlier, had no intention of risking heavy losses with a direct assault on New York. Instead, Howe's plan called for his army to outmaneuver Washington and strike the Americans where they were weak. After weeks of reconnaissance, Howe chose his objective, Long Island.

The British invasion of Long Island began at sunrise on August 22nd, when 15,000 British and Hessian troops landed unopposed at Gravesend Bay.[3] Weeks earlier, General Washington had posted half of his army along two defensive lines on the western end of Long Island in anticipation of a possible British landing. Washington's main defensive line on Long Island comprised a series of earthworks and redoubts along Brooklyn Heights. These heights, which overlooked the East River and New York City, were vital to the city's defense. From this position cannon could shower New York with shot and shell and make the town untenable for the Americans.

The other American defensive line on Long Island stretched along a series of hills and ridges a few miles east of the Brooklyn line. The position, called Gowanus Heights, was heavily wooded and formed a natural barrier between the British and Americans. Roads cut through the heights in a few gaps, or passes, which the Americans fortified. Each pass was defended by approximately 800 men, and pickets were stationed in the woods between the passes.[4] Colonel Samuel Miles's Pennsylvania state rifle regiment was posted in the woods on the far left flank of the American line. To their left,

---

[2] Goold, "Col. James Scamman's 30th Regiment of Foot, 1775," *Collections of the Maine Historical Society, 2nd Ser. Vol. 10*, 375, 397-398
[3] Henry P. Johnson, *The Campaign of 1776 Around New York and Brooklyn*, (New York: Da Capa Press, 1971), 140
(Originally published in 1878)
[4] Johnson, 156

about two miles away, was an unguarded road through Gowanus Heights called the Jamaica Pass.[5]

Colonel Miles was deeply troubled by the lack of American troops to his left, but his concerns went largely unheeded because the Americans had no men to spare. The best General Washington could do was post a handful of cavalrymen at Jamaica Pass.

Battle of Long Island

General Howe's battle plan called for two large detachments, commanded by General James Grant and General von Heister, to approach the American line at Gowanus Heights to draw Washington's attention to his center and right flank, while a 10,000 man force led by General Henry Clinton and General Charles Cornwallis marched around the American left flank via the Jamaicia Pass to strike the Americans in the rear.[6] If all went as planned, the Americans would be crushed between two British forces.

Howe's flanking force commenced its march toward Jamaica Pass early in the evening of August 26th. They reached the pass around 2:00 a.m. and captured the American cavalrymen posted there.[7] While the British flanking party secured Jamaica Pass, General Grant advanced his detachment toward the right wing of the American line. General William Stirling rushed 2,000 men from the Brooklyn line to bolster the American troops confronting General Grant. Stirling's men helped stop Grant's advance. Unbeknownst to them, General Grant was content to employ his artillery to hold the Americans in place until the British right wing enveloped them.[8]

---

[5] Johnson, 154 - 160
[6] Mark Boatner III, *The Encyclopedia of the American Revolution*, (Stackpole Books, 1994), 651
[7] Johnson, 176-177
[8] Johnson, 161- 167

On the American left flank, Colonel Miles and his Pennsylvania riflemen were in trouble. The British had flanked their line and were bearing down on their rear. Colonel Miles ordered his men to retreat, but only a portion managed to escape the British envelopment. Sergeant James McMichael was attached to the rifle battalion and described his escape:

> *We numbered just 400. We at first thought it prudent to retire to a neighboring thicket, where we formed and gave battle.... Their superior numbers forced us to retire for a short distance, when we again formed and fought with fortitude until we were nearly surrounded. Having by this time lost a great number of men, we were again forced to retreat, when we found that the enemy had got between us and the fort* [Brooklyn Heights]....*we were drove from place to place 'till 3 o'clock p.m., when we agreed to attempt crossing the mill-pond, that being the only way left for our escape. Here numbers were drowned, but it was the will of Providence that I should escape, and at half past three, we reached the lines, being much fatigued.* [9]

While these events transpired on the far left of the American line, the rest of the American troops at Gowanus Heights held firm, unaware of the danger to their flank and rear. The shocking news that the British were about to encircle them arrived with the British troops themselves. The American center quickly collapsed, and the panicked troops raced for the safety of the Brooklyn lines. Scores of Americans were bayoneted and many more, including General John Sullivan, were captured.

---

[9] James McMichael "The Diary of Lt. James McMichael of the Pennsylvania Line, 1776-1778," *The Pennsylvania Magazine of History and Biography, Vol. 16, no. 2,* (1892), 134

Battle of Long Island

All that remained of the American line at Gowanus Heights was General Stirling's force on the right. Stirling's men held the British in check all morning, but the sound of combat in their rear worried them. Unaware that the rest of the American line had collapsed, Stirling fought on, unwilling to retreat without orders. He eventually realized his perilous situation. With nearly every avenue of escape to the Brooklyn lines blocked, Stirling ordered his men to break ranks and cross Gowanus Creek as best they could. To buy time for his men, General Stirling personally led an attack against the British with half of the 1st Maryland Regiment. The conduct of the Maryland troops earned them universal esteem and saved hundreds of Americans from capture. The Marylanders with Stirling were not so fortunate. Most of them, along with General Stirling, were captured.

The battle of Long Island was a disaster for the Americans, yet the result was less decisive than it could have been. Although the British routed Washington's advance line at Gowanus Heights, General Howe's troops approached the main American line at Brooklyn with caution. Howe decided to avoid a bloody frontal assault and commenced a siege instead. His indecisive action on the heights of Brooklyn provided General Washington with the time he needed to evacuate his army across the East River two nights later. Colonel Prescott's Massachusetts men played an important role in this movement by helping to keep the British navy at bay. Had the navy discovered the evacuation, the result could have been disastrous. Instead, General Washington salvaged the bulk of his army, including Prescott's 7th Continentals, who evacuated Governors Island with most of their supplies after the last American boats left Brooklyn.

Kip's Bay

For two weeks the only thing that separated the British and American armies was the East River. The Americans on Manhattan could see the British preparing to attack, but could do nothing to stop it. General Howe's troops struck in mid-September with an amphibious landing on the east shore of Manhattan a few miles north of New York at Kip's Bay. Joseph Plum Martin, a young private posted at Kip's Bay with the Connecticut militia, recalled the engagement:

> *All of a sudden there came such a peal of thunder from the British shipping that I thought my head would go with the sound. I made a frog's leap for the ditch and lay as still as I possibly could and began to consider which part of my carcass was to go first.... We kept the lines until* [the British were almost ashore] *when our officers, seeing that we could make no resistance and no orders coming from any superior officer and that we must soon be entirely exposed to the rake of their guns, gave the orders to leave the lines. In retreating we had to cross a level, clear spot of ground forty or fifty rods wide, exposed to the whole of the enemy's fire, and they gave it to us in prime order. The grapeshot and* [lead] *flew merrily, which served to quicken our motions.*[10]

General Washington arrived on the scene and was dismayed at what he saw:

---

[10] Joseph Plum Martin, *Private Yankee Doolittle: Being a Narrative of Some of the Adventures, Dangers and Sufferings of a Revolutionary Soldier*, (Eastern Acorn Press, 1962), 34-35 (First published in 1840)

> *As soon as I heard the Firing, I rode with all possible dispatch towards the place of landing when to my great surprize and Mortification I found the Troops that had been posted in the Lines retreating with the utmost precipitation.*[11]

Perhaps even more distressing to Washington was the disintegration of two brigades of continentals that he ordered to Kip's Bay to support the militia. One of those brigades, under General Holden Parsons, included Colonel William Prescott's 7th Continentals. They arrived on the scene in a disorderly manner and were soon overwhelmed by the chaos of battle. Washington reported to Congress:

> *Parson's & Fellow's Brigades* [were] *flying in every direction and in the greatest confusion, notwithstanding the exertions of their Generals to form them. I used every means in my power to rally and get them into some order but my attempts were fruitless and ineffectual, and on the appearance of a small party of the Enemy, not more than Sixty or Seventy, their disorder increased and they ran away in the greatest confusion without firing a Single Shot.*[12]

General Washington left the scene in disgust and raced to the north end of Manhattan to secure Harlem Heights. Behind him marched thousands of frightened and demoralized American troops desperately trying to reach Harlem Heights before the British cut them off. Most were successful, but in

---

[11] Philander D. Chase and Frank E. Grizzard, "General Washington to John Hancock, 16 September, 1776," *The Papers of George Washington: Revolutionary War Series, Vol. 6*, 313
[12] Ibid.

doing so they abandoned one of America's most important cities without a fight.

Throg's Neck

Although the American position at Harlem Heights was strong, Washington's army was concentrated on the northern end of an island with only one secure crossing point, King's Bridge. It was vital, therefore, that the Americans protect the bridge. General William Heath commanded the American troops in the vicinity of King's Bridge, and one of the units placed under his command was Colonel William Prescott's 7th Continentals. Prescott's men would soon get a chance to redeem themselves for their poor performance at Kip's Bay.

General Howe resumed his offensive against the Americans on October 12th with a movement against King's Bridge. A large British force landed on a peninsula a few miles east of the bridge called Throg's Neck. Howe's plan was to seize the bridge and trap the bulk of Washington's army on Manhattan. His choice of a landing site, however, was poor.

To reach the mainland and ultimately King's Bridge from Throg's Neck, one had to pass a creek and marshland that flooded at high tide. There were only two routes over these obstacles: one was a causeway and bridge, and the other was a ford near the headwaters of the creek. Both locations were ideal defensive positions, and General Heath had both spots strongly defended.

When the British advanced towards the mainland, a detachment of riflemen and Colonel Prescott's 7th Continental regiment stopped them in their tracks. General Heath described the encounter:

The [British] *troops landed at Frog's Neck, and their advance pushed towards the causeway and bridge, at West Chester mill. Col. Hand's riflemen took up the planks of the bridge, as had been directed, and commenced a firing with their rifles. The British moved towards the head of the creek, but found here also the Americans in possession of the pass. Our General* [Heath] *immediately (as he had assured Col. Hand he would do) ordered Col. Prescott, the hero of Bunker Hill, with his regiment, and Lieut. Bryant of the artillery, with a 3 pounder, to reinforce the riflemen at West Chester causeway; and Col. Graham of the New-York line, with his regiment, and Lieut. Jackson of the artillery, with a 6 pounder, to reinforce at the head of the creek; all of which was promptly done, to the check and disappointment of the enemy. The British encamped on the Neck. The riflemen and Jagers kept up a scattering popping at each other across the marsh; and the Americans on their side, and the British on the other, threw up a work at the end of the causeway. Capt. Bryant, now and then, when there was an object, saluted the British with a field-piece.*[13]

By the end of the day, 1,800 Americans faced the British.[14] For five days, Howe's men sat at Throg's Neck unable to cross onto the mainland, but unwilling to withdraw. Finally, General Howe moved his troops across a cove to Pell's Point. This was only a short distance away, but was a much better landing area.

---

[13] William Heath, *Memoirs of Major General William Heath*, (NY: William Abbatt, 1901), 62
[14] Boatner, 1101

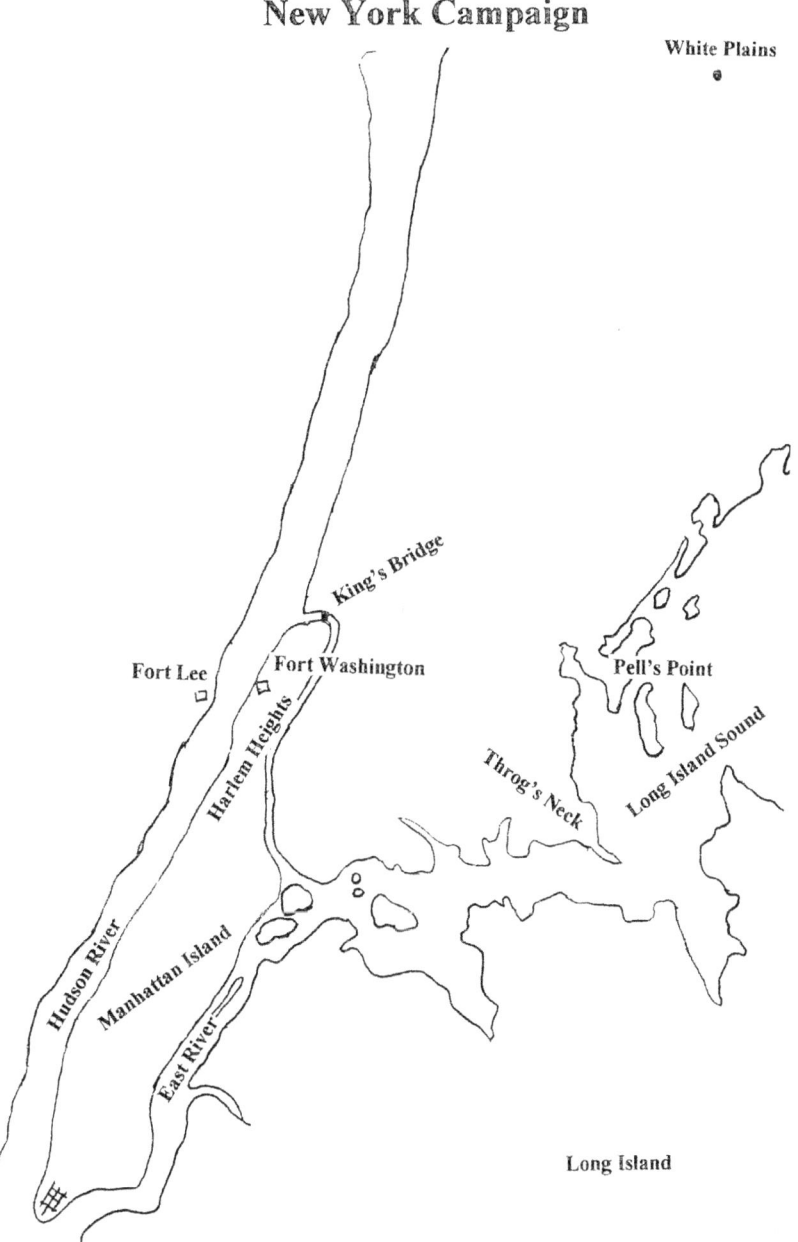

The new American commander on the scene, General Charles Lee, had anticipated this move and placed Colonel John Glover's Massachusetts brigade in the area to contest Howe's advance inland. When the British began their march, Glover's 750 musket-men ripped into them from behind stone walls and trees.[15] Although they were outnumbered more than five to one, Glover's men extracted a heavy toll in British casualties for their advance onto the mainland.

American resistance at Throgs Neck and Pell's Point allowed General Washington to remove the bulk of his army from Manhattan Island. He posted his troops on the hills outside of White Plains, New York, where a large, but inconclusive battle was waged on October 28th. The two armies remained in the area for another week without incident when General Howe suddenly withdrew back to New York. General Washington and his men hoped that Howe's withdrawal marked an end to British operations for 1776.

Defense of Lake Champlain

Two hundred miles to the north, thousands of Americans had similar hopes. The upper reaches of New York had seen little fighting since the American withdrawal from Canada in June; instead, each side had spent the summer constructing a naval force for Lake Champlain. American efforts were centered at Skenesborough, a small settlement at the southern end of the lake. Carpenters and shipwrights gathered there to construct gondolas and galleys (fifty to eighty foot long flat bottom boats with sails and oars and cannon). Eleven of these vessels sailed to Fort Ticonderoga over the summer where they joined four larger ships that the Americans captured in Canada a year earlier. All told, the American fleet under the command of Benedict Arnold numbered 15 ships and 78

---

[15] Ibid., 850

cannon.[16] The vessels were manned by over 750 volunteers and draftees taken from the ranks of the army at Fort Ticonderoga.[17] Men from Maine commanded the 54 foot gondolas *New York* and *Connecticut*, and comprised part of the 44 man crews of the gondolas *Philadelphia*, *Spitfire*, and *Providence*.[18]

The British, who were at the northern end of the lake, built an even larger naval force which included two large sailing ships bristling with cannon that easily outgunned anything the Americans had. These ships were disassembled at Chambly and hauled twelve miles by land (past the rapids of the Richeleau River) to St. John's where they were reassembled. Twenty-seven gunboats armed with a single cannon in the bow (ranging from 9 to 24 pounders) and several larger vessels filled out the British fleet of 32 vessels.[19] Carleton's fleet mounted 89 cannon and was manned by experienced sailors and artillerists.[20] General Carleton also had thousands of British and Hessian soldiers and hundreds of Canadian militia and Indians at his disposal.

Bracing for the expected British attack were 7,000 American troops at Fort Ticonderoga and Mount Independence under General Horatio Gates. They included seasoned veterans from the Canadian campaign like fifer John Greenwood and the 15th Continentals, as well as reinforcements from New England such as Colonel Edmund Phinney's 18th Continental Regiment (all from Maine). Colonel Paterson's 15th Continentals were posted at Mount Independence, a steep hill across the lake from Fort

---

[16] James Nelson, *Benedict Arnold's Navy* (McGraw Hill, 2006), 293
[17] Boatner, 1136 and Nelson, 258
[18] Philip K. Lundeberg, *The Gunboat Philadelphia And the Defense of Lake Champlain in 1776*, (Lake Champlain Museum, 1995), 30, 49 and *Massachusetts Soldiers and Sailors in the War of the Revolution*, 17 vol. (1896)
[19] Nelson, 293
[20] Ibid.

Ticonderoga. They worked all summer to clear timber and construct earthworks. Hundreds of their fellow soldiers toiled across the lake to strengthen Fort Ticonderoga's defenses. A floating bridge and protective boom were also built to connect the two American positions.

Supplying this large force with the necessary provisions was a significant challenge, one that required a lot of labor. Colonel Edmund Phinney's 18th Continentals, who arrived from Boston in September, spent most of that month shuttling supplies by bateau from Fort George (which was located at the southern tip of Lake George) to Fort Ticonderoga.[21] In October, they returned to Mount Independence and waited with the rest of the American army for the British to attack.

Battle of Valcour Island

General Carleton resumed his offensive on Lake Champlain in October by sending his naval force down the lake to confront the American squadron under Benedict Arnold. On October 11th, General Arnold's 15 vessels met the superior British fleet near Valcour Island and engaged in a heated battle that raged until nightfall. Captain George Pausch, a German artillery officer attached to one of the British gunboats, described the engagement:

> *Our attack with about 27 batteaux with 24, 12, and 6 pound cannon and a few howitzers became very fierce; and, after getting to close quarters, very animated.... The cannon of the Rebels were well served; for, as I saw afterwards, our ships were pretty well mended and patched up with boards and stoppers.*[22]

---

[21] Goold, "Col. Edmund Phinney's 18th Continental Regiment," *Collections of the Maine Historical Society, Ser. 2, Vol. 9*, 65

[22] Morgan, "Journal of Captain George Pausch", *Naval Documents of the American Revolution Vol. 6*, 1259

At one point in the fight Pausch risked his own life, and that of his crew, to rescue the crew of a burning British gunboat:

> *Close to one o'clock...this naval battle began to get very serious. Lieut. Dufais came very near perishing with all of his men; for a cannon ball from the enemy's guns going through his powder magazine, it blew up.... Dufais's bateau came back burning; and I hurried toward it to save...the Lieutenant and his men.... All that could jumped on board my batteau, which being thus overloaded, came near sinking.*[23]

Lieutenant Dufais and a few of his men transferred to a second bateau which allowed Pausch to retire with the rest of the British gunboats without swamping his vessel. Darkness ended the battle, which cost the British twenty men.[24]

The American fleet was severely battered in the fight. General Arnold described the engagement and the damage done to his ships in a letter to General Gates the next day:

> *At half past 11 the engagement became General & very warm. Some of the Enemies Ships & all their Gondolas beat & rowed up within musquet shott of us. They, Continued a very hot fire with Round and Grape Shott until five OClock.... The Congress and Washington have Suffered, greatly, the Latter Lost her first Lieut killed, & Capt. & Master wounded, the New York lost all of her Officers except her Captain. The Philada was hulled in so many Places that She Sank About One hour after the engagement was over, the whole killed & wounded, amounts to about Sixty.*[25]

---

[23] Ibid.
[24] Nelson, 306
[25] Morgan, "General Arnold to General Gates, 12 October, 1776," *Naval Documents of the American Revolution, Vol. 6,* 1235

Defense of Lake Champlain

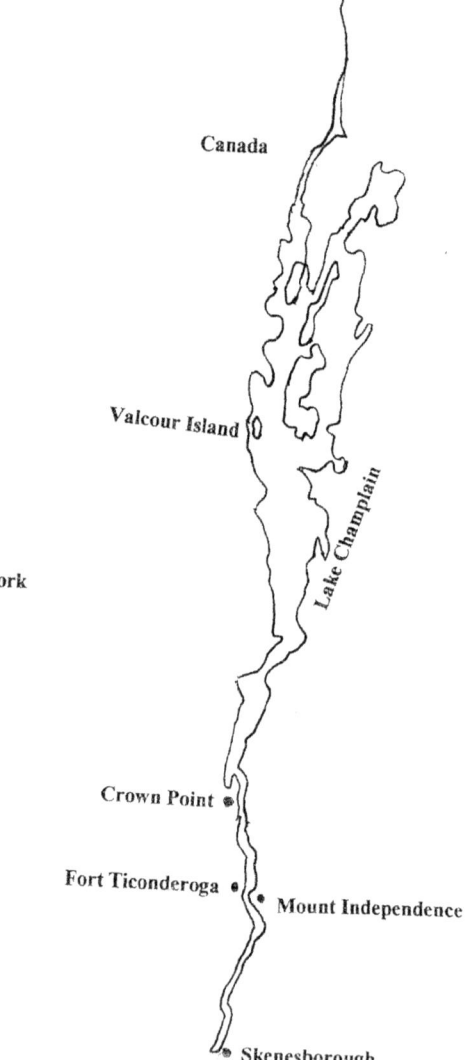

Although the damage to the American fleet was extensive, it could have been a lot worse. They were fortunate that the wind and their placement on the lake prevented Carleton's most powerful ships, with their 24 and 18 pound cannon, to maneuver into position to pound the Americans. Arnold worried that he would not be so lucky when the battle resumed in the morning, so he ordered his battered fleet to slip past the British (who were positioned between Arnold's fleet and Fort Ticonderoga) in the middle of the night. His goal was to reach the American garrison at Crown Point, twelve miles north of Fort Ticonderoga, in order to re-supply his depleted ammunition chests and, with the assistance of the garrison's shore batteries, make another stand against Carleton's fleet.[26]

Although Arnold's fleet successfully slipped past the British, most of the American ships, including Arnold's flagship the *Congress*, were overtaken by Carleton the next day before they reached Crown Point. General Arnold described what happened:

> *The Washington and Congress were in the Rear, the Rest of our fleet a head except two Gondolas* [that] *sunk* [enroute]. *The Washington Galley was in such a shattered Condition and had so many Men killed and wounded she struck to the Enemy after receiving a few Broadsides. We were then attacked in the Congress Galley by a Ship mounting twelve Eighteen Pounders, a Schooner of fourteen Sixes and one of twelve Sixes, two under our Stern and one on our Broadside within Musquet Shot. They kept up an incessant Fire on us for about five Glasses with Round and Grape Shot, which we returned as briskly – the Sails, Rigging and Hull of the Congress was shattered and torn in Pieces, the first Lieutenant and 3 Men killed, when to prevent her falling into the*

---

[26] Ibid.

Enemy's hands, who had seven Sail around me, I ran her ashore in a small Creek ten Miles from Crown Point on the East Side when after saving our small Arms, I set her on Fire with four Gondolas, with whose Crews I reached Crown point thro' the Woods that Evening, and very luckily escaped the Savages....[27]

Arnold reached Fort Ticonderoga early in the morning of October 14th "*exceedingly fatigued and unwell*" having gone without food or rest for three days.[28] Eleven of Arnold's fifteen ships were captured or destroyed in the two engagements, and over 100 Americans were captured by the British. General Arnold estimated his total casualties in killed and wounded at 80.[29]

When word of Arnold's defeat reached Fort Ticonderoga, its defenders resolutely waited for the British to attack. Carleton settled at Crown Point after the Americans abandoned it, but his army went no further. A few anxious weeks passed before it was learned that General Carleton abandoned Crown Point and returned to Canada. Carleton had decided that despite his victory over Arnold's fleet, it was too risky to continue the offensive so late in the year. Weather conditions were already bad and sure to get worse. Carleton believed that it was best to return to Canada and allow his troops to pass the coming winter in comfortable quarters. Although most of Benedict Arnold's fleet had been destroyed, its existence had delayed the British long enough to thwart their plans. The British objective to reach Albany from Canada and separate New England from the rest of the colonies would have to wait until 1777.

---

[27] Morgan, "General Benedict Arnold to General Philip Schuyler, 15 October, 1776," *Naval Documents of the American Revolution, Vol. 6*, 1275-76
[28] Ibid.
[29] Ibid.

Times That Try Men's Souls

In southern New York the brief pause in British military operations ended in November when General Howe attacked Fort Washington. The fort was constructed in the summer of 1776 on the northern end of Manhattan Island to prevent British ships from sailing up the Hudson River. A garrison of 1,200 men originally manned the fort and, despite Washington's withdrawal from Harlem Heights in October, the garrison's numbers swelled to nearly 3,000 men prior to Howe's attack; however, they were no match for the 8,000 British and Hessian troops that attacked on November 16th and, in one of the biggest American defeats of the war, the garrison surrendered before nightfall.[30]

Across the Hudson River, a shocked General Washington commanded over 4,000 troops detached from the army at White Plains. They were mostly "southern" troops from Pennsylvania, Delaware, Maryland, and Virginia that Washington had led across the river a few days before the fall of Fort Washington as a precaution against a British move towards New Jersey. General Charles Lee remained at White Plains with most of the troops from New England, 7,500 in all. Many were due to leave the army on December 1st, and all of them were fatigued by months of hard service. A third detachment from Washington's army, numbering 4,000 men, marched north from White Plains under General William Heath to defend the New York Highlands. Colonel William Prescott's 7th Continentals were attached to this detachment.

The fall of Fort Washington, on November 16th, was a major blow to the American army. General Howe followed his victory at Fort Washington with an attack on Fort Lee (across the Hudson River) four days later. The American garrison abandoned the fort without a fight and fled with the

---

[30] Johnson, 277

rest of Washington's small force into New Jersey. The British followed in their wake.

By late November, General Washington and his troops were in serious trouble. Significantly outnumbered by the British, Washington was powerless to stop Howe's pursuit. Captain John Chilton of the 3rd Virginia Regiment described the American retreat across New Jersey:

> *Our Regmt. brought up the rear. This was a melancholy day,* [November 27] *deep miry road and so many men to tread it made it very disagreeable marching, we came 8 or 10 miles and encamped....How long we shall stay, I can't say, but expect we shall make a stand near this place* [New Brunswick] *if not at it, but no certainty when the Enemy are advancing on and an engagement may happen before tomorrow night. We must fight to a disadvantage. They exceed us in numbers greatly.*[31]

Sergeant James McMichael, with the Pennsylvania state rifle regiment, made a similar observation in his diary:

> *Intelligence that the enemy are marching for Brunswick causing us to prepare to meet them but we are reduced to so small a number we have little hopes of victory.*[32]

Fortunately for the Americans, the British pursuit was sluggish. Washington's exhausted and demoralized troops retreated across New Jersey and crossed the Delaware River into Pennsylvania ahead of the British on December 7th.

---

[31] Lyon Tyler, "John Chilton to his brother, 30 November, 1776," *Tyler's Quarterly Historical and Genealogical Magazine, Vol. 12,* (Richmond, VA: Richmond Press Inc., 1931), 98

[32] McMichael Diary, 139

Retreat Across New Jersey

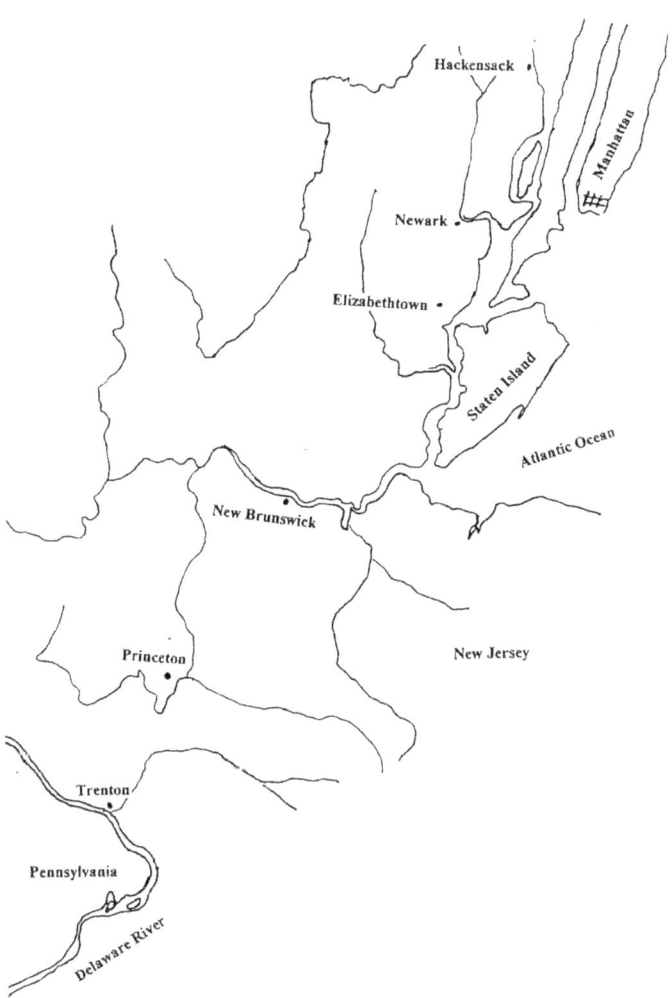

Washington posted his men along the west bank of the river to guard against an attempted crossing by the British. Lacking proper shelter and winter clothing, the men struggled to stay warm. Lieutenant Enoch Anderson of the Delaware Regiment described his first night in Pennsylvania:

> *We lay amongst the leaves without tents or blankets, laying down with our feet to the fire. It was very cold. We had meat, but no bread. We had nothing to cook with but our ramrods, which we run through a piece of meat and roasted it over the fire, and to hungry soldiers it tasted sweet.*[33]

David Griffith, the regimental surgeon for the 3rd Virginia, also described the dire situation facing the Americans:

> *We have much need for a speedy re-inforcement. I am much afraid we shall not have it in time to prevent the destruction of American affairs... Everything here wears the face of despondency...A strange consternation seems to have seized everybody in this country. A universal dissatisfaction prevails, and everybody is furnished with an excuse for declining the publick service.*[34]

For almost three weeks Washington's men braced themselves for an anticipated British crossing. Rumors spread that General Howe was waiting for the river to freeze so his men could walk across. Many wondered if there would be an American army left to challenge them. Even General

---

[33] "Personal Recollections of Captain Enoch Anderson, an Officer of the Delaware Regiment in the Revolutionary War," *Papers of the Historical Society of Delaware, Vol. 16*, (Wilmington: The Historical Society of Delaware, 1896), 28

[34] Tyler, "David Griffith to Major Powell, 8 December, 1776," *Tyler's Quarterly*, 101

Washington's Position Along the Delaware River

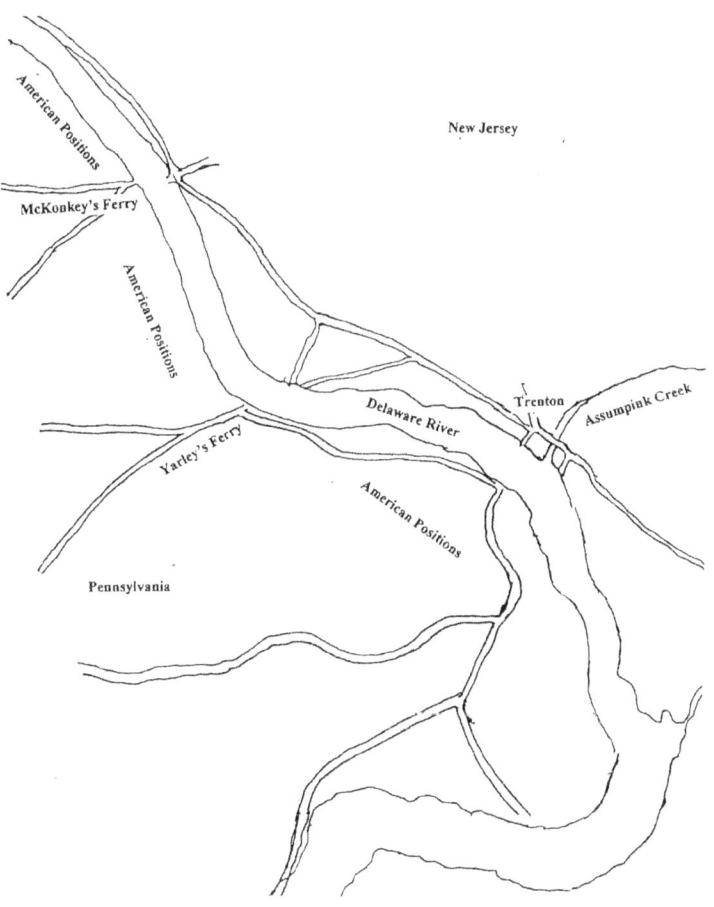

Washington was concerned. He wrote to his brother on December 18th :

> *Our Affairs are in a very bad situation...In a word my dear Sir, if every nerve is not strain'd to recruit the New Army with all possible expedition, I think the game is pretty near up.*[35]

Washington sent urgent appeals to General Lee in New York to march his men to Pennsylvania, but Lee, citing the dismal condition of his troops, was slow to respond. Gradually, and perhaps reluctantly, Lee led his force, which had shrunk to 2,000 men due to expired enlistments, across New Jersey. Along the way, Lee had the embarrassing misfortune to be captured by a British patrol after he foolishly spent the night away from camp. Command of Lee's force fell to General John Sullivan, who returned to the army in a prisoner exchange in September. General Sullivan led Lee's troops into Pennsylvania and joined Washington's army on December 21st. General Horatio Gates arrived the next day from Fort Ticonderoga with an additional 600 soldiers, including approximately 100 men in Colonel John Paterson's 15th Continentals.[36]

Service in the northern army had taken a heavy toll on Paterson's regiment. Fifer John Greenwood recalled,

> *Out of the 500 men we had in our regiment upon entering Canada* [in May], *but 100 were left when* [the] *order came* [to join Washington's army in] *November...With no tents to shelter us from the snow and rain, we were obliged to get through* [the march] *as well as we could.*[37]

---

[35] Chase, "Gen. Washington to John A. Washington, 18, December, 1776," *The George Washington Papers at the Library of Congress* : Online
[36] Greenwood, 79
[37] Ibid.

The arrival of these vital reinforcements, combined with General Howe's decision a week earlier to place his army in small garrisons throughout New Jersey for the winter, presented General Washington with a crucial opportunity to boost the morale of his men and the nation.

Washington's bold plan called for an early morning attack upon the 1500 man Hessian garrison across the Delaware River in Trenton. This would require a night crossing of the river, nine miles above Trenton, to avoid detection. Another detachment of militia and continentals were to cross the Delaware a few miles below Trenton. These two forces would then converge on Trenton from the north and south and hopefully catch the Hessians by surprise at dawn.

Battle of Trenton

On Christmas Day Washington ordered his troops, who were spread out for miles along the western bank of the Delaware River, to cook three days provisions, draw new flints and ammunition, and prepare to march.[38] Their destination was McKonkey's Ferry, nine miles upriver from Trenton. Only 2,400 men answered Washington's call, the rest were too sick or fatigued to join the attack. As the men gathered along the riverbank and waited their turn to cross, the weather began to deteriorate. An officer on Washington's staff described the crossing in his diary:

> *Christmas, 6 p.m. -- ...It is fearfully cold and raw and a snow-storm settig in. The wind is northeast and beats in the faces of the men. It will be a terrible night for the soldiers who have no shoes. Some of them have tied old rags around their feet; others are barefoot, but I have not heard a man complain* [39]

---

[38] William Stryker, "General Mercer to Colonel Durkee, 25 December, 1776," *The Battles of Trenton and Princeton*, 362
[39] Stryker, "Diary of an American Officer on Washington's Staff," 360

General Adam Stephen's brigade of Virginians was sent across the river first to form a defensive perimeter around the landing area. They were to watch for enemy patrols and curious civilians.

Young John Greenwood and his comrades in Colonel Paterson's regiment crossed the river soon after Stephen's brigade. Greenwood recalled,

> *As I was with the first that crossed, we had to wait for the rest and so began to pull down the fences and make fires to warm ourselves, for the storm was increasing rapidly. After awhile it rained, hailed, snowed, and froze, and at the same time blew a perfect hurricane; so much so that...when I turned my face towards the fire my back would be freezing. However...by turning round and round I kept myself from perishing before the large bonfire.*[40]

Colonel John Glover's regiment of Marbleheaders manned many of the boats used in the crossing. They had plenty of experience with night crossings having manned the boats used in Washington's escape from Brooklyn four months earlier. Their new task, to deliver 2,400 men and eighteen cannon across a swift flowing, ice choked river in deteriorating weather was daunting, and they steadily fell behind schedule. They finished ten hours after they began, exhausted, but determined to join the attack.

The Americans started their march on Trenton around 4:00 a.m., four hours behind schedule.[41] The storm made the march very difficult on the men. Fifer Greenwood recalled,

---

[40] Greenwood, 80
[41] Stryker, 139

After our men had all crossed...we began an apparently circuitous march, not advancing faster than a child ten years old could walk, and stopping frequently.... During the whole night it alternately hailed, rained, snowed, and blew tremendously. I recollect very well that at one time, when we halted on the road, I sat down on the stump of a tree and was so benumbed with cold that I wanted to go to sleep; had I been passed unnoticed I should have frozen to death without knowing it....We were all...nearly half dead with cold for the want of clothing...many of our soldiers had not a shoe to their feet and their clothes were ragged as those of a beggar.[42]

About mid-way to Trenton, the column split. General Sullivan led his division down the River Road, and General Nathanael Greene led his along the Pennington Road. The plan called for both columns to enter Trenton from two directions simultaneously at sunrise. Another detachment of continentals and militia under General John Cadawalder was expected to cross the river south of Trenton and attack the Hessians from that direction. Unfortunately for the Americans, Cadwalader's men had a very difficult time crossing the river and did not attack Trenton. Victory rested solely on the shoulders of General Washington's detachment; as dawn broke, they were still miles from town, and the element of surprise was in jeopardy.

Fortunately for the Americans, the same storm that delayed their march caused the Hessians to let their guard down and allowed the Americans to march to the outskirts of Trenton undetected. The first contact between the two sides occurred at the Hessian picket line just outside Trenton around 8:00

---

[42] Greenwood, 81

a.m. An aide to General Washington recorded what happened in his diary:

> *It was just 8 o' clock. Looking down the road I saw a Hessian running out from the house. He yelled in Dutch and swung his arms. Three or four others came out with their guns. Two of them fired at us, but the bullets whistled over our heads. Some of General Stephens men rushed forward and captured two.*[43]

The Americans quickly pushed the Hessian pickets into Trenton and took position of the high ground overlooking the town. Colonel Edward Hand's 1st Continental riflemen (attached to General Greene's division) moved to the left and helped secure the road to Princeton, severing that escape route, while Colonel Henry Knox's artillery unleashed a barrage of cannon fire into the town.

The startled Hessians attempted to form in the streets, but they were harassed first by Knox's artillery and then by Washington's infantry, who pressed into town from the north and west. Fifer John Greenwood and the 15th Continentals were attached to Colonel Arthur St. Clair's brigade of General Sullivan's column. Greenwood recalled that the wet weather disabled their muskets and forced the Americans to charge the Hessians:

> *As we had been in the storm all night we were not only wet through and through ourselves, but our guns and powder were wet also, so that I do not believe one would go off, and I saw none fired by our party...and, although there was not more than one bayonet to five men, orders were given to "Charge bayonets and rush on!" and rush on we did. Within*

---

[43] Stryker, "Diary of an American Officer on Washington's Staff," 363

> *pistol-shot* [the Hessians] *fired point-blank at us; we dodged and they did not hit a man, while before they had time to reload we were within three feet of them, when they broke in an instant and ran like so many frightened devils into the town, which was at a short distance, we after them pell-mell.*[44]

Colonel Knox's artillery maintained a steady barrage into the town and disrupted Hessian efforts to form their regiments. The scene made a strong impression on Knox:

> *The hurry, fright, and confusion of the enemy was (not) unlike that which will be when the last trumpet shall sound. They endeavoured to form in streets, the heads of which we had previously the possession of with cannon and howitzers; these, in a twinkling of an eye, cleared the streets. The backs of the houses were resorted to for shelter. These proved ineffectual:* [our] *musketry soon dislodged them.*[45]

Some of the Hessians sought refuge in town buildings, but most retreated to an apple orchard where their officers desperately re-formed their lines. Colonel Rall rallied his men and attempted to attack Washington's left flank near the Princeton Road, but General Washington acted quickly and shifted more troops to that position to secure it.[46]

---

[44] Greenwood, 83-84
[45] Stryker, "Colonel Knox to his Wife, 28 December, 1776," 371
[46] Fischer, 246

Battle of Trenton

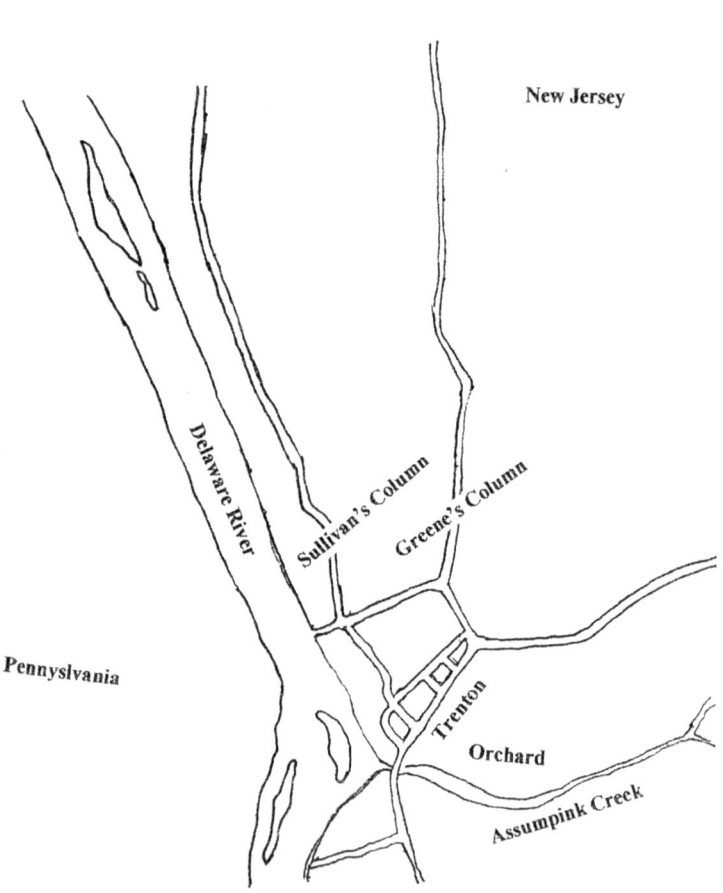

With large numbers of hostile troops to his front and flanks, Colonel Rall's next move should have been a retreat across the Assunpink bridge, the only avenue of escape still available; instead, Rall ordered his men back into town to recapture two abandoned cannon. The outnumbered Hessians endured heavy artillery fire from the Americans as they bravely advanced back into town to re-gain their cannon, however, Captain William Washington and Lieutenant James Monroe of the 3rd Virginia Regiment charged forward and seized the disputed cannon for good. The two Virginian officers were seriously injured in the attack, but the guns were securely in American hands.

Rall's men were forced back to the orchard, closely pursued by the Americans who pressed them on three sides. Trapped by the Assunpink Creek to their rear and the Americans on their front and flanks, the Hessians had little choice but surrender. They suffered over a hundred casualties, including their commander, Colonel Rall, who died of his wounds the next day.[46] The attack was a staggering success for the Americans. At the cost of a handful of men, the Americans captured over 900 Hessian prisoners and tons of much needed supplies.[47] More importantly, the victory provided a huge boost to American morale.

General Washington worried that General Howe might counterattack to rescue the Hessian prisoners so he withdrew back across the Delaware River. The weary American troops marched back to their boats and arrived in their camps at nightfall, exhausted, but pleased with the day's results. While they rested, General Washington learned that General Howe had abandoned his other outposts in western New Jersey.

---

[46] David Hackett Fischer, *Washington's Crossing*, (Oxford University Press, 2004), 405
[47] Ibid.

Hoping to prolong the morale boost from Trenton, General Washington re-crossed the river and occupied the town.

Although Washington hoped that the rejuvenation in American morale would translate into additional troops for his army, he realized that it would be weeks before new recruits arrived in large numbers. It was crucial, therefore, that he keep the present army intact as long as possible. The Virginia and Maryland troops under his command were committed to another year of service, but most of the troops north of Pennsylvania, including the Maine troops in Colonel Paterson's 15th Continental Regiment, were due to go home on January 1st. General Washington had to convince these men to extend their enlistment until replacements arrived, so on December 31st he appealed directly to them to stay. A witness, known to history as Sergeant R, recalled Washington's address:

> *At this trying time General Washington, having now but a little handful of men and many of them new recruits in which he could place but little confidence, ordered our regiment to be paraded, and personally addressed us, urging that we should stay a month longer. He alluded to our recent victory at Trenton; told us that our services were greatly needed, and that we could now do more for our country than we ever could at any future period; and in the most affectionate manner entreated us to stay. The drums beat for volunteers, but not a man turned out. The soldiers worn down with fatigue and privations, had their hearts fixed on home and the comforts of the domestic circle, and it was hard to forego the anticipated pleasures of the society of our dearest friends.*

> The General wheeled his horse about, rode in front of the regiment, and addressing us again said, 'My brave fellows, you have done all I asked you to do, and more than could be reasonably expected; but your country is at stake, your wives, your houses, and all that you hold dear. You have worn yourselves out with fatigues and hardships, but we know not how to spare you. If you will consent to stay only one month longer, you will render that service to the cause of liberty, and to your country, which you probably never can do under any other circumstances. The present is emphatically the crisis, which is to decide our destiny.'
>
> The drums beat the second time. The soldiers felt the force of the appeal. One said to another, 'I will remain if you will.' Others remarked, 'We cannot go home under such circumstances.' A few stepped forth, and their example was immediately followed by nearly all who were fit for duty in the regiment, amounting to about two hundred volunteers.[48]

Similar results occurred among the other regiments that Washington addressed.

It was fortunate that so many men agreed to stay because when General Howe learned that Washington was encamped in Trenton, he sent approximately 8,000 men under General Charles Cornwallis to destroy Washington's army once and for all.[49]

---

[48] Sergeant R ----- "The Battle of Princeton," *Pennsylvania Magazine of History and Biography* Vol. 20 No. 1, (1896), 515-516

[49] Samuel S. Smith, *The Battle of Princeton*, (Monmouth Beach, NJ : Philip Freneau Press, 1967), 12

Princeton

General Washington anticipated a British attack on his army at Trenton and posted a large detachment of light troops on the road to Princeton to slow their advance. They confronted Cornwallis's force on January 2nd, and skirmished with them for most of the day. The stubborn resistance of the Americans delayed the British long enough to prevent Cornwallis from launching an all out attack against Washington's army at Trenton. It was nearly sunset when the British reached the town, and their attempt to cross the Assumpink Bridge to reach Washington's lines was repulsed with significant loss. General Cornwallis ended his assault and confidently declared that he would finish off Washington and his army in the morning. General Washington had other ideas and used the brief reprieve to turn the tables on General Cornwallis.

After a few hours of tense rest, most of the American army quietly withdrew from their defensive lines along the Assumpink Creek and marched to Princeton via a little used back road. General Washington hoped to surprise the small British garrison that Cornwallis had left there with a dawn attack. The maneuver required stealth and deception, so 400 local militia stayed in the Trenton lines to keep the campfires burning and convince the British that Washington was still there.[50] Major James Wilkinson reported that General Washington

> *Ordered the guards to be doubled, a strong fatigue party to be set to work on an intrenchment...within hearing of the sentinels of the enemy, the baggage to be sent to Burlington, the troops to be silently filed off by detachments, and the neighboring fences to be used for fuel to our guards, to keep up blazing until toward day when they had orders to retire. The*

---

[50] Stryker, 275

> *night, although cloudless, was exceedingly dark, and, though calm, most severely cold, and the movement was so cautiously conducted as to elude the vigilance of the enemy.*[51]

For the most part, the ruse worked. Only a handful of British sentries reported movement in the American camp, but these reports went unheeded.

The route the Americans took to Princeton barely qualified as a road and was very difficult on the horses and men. One soldier recalled,

> *The horses attached to our cannon were without shoes, and when passing over the ice they would slide in every direction, and could advance only by the assistance of the soldiers. Our men too, were without shoes or other comfortable clothing; and as traces of our march towards Princeton, the ground was literally marked with the blood of the soldiers feet.*[52]

As the Americans approached the outskirts of Princeton, General Washington split his force. General Greene was sent west to secure a bridge at Stony Brook and enter Princeton along the Post Road, while General Sullivan continued north along the back road with the bulk of the army. General Greene's column consisted of a brigade under General Hugh Mercer (between 300-350 men) and a much larger brigade under General Cadwalader (approximately 1,150).[53]

---

[51] James Wilkinson, *Memoirs of My Own Times, Vol. 1*, (Philadelphia: Abraham Small, 1816), 140

[52] Sergeant R, "The Battle of Princeton," *The Pennsylvania Magazine of History and Biography, Vol. 20, No. 1*, 515

[53] Wilkinson, 141, See also:
Caesar Rodney, *The Diary of Captain Thomas Rodney, 1776-1777*, (Wilmington: The Historical Society of Delaware, 1888), 33
David Hackett Fischer, *Washington's Crossing* 408 and
Samuel Smith, 34

At almost the same moment that Washington divided his army, a British column about a mile to the west crossed the Stony Brook Bridge and ascended a hill on their way to Trenton. They were reinforcements (over 400) from the 17th and 55th British Regiments under Lieutenant Colonel Charles Mawhood.[54] As they climbed the hill, some of Mawhood's horsemen caught a glimpse of Sullivan's column moving towards Princeton. Mawhood could not determine the size of the American force, but he realized that the lone British regiment left in Princeton was in danger, so he reversed direction and rapidly marched back to town. General Washington, who was with Sullivan, soon learned about Mawhood's column. He assumed that it was only a British reconnaissance force from Princeton and ordered General Mercer to intercept and attack it before Mawhood warned the town's garrison.[55] Mercer responded quickly; he marched his brigade northwestward up a hill and attempted to head off the British.[56]

The two forces collided on a farm southwest of Princeton. Lieutenant James McMichael was attached to Mercer's brigade and recalled,

> *Gen. Mercer, with 100 Pennsylvania riflemen and 20 Virginians, was detached to the front to bring on the attack. The enemy then consisting of 500 paraded in an open field in battle array. We boldly marched to within 25 yards of them, and then commenced the attack, which was very hot. We kept up an incessant fire until it came to pushing bayonets, when we were ordered to retreat.*[57]

---

[54] Smith, 19
Note: Fischer contends that the Mawhood's column was closer to 700 men, 329
[55] Smith, 20
[56] Ibid.
[57] McMichael, 141

March to Princeton

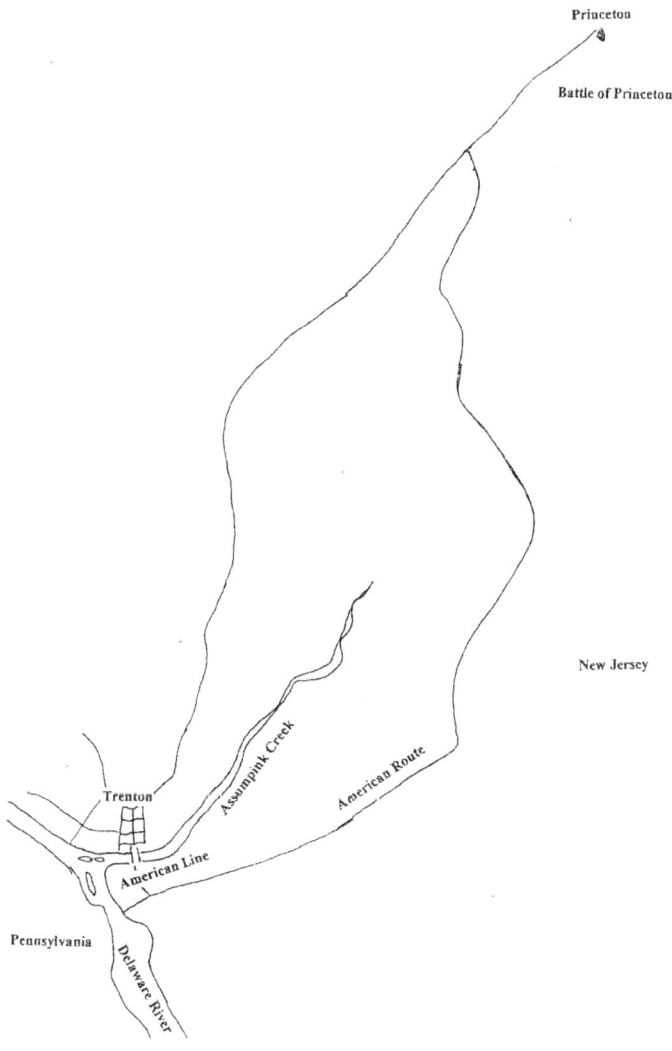

Mercer's men broke and fled to the rear. They abandoned two cannon and their commander, who was struck down and mortally wounded by British bayonets.

Help soon arrived for Mercer's scattered troops in the form of General Cadwalader's militiamen and a two cannon battery under Captain William Moulder. Their appearance on the field momentarily checked the British. General Cadwalader ordered his brigade to advance, and they closed to within 50 yards of the enemy. Unfortunately, this proved too much for Cadwalader's inexperienced men. A witness recalled,

> *The fire of the enemy was so hot, that, at the sight of troops running to the rear, the militia gave way and the whole brigade broke and most of them retired to a woods about 150 yards in the rear, but two pieces of artillery stood their ground and were served with great skill and bravery.*[58]

The battery that held its ground was Captain Moulder's, and for a few minutes, his two cannon and a handful of intrepid infantry were the only Americans on the battlefield. Captain Thomas Rodney of Delaware commanded a portion of the infantry still on the field and recalled,

> *We...took position behind some [hay] stacks just to the left of the artillery; and about 30 of the Philadelphia Infantry were under cover of a house on our left and a little in the rear. About 15 of my men came to this post, but I could not keep them all there, for the enemies fire was dreadful....From these stacks and buildings we, with the two pieces of artillery kept up a continuous fire on the enemy; and in all probability it was this circumstance that prevented the enemy from advancing, for they could not tell the*

---

[58] Ibid. 35

> *number we had posted behind these covers and were afraid to attempt passing them; but if they had known how few there were they might easily have advanced while the two brigades were in confusion and routed the whole body for it was a long time before they could be reorganized again, and indeed many, that were panic struck, ran quite off.*[59]

The determined stand of Moulder, Rodney, and their men not only allowed Cadwalader's and Mercer's brigades to reform, but also allowed reinforcements to take a strong position on the battlefield. These reinforcements, continentals from New England and Virginia and Pennsylvania riflemen, rushed to the fight from General Sullivan's column. They were joined on the battlefield by General Washington, who rallied Cadwalader's and Mercer's men. Sergeant R observed Washington's efforts:

> *Washington appeared in front of the American army, riding towards those of us who were retreating, and exclaimed 'Parade with us, my brave fellows, there is but a handful of the enemy, and we will have them directly'*[60]

The effect of his appeal was electric. Sergeant R recalled, "*I immediately joined the main body, and marched over the ground again.*"[61] Washington led the restored American line, which significantly outflanked the British, towards Mawhood's troops. The British momentarily stood firm and then began an orderly retreat. When the American riflemen moved against their left flank, the British retreat turned into a rout. The pursuing Americans were urged on by General

---

[59] Rodney, 35-36
[60] Sergeant R, 517
[61] Ibid.

Washington, who gleefully exclaimed, "*It's a fine fox chase, boys!*"[62]

Some of Colonel Mawhood's scattered force fled towards Trenton while others withdrew towards Princeton where they found General Sullivan's column pushing the 40th and part of the 55th Regiments. Many of the British fugitives sought shelter in Nassau Hall, a large brick building in town. A blast of artillery quickly convinced them to surrender, however, and Washington's victory was complete. At the cost of less than forty men killed, including General Mercer who died of his wounds a few days later, and another forty wounded, the Americans inflicted a second stunning defeat on General Howe's army. British losses in killed, wounded, and captured numbered between 400 to 500 men.[63]

General Washington was tempted to stage one more daring act, an assault on the vital British supply depot at New Brunswick fifteen miles to the east. He reported to Congress after the battle:

> *My Original plan when I set out from Trenton was to have pushed on to Brunswic, but the harassed State of our own Troops (many of them having no rest for two nights & a day) and the danger of losing the advantage we had gained by aiming at too much induced me...to relinquish the attempt.*[64]

Instead, Washington reluctantly headed north, towards Morristown, and the safety of New Jersey's mountains.

---

[62] Ibid.
[63] Fischer, 414-415
[64] Chase, "General Washington to John Hancock, 5 January, 1777," *The Papers of George Washington: Revolutionary War Series, Vol. 7*, 523

Chapter Seven

"Everything Shall Be Done...To Frustrate the Enemy's Designs" 1777

General Washington's "barefoot and ill clad" army reached Morristown three days after its victory at Princeton.[1] After weeks of hardship in the field, often with no shelter from the weather, the troops were eager to settle into winter quarters.

With the campaign on winter hiatus, most of the New England troops still with Washington prepared to return home. Many departed before their extended enlistments expired. General Washington informed Congress in mid-January that only 800 New England continentals remained out of the 1,200 to 1,400 that originally agreed to stay through January.[2] By mid-February all of the New England continentals had returned home. They found local leaders in Massachusetts scrambling to recruit new continental regiments.

As in previous years, the start of a new year necessitated a reorganization of the American army. While General Washington encamped at Morristown with Virginia and Maryland continentals and short term militia (including militia troops from Massachusetts), the entire Massachusetts continental line underwent another overhaul. Veteran commanders like John Nixon, John Glover, John Paterson, and Ebenezer Learned were promoted by the Continental Congress to brigadier generals and placed in charge of brigades made up of restructured Massachusetts regiments. Most of these continental regiments included a core of seasoned veterans

---

[1] Chase, "General Washington to John Hancock, 5 January, 1777," *The Papers of George Washington, Revolutionary War Series*, Vol. 7, 523
[2] Grizzard, Jr., "General Washington to John Hancock, 19 January, 1777," *The Papers of George Washington, Revolutionary War Series*, Vol. 8, 102

who, like the new recruits, agreed to serve for three years or the duration of the war. Although it is probable that men from Maine served in all 15 Massachusetts regiments, the 11th, 12th, 13th, 1st, 2nd, 7th, and 8th, Massachusetts regiments held significant numbers of Maine troops.[3] Colonel Ebenezer Francis's 11th Massachusetts and Colonel Samuel Brewer's 12th Massachusetts held the largest proportion of Maine troops with nearly half of each regiment consisting of Maine men.[4]

General William Heath, who returned to Massachusetts in February, was ordered by General Washington to organize the new Massachusetts regiments and send them, as soon as possible, to Peekskill, New York (an important supply depot on the Hudson River) and Fort Ticonderoga. Heath reported in mid-March that detachments of troops from the new regiments were on the march:

> *Part of four regiments vizt Colo. Marshalls, Brewers Bradfords, and Frances have marched, and some of them I suppose by this Time have reached* [Fort Ticonderoga].[5]

Heath expected additional detachments to march west within the week but reported that they lacked important articles:

> *The Colonels Are much Embarrassed in procuring Arms & Blankets for their men, this State having been much drained of those Articles heretofore.*[6]

Committees throughout Massachusetts were collecting blankets, and General Heath was hopeful for their success, but he was discouraged about arming all of the troops:

---

[3] *Maine at Valley Forge: Proceedings at the Unveiling of the Maine Marker*, October 17, 1907, (Augusta: Burleigh & Flynt, 1910), 9
[4] Ibid.
[5] Grizzard, Jr., "General Heath to General Washington, 16 March, 1777," *The Papers of George Washington, Revolutionary War Series, Vol. 8*, 586
[6] Ibid.

> *As to Arms I cannot See that they can be Obtained here in Sufficient numbers, being Informed that a number were returned into the Store at Tyconderoga, I have Directed Some of the Officers to March part of their recruits without Arms.*[7]

The recruitment process stretched into April, and detachments departed camp nearly every week for Peekskill and Fort Ticonderoga. General Washington was unsure of British plans for the upcoming campaign, so he ordered eight Massachusetts regiments to Peekskill and seven to Fort Ticonderoga as a precaution. Washington explained to General Heath that

> *A respectable force at Peekskill secures the passage of the North River, and keeps a Body of Men, in our Centre, ready to move North or South as there may be occasion.*[8]

General Washington viewed the men at Peekskill as reinforcements for either his army in New Jersey or the northern army at Fort Ticonderoga, depending on the actions of the British. The regiments at Peekskill included the 1st, 3rd, 4th, 5th, 6th, 7th, 13th, and 15th Massachusetts Regiments of which Colonel Vose's 1st Massachusetts, Colonel Alden's 7th Massachusetts, and Colonel Wigglesworth's 13th Massachusetts, each had over a hundred Maine troops in them.[9] The regiments were organized into two brigades under General John Nixon and General John Glover. Nixon's brigade consisted of the 3rd, 5th, 6th, and 7th Regiments and Glover's consisted of the 1st, 4th, 13th, and 15th Regiments.

The remaining seven Massachusetts regiments that were assigned to Fort Ticonderoga included the 2nd, 8th, 9th, 10th,

---

[7] Ibid.
[8] Grizzard, Jr., "General Washington to General Heath, 13 March, 1777," *The Papers of George Washington, Revolutionary War Series, Vol. 8,* 564
[9] *Maine at Valley Forge,* 9

11th, 12th, and 14th Massachusetts Regiments. The 2nd, 8th, and 9th Regiments under Colonels Bailey, Jackson, and Wesson were brigaded under General Ebenezer Learned. His brigade held over one hundred men from Maine.[10] The 10th, 11th, 12th, and 14th Regiments, under Colonels Marshall, Francis, Brewer, and Bradford were brigaded under General John Paterson and included over 500 men from Maine.[11] While Learned's brigade was distributed among the forts south of Fort Ticonderoga (specifically Fort George on the southern end of Lake George and Fort Edward along the Hudson River), Paterson's brigade, along with a brigade of New Hampshire continentals under General Enoch Poor, took post at Fort Ticonderoga and Mount Independence.[12]

The arrival of Paterson's and Poor's continentals provided a small measure of relief to Fort Ticonderoga's beleaguered commander, Colonel Anthony Wayne of Pennsylvania. He had struggled all winter to maintain a garrison built largely around militia troops and had confided to a friend that

> *This post has been most shamefully neglected – all the old and good Troops are gone – none here but a few wretched militia – badly armed and worse Disciplined. This Garrison at this time Ought to Consist of at least 5000 Effective men – with a well trained Corps of Artillery – perhaps Congress thinks it does. I have not One fifth part of that number on the Ground – and I would much Rather Risque my life, Reputation, and the fate of America on 400 Good Troops, than the Whole of the present Garrison.*[13]

---

[10] Ibid.
[11] *Maine at Valley Forge,* 9
[12] "General Return of the Troops at Fort Ticonderoga, May 24, 1777," in "Nathanael Greene to George Washington, May 24, 1777, with Report on Troop Strength," George Washington Papers at the Library of Congress (Online)
[13] Stille, "Colonel Wayne to Sharp Delany – Extract, 20 Feb. 1777," 49-50

When Wayne returned to New Jersey to command a brigade of Pennsylvanian continentals in the spring, responsibility for the defense of Fort Ticonderoga passed to General Enoch Poor of New Hampshire. Poor reported in late May that he had just over 2,000 men fit for duty, about a quarter of which were from Paterson's brigade.[14]

On June 12th, General Arthur St. Clair assumed command of Fort Ticonderoga. Like all of the fort's commanders before him, St. Clair's immediate superior was General Philip Schuyler in Albany. Schuyler had been placed in command of the northern department two years earlier and had organized the invasion of Canada in 1775 and the defense of Lake Champlain in 1776. The approach of a new campaign season worried General Schuyler. On June 14th, he wrote to General Washington and hinted at the need for reinforcements:

> *Our Numbers are so few to the Northward; and we have so little prospect of their increasing, that should a Disaster befall us at Tyconderoga, we should have very few Troops indeed to oppose them – If the Enemy should make an Attempt to penetrate into the Country, I shall probably be under the Necessity of calling for Assistance from Peek's Kill.*[15]

Unbeknownst to Schuyler, British movements in New Jersey had prompted General Washington to order the very troops Schuyler desired at Peekskill to join Washington's army in New Jersey. General Glover's brigade was part of this force, but they were so poorly clothed they were forced to delay their march.[16] The delay was fortuitous because General

---

[14] Chase, "General Horatio Gates to General Washington, 30 May, 1777," *The Papers of George Washington, Vol. 9,* 561
[15] Grizzard, Jr. "General Schuyler to General Washington, 14 June, 1777," *The Papers of George Washington, Vol.10,* 39
[16] Grizzard, Jr. "General Putnam to General Washington, 19 June, 1777," *The Papers of George Washington, Vol.10,* 76 *The Papers of George Washington, Vol. 9,* 561

Washington rescinded his order when General Howe led the British army back to New York after just a few days in the New Jersey countryside. Howe's movements mystified General Washington, who grew even more perplexed in July when General Howe loaded the bulk of his army aboard British ships and sailed out to sea. It was not until Howe's fleet was spotted entering Chesapeake Bay in late August that his objective became clear. General Howe intended to land his army at the head of the bay and march on Philadelphia from the south.

While General Howe's designs were unclear to the Americans for most of the summer, such was not the case for the other British army in North America. General John Burgoyne and an army of over 7,000 British, Hessian, and Canadian troops, accompanied by hundreds of Indians, moved south along Lake Champlain in early summer. Their objective was Albany. Standing in their way at Fort Ticonderoga and Mount Independence was General Arthur St. Clair and approximately three thousand Americans including hundreds of men from Maine.[17]

Fall of Fort Ticonderoga

General St. Clair received detailed information on Burgoyne's intentions through the interrogation of two prisoners captured by the Americans in mid-June. They informed St. Clair that not only was a large British force under General Burgoyne about to attack the Americans from the north, but a second force of British and Canadian troops and Indians were marching on Albany from the west along the

---

[15] Grizzard, Jr. "General Schuyler to General Washington, 14 June, 1777," *The Papers of George Washington, Vol.10,* 39
[16] Grizzard, Jr. "General Putnam to General Washington, 19 June, 1777," *The Papers of George Washington, Vol.10,* 76
[17] Grizzard, Jr. "General Schuyler to General Washington, 5 July, 1777," Troop Return *The Papers of George Washington, Vol.10,* 201

Mohawk River.[18] General St. Clair relayed this information to General Schuyler who promptly requested reinforcements from General Washington. On June 25th, General St. Clair described a bleak scenario to General Schuyler and predicted that unless significant reinforcements arrived soon, Fort Ticonderoga and Mount Independence would likely fall to General Burgoyne:

> *I cannot help repeating to you the disagreeable Situation we are in, nor can I see the least prospect of our being able to defend the post unless the Militia come in, and should the Enemy...invest us & content themselves with a simple Blockade we are infallibly ruined. I have Thoughts of calling for the Berkshire Militia, which are nearest to us, and will probably be the most alert to come to our assistance....This however is clear to me, that we shall be obliged to abandon this Side* [Fort Ticonderoga] *and then they will soon force the other from us* [Mount Independence] *nor do I see that a Retreat will in any Shape be practicable. Every Thing however shall be done that is possible to frustrate the Enemy Designs, but what can be expected from Troops ill armed naked and unaccoutered.*[19]

General St. Clair's dire prediction unfolded a few days later when General Burgoyne's army arrived and began to encircle Fort Ticonderoga and Mount Independence. Hessian troops worked their way along the east bank of Lake Champlain in an effort to sever the only road to Mount Independence while British troops blocked Fort Ticonderoga's access to Lake

---

[18] Grizzard, Jr. "General Schuyler to General Washington, 16 June, 1777," *The Papers of George Washington, Vol.10,* 55-57
[19] Grizzard, Jr. "General St. Clair to General Schuyler, 25 June 1777," enclosed in a letter to General Washington from General Schuyler dated 28 June, 1777," *The Papers of George Washington, Vol.10,* 141-142

Fort Ticonderoga and Mount Independence

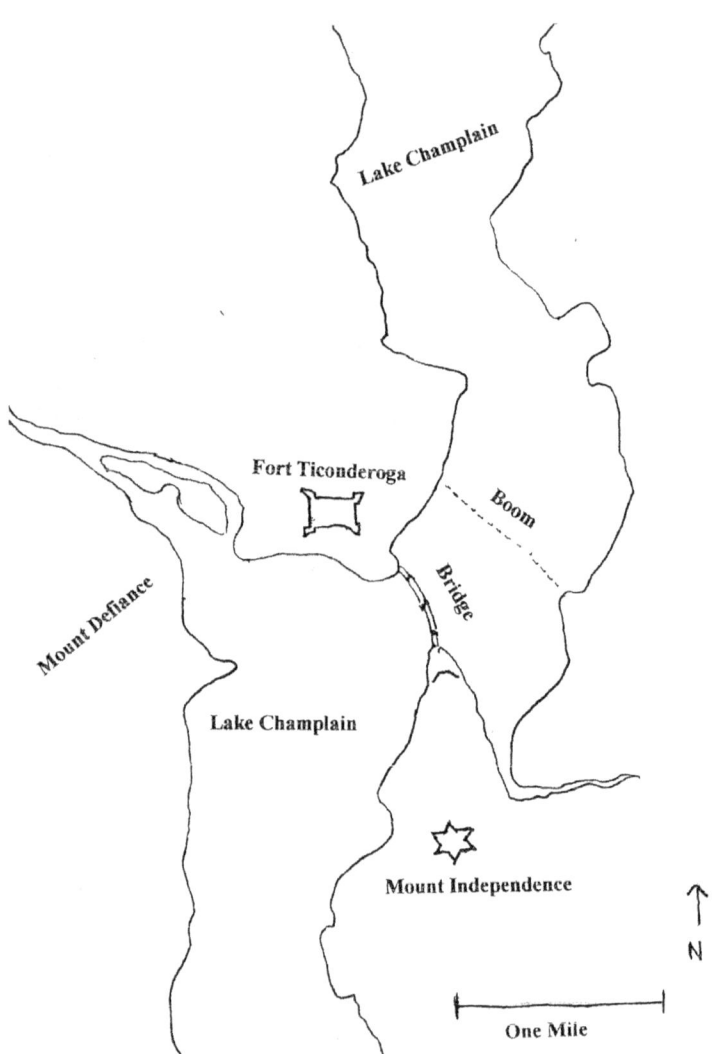

George (and the American forts to the south). The noose around the Americans tightened further on July 5th when Burgoyne's troops successfully hauled cannon to the top of Mount Defiance, a position that commanded Fort Ticonderoga and threatened Mount Independence.

General St. Clair convened a council of war which unanimously agreed that the presence of the British cannon on Mount Defiance made Fort Ticonderoga untenable. The council considered making a stand at Mount Independence but determined that such an attempt against a force more than twice their number would be futile. The council voted instead to abandon both positions and retreat southward before the Hessians cut the road from Mount Independence.[20]

General St. Clair agreed and commenced the retreat under cover of darkness. His order caught much of the garrison by surprise. James Thacher, a surgeon's mate attached to the hospital, described the hectic withdrawal:

At about twelve o' clock...I was urgently called from sleep, and informed that our army was in motion, and was instantly to abandon Ticonderoga and Mount Independence. I could scarcely believe that my informant was in earnest, but the confusion and bustle soon convinced me that it was really true.... It was enjoined on me immediately to collect the sick and wounded, and as much of the hospital stores as possible, and assist in embarking them on board the bateaux and boats at the shore. Having with all possible dispatch completed our embarkation, at three o' clock in the morning...we commenced our voyage...to Skeensboro, about thirty miles. Our fleet consisted of five armed gallies and two hundred bateaux and boats deeply laden with cannon, tents,

---

[20] Grizzard, Jr. "General St Clair to General Washington, 17 July, 1777," *The Papers of George Washington, Vol.10,* 309

> *provisions, invalids and women. We were accompanied by a guard of six hundred men, commanded by Colonel Long, of New Hampshire.*[21]

As Thacher fled south by boat with the invalids, women, and what little provisions and military stores could be secured from the forts, the bulk of General St. Clair's army marched south on foot. St. Clair planned to reunite with his fleet of bateaux at Skenesborough and continue on to join General Schuyler at Fort Edward where he expected they might make a stand against Burgoyne.[22] To do so, St. Clair's men had to endure a forced march with British troops at their heels.

The American column was led by General Poor's New Hampshire continentals followed by the militia, then General Paterson's and General Fermoy's continental brigades.[23] A rear guard, charged with shielding the column from the pursuing British, trailed behind. This detachment was commanded by Colonel Ebenezer Francis of the 11th Massachusetts Regiment. It numbered 450 men (including scores of men from Maine), and comprised select elements from several regiments including his own. Along with protecting the column, the rear guard was ordered to collect all the stragglers who failed to keep up with the march.[24]

St. Clair's men began the march in the early morning hours of July 6th, anxious to put some distance between themselves and General Burgoyne's army. American officers were hard pressed to keep the troops in formation and the column gradually dissolved into separate parties of men stretched out over miles. The warm weather and rough road took a toll on

---

[21] James Thacher, *Military Journal of the American Revolution: 1775-1783*, 82-83

[22] Richard M. Ketchum, *Saratoga: Turning Point of America's Revolutionary War*, (NY: Holt & Co., 1997), , 181

[23] Ibid.

[24] John Williams, *The Battle of Hubbardton: The American Rebels Stem the Tide*, (Vermont Division of Historic Preservation, 1988), 8

many men causing a large number to fall out of the march. They were swept up by Colonel Francis and the rearguard, who prodded them along as best they could.

By early afternoon, the lead elements of St. Clair's scattered force reached Hubbardton, a small settlement seven miles north of Castleton. St. Clair halted at Hubbardton for several hours to give his footsore and exhausted men some much needed rest and allow stragglers and Francis's rearguard to catch up.[25] When General St. Clair resumed his march, he left Colonel Seth Warner and his regiment of Green Mountain Boys behind to reinforce the rearguard. Warner was ordered to assume command of the reinforced rearguard from Francis and lead it to the outskirts of Castleton. Colonel Nathan Hale's 2nd New Hampshire Regiment also joined the rearguard at Hubbardton. Hale was burdened with several hundred sick and disabled men attached to his command.[26]

The condition of Hale's invalids, along with the many stragglers that Colonel Francis brought in when he finally arrived at Hubbardton, made it impossible for Colonel Warner to proceed to Castleton without abandoning scores of men, so he decided to disregard St. Clair's orders and encamp at Hubbardton for the evening. The bulk of the American rearguard, which numbered approximately 1200 men including the invalids and stragglers, camped on a hill along the Castleton Road.[27] A large number of Hale's invalids, as well as a company of 2nd New Hampshire men under Captain James Carr, bivouacked along a brook below the hill.

Three miles away, 850 British troops under General Simon Fraser also made camp.[28] They had pursued the Americans all day and had captured a number of exhausted American stragglers who dropped out of the American march. Three

---

[25] Ibid., 9
[26] Ibid.
[27] Ibid., 60
[28] Ibid., 14

miles behind Fraser were over one thousand German soldiers under General Friedrich Von Riedesel.[29] General Burgoyne had sent these reinforcements to join Fraser as a precaution, and they were destined to play a key role in the upcoming battle.

Battle of Hubbardton

The British and German troops resumed their pursuit of the Americans early the next morning. Two companies from Fraser's 24th Regiment led the march. They were followed by a battalion of light infantry (ten companies) and a battalion of grenadiers (ten companies).[30] Thomas Anburey, an officer in the 24th Regiment, recalled,

> *At three in the morning our march was renewed, and about five we came up with the enemy, who were busily employed in cooking their provisions. Major Grant of the 24th Regiment, who had the advance guard, attacked their pickets, which were soon driven into the main body.... Upon [Grant's] coming up with the enemy, he got upon the stump of a tree to reconnoiter, and had hardly given the men orders to fire when he was struck by a rifle ball, fell off the tree, and never uttered another syllable.*[31]

Although the arrival of the British caught the Americans by surprise, some of the startled American rear guard stood their ground. Sixteen year old Ebenezer Fletcher, a fifer in Captain

---

[29] Ibid., 15
[30] Ibid., 14
[31] Sydney Jackman, *With Burgoyne from Quebec: An Account of the Life at Quebec and of the Famous Battle at Saratoga*, (Toronto: Macmillan of Canada, 1963), 140
Henceforth referred to as Anburey.
First published as *Travels Through the Interior Parts of North America*, by Thomas Anburey.

Battle of Hubbardton

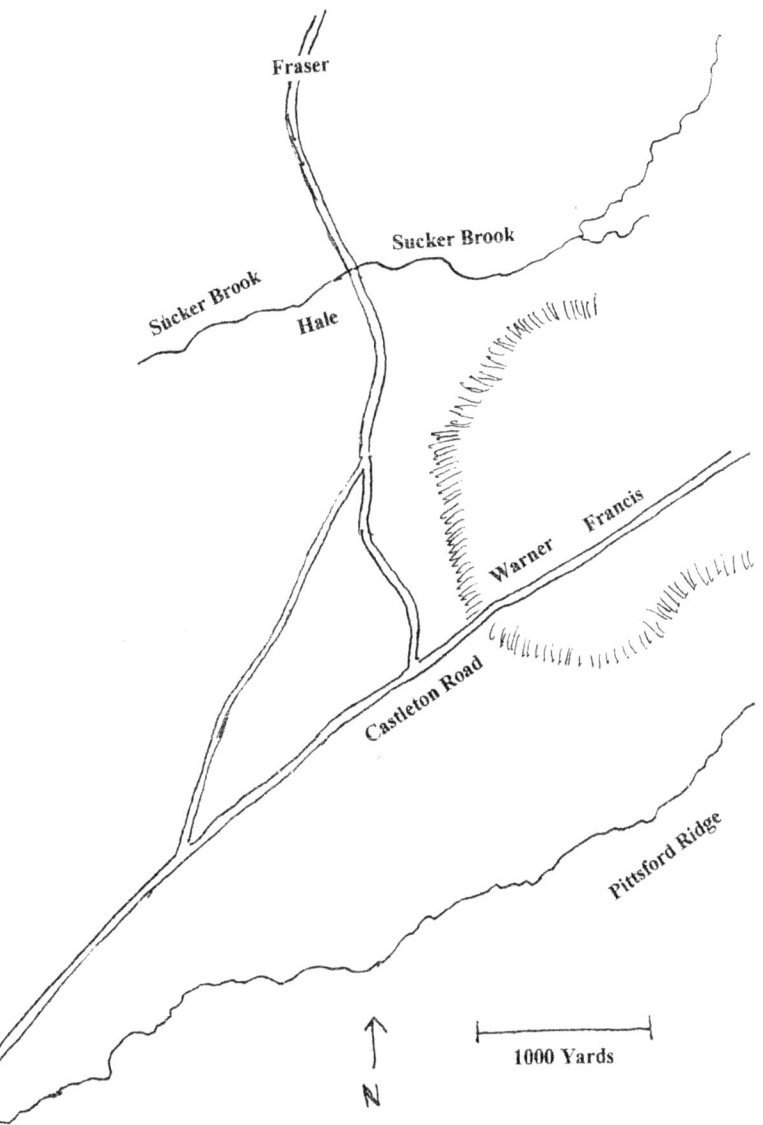

James Carr's company of New Hampshire continentals, recalled the start of the battle:

> *The morning after our retreat, orders came very early for the troops to refresh and be ready for marching. Some were eating; some were cooking, and all in a very unfit posture for battle. Just as the sun rose, there was a cry; " the enemy are upon us." Looking round I saw the enemy in line of battle. Orders came to lay down our packs and be ready for action. The fire instantly began. We were but few in number compared to the enemy. At the commencement of the battle, many of our party retreated back into the woods. Capt. Carr came up and says, "My lads advance, we shall beat them yet." A few of us followed him in view of the enemy. Every man was trying to secure himself behind girdled trees, which were standing on the place of action. I made shelter for myself and discharged my piece. Having loaded again and taken aim, my piece missed fire. I brought the same a second time to my face; but before I had time to discharge it, I received a musket ball in the small of my back, and fell with my gun cocked. My uncle, Daniel Foster, standing but little distance from me, I made out to crawl to him and spoke to him. He and another man lifted me and carried me back some distance and laid me down behind a large tree, where was another man crying out most bitterly with a grievous wound. By this time I had bled so freely, I was very weak and faint. I observed the enemy were like to gain the ground. Our men began to retreat and the enemy to advance. Having no friend to afford me any relief, every one taking care of himself, all things looked very shocking to me; to remain where I was and fall into the hands of the enemy, especially in the condition I*

> was in, expecting to receive no mercy, it came into my mind to conceal myself from them if possible. I made use of my hands and knees, as well as I could, and crawled about two rods among some small brush, and got under a log. Here I lay concealed from the enemy, who came instantly to the place I lay wounded at. What became of my distressed partner I know not. The enemy pursued our men in great haste. Some of them came over the log where I lay. Some came so near I could almost touch them. I was not discovered by the enemy till the battle was over.[32]

After a brief but intense firefight along Sucker Brook, Fraser's troops scattered the Americans and swung left towards the hill on which the bulk of the American rearguard was posted. General Fraser recalled,

> I was at the head of the Light Infantry Battalion, it had then a pretty steep hill on the left flank; I halted the Light Infantry, faced them to the left and with the whole in front I ran up the hill with them....[33]

While Fraser's light infantry scaled the steep hill, the two companies of the 24th Regiment moved around the hill to the right of the British light infantry and engaged Colonel Warner's Green Mountain Boys. Warner's men fought hard and forced Fraser to reinforce his right with the grenadier battalion, which was held in reserve, and a detachment of light infantry. These reinforcements overwhelmed Warner's men and pushed them across the Castleton Road, blocking the American march route south.

---

[32] Ebenezer Fletcher, *Narrative of the Captivity & Sufferings of Ebenezer Fletcher of New Ipswich*, (New Ipswich, NH: S. Wilder, 1827), 12-13
[33] Simon Fraser, Gen. Fraser's Account of Burgoyne's Campaign on Lake Champlain and the Battle of Hubbardton, "Letter to John Robinson, 13 July, 1777," *Proceedings of the Vermont Historical Society*, (1898), 145

While the American left flank was forced across the road, Colonel Francis's detachment and part of the 2nd New Hampshire Regiment engaged General Fraser's light infantry battalion for control of the hill. Fraser's light troops scaled the steep hill and forced the Americans from the crest, but they failed to drive the rebels completely off the hill. Colonel Francis's men reformed behind a sturdy rail fence along the Castleton Road. Joseph Bird of the 6th Massachusetts Regiment fought in Colonel Francis's detachment and recalled,

> *While the enemy were forming, Capt.* [Enos] *Stone went forward, and from the rail fence...next to the Selleck House, on the west side of the* [Castleton] *road, removed the three top rails, for seven or eight lengths, so that we could have a better chance at them. We drove them back twice, by cutting them down fast. We didn't leave* [the] *log fence or charge them...I was near the centre...under Col. Francis...We fought before they drove us till I had fired 20 cartridges.*[34]

Bird's description of the intensity of the fight is confirmed by others. Joshua Pell, a loyalist officer at the battle, noted that the British "*ascended the Hill within thirty yards of the Rebels and immediately began a brisk fire.*"[35] Captain Enos Stone of the 12th Massachusetts Regiment described the engagement as "*as hot a fire as ever was kept up.*"[36] As Colonel Francis's men struggled to hold the center of the American position at

---

[34] Henry Hall, Battle of Hubbardton (1877) Vermont Historical Society, John Williams Papers, MS 149, 20

[35] Joshua Pell, Jr., "Diary of Joshua Pell Jr., An Officer of the British Army in America: 1776-1777," *Bulletin of the Fort Ticonderoga Museum*, Vol. 1, No. 6, July 1929, 9

[36] Enos Stone, "Capt. Enos Stone's Journal," *New England Historical and Genealogical Register*, Vol. 15, October, 1861, Vermont Historical Society, John Williams Papers, MS 149

the fence line, elements of the 2nd New Hampshire moved against the British left flank. General Fraser recounted that the Americans "*observed the weakness of my left* [flank] *and made some demonstrations to renew the attack,* [which] *they began pretty briskly.*"[37] The Americans were about to turn Fraser's left flank when General Riedesel's German troops arrived. Riedesel's vanguard smashed into the right flank of the attacking Americans and drove them back. The shock of these German reinforcements was more than the Americans could handle, and the entire American line broke to the rear.

With the road to Castleton blocked and the enemy converging on them from three sides, the only choice for the Americans was to flee over Pittsford Ridge. A running battle ensued as the Americans scrambled and fought their way up and over the ridge. It was during this stage of the battle that Colonel Francis was killed by a British volley. Captain Moses Greenleaf of the 11th Massachusetts described the colonel's death:

> *Numbers fell on both sides, among ours the brave and ever to be lamented Col. Francis, who fought bravely to the last. He first received a ball through his right arm, but still continued at the head of our troops, till he received the fatal wound through his body, entering his right breast, he dropped on his face.*[38]

Captain Greenleaf and most of the Americans managed to escape and gradually made their way to rejoin the American army, which was now headed for Rutland. Nearly 400 of their comrades were left behind, over 40 of whom died on the battlefield and nearly a hundred others were wounded.

---

[37] Fraser, 146
[38] Donald Wickman, ed. "Breakfast on Chocolate: The Diary of Moses Greenleaf, 1777," *The Bulletin of the Fort Ticonderoga Museum*, 497

New York Campaign of 1777

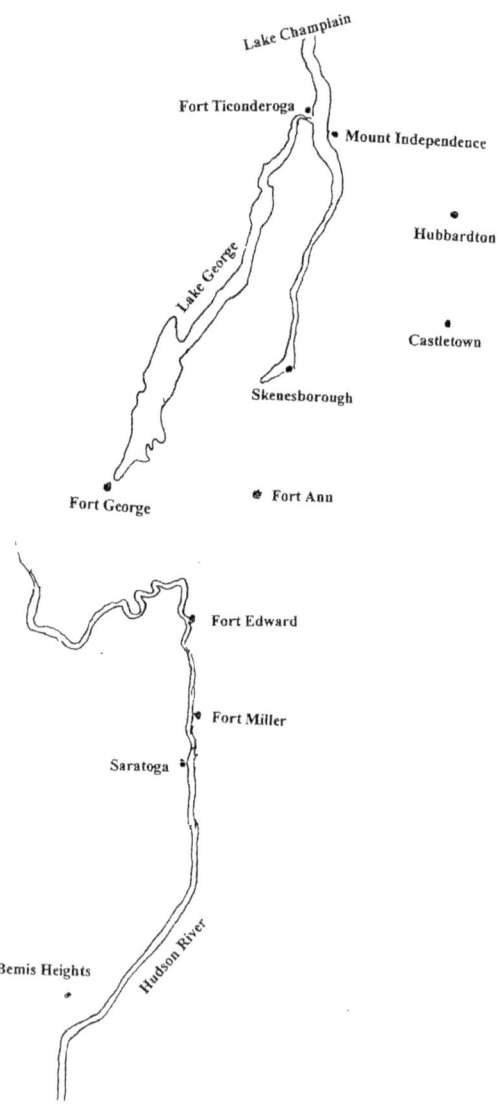

British and Germans losses were approximately half that of the Americans.

The situation was equally grim for the Americans who fled by bateaux to Skenesborough. Within hours of the American retreat from Fort Ticonderoga, General Burgoyne's army broke through the log boom and bridge that stretched across the lake. Burgoyne's fleet quickly caught up to Colonel Long and the American baggage train at Skenesborough. Many of the Americans panicked upon Burgoyne's approach, and Colonel Long struggled to destroy what supplies he could before he fled with his troops to Fort Anne. The next morning, General Burgoyne ordered a regiment under Lieutenant Colonel John Hill to march towards Fort Anne.

The situation at Fort Anne was chaotic as members of Colonel Long's force wandered in all night. The arrival of 400 New York militia from Fort George helped calm the garrison, and the Americans very nearly defeated Colonel Hill's force in a heated battle outside the fort on July 8th. Their success was undermined by the quick thinking of a British officer who yelled out an Indian war hoop that tricked the Americans into thinking that enemy reinforcements were approaching. Low on ammunition and discouraged at the prospect of fighting British and Indian reinforcements, the Americans disengaged and returned to Fort Anne. They abandoned the fort the next day and withdrew to Fort Edward, sixteen miles to the south.

General Arthur St. Clair was also trying to reach Fort Edward with the bulk of his army, but the British presence in Skenesborough forced him to take a circuitous route around that settlement to the Hudson River. St. Clair's exhausted and demoralized troops finally reached Fort Miller, a few miles south of Fort Edward on July 12th. St. Clair continued on to Fort Edward to meet with General Schuyler. Two days later, Schuyler wrote to General Washington to update him on the dire situation in New York:

> *Desertion prevails and Disease gains Ground nor is it to be wondered at, for we have neither Tents, Houses, Barns, Boards or any Shelter, except a little Brush – Every Rain that falls, and we have it in great Abundance almost every Day, wets the Men to the Skin – We are besides in great Want of every Kind of Necessaries, provisions excepted – Camp Kettles we have so few that we cannot afford above one to twenty Men. Altho' we have near fifteen Tons of powder, yet we have so little Lead, that I could not give each Man above fifteen Rounds, and altho' I have saved about thirty pieces of light Artillery yet I have not a single Carriage for them.... In this Situation, I have only to look up to your Excellency for Relief, and permit me to entreat you to send a Reinforcement of Troops and such a Supply of Artillery, Ammunition and every other Necessary (except provisions and powder) as an Army ought to have, if it can possibly be spared.*[39]

General Schuyler reported that General John Nixon's Massachusetts brigade from Peekskill arrived on July 12th but amounted to only 575 men fit for duty. Schuyler sent them, along with 600 militia, to cut trees and obstruct Wood Creek and the road from Fort Anne to Fort Edward.[40]

Bloody skirmishes occurred almost daily between General Nixon's continentals and Burgoyne's Indians and Tories. On July 21st a scouting party from the 7th Massachusetts Regiment was ambushed and nearly wiped out by a large party of Indians.[41] Two days later, Indians attacked General Nixon's picket, killing and wounding nearly twenty men and a few days later a lieutenant, two sergeants, and a young lady named

---

[39] Grizzard, Jr., "General Schuyler to General Washington, 14 July, 1777," *The Papers of George Washington, Vol. 10*, 280
[40] Ibid., 280-81
[41] Ketchum, 278

Jane McCrea were killed and scalped in separate incidents.[42] McCrea's murder was widely reported and provoked much outrage towards Burgoyne and his Indian allies. This outrage was slow to manifest itself into increased militia support for General Schuyler, so for the rest of July and most of August Schuyler had to make due with the troops he had and the few reinforcements General Washington sent.

Washington's ability to assist Schuyler was limited to sending General John Glover's Massachusetts brigade northward from Peekskill in late July. These troops were barely enough to replace General Ebenezer Learned's brigade – which was sent into western New York in August under General Benedict Arnold to reinforce Fort Stanwix against Lieutenant Colonel Barry St. Leger's large British and Indian force that was attacking from the west.

Fort Stanwix and Oriskany

St. Leger's force of nearly 2,000 men, half of which were Indians, a third of which were Tories, and the remainder British and German troops, planned to march from Canada along the Mohawk Valley and link up with General Burgoyne in Albany.[43] Approximately 550 New York continentals under Colonel Peter Gansevoort stood in St. Leger's way at Fort Stanwix.[44] Two hundred reinforcements joined the garrison on August 1st, the day before St. Leger's force arrived and commenced a siege.[45]

On August 5th, St. Leger learned that an 800 man American relief force of militia under General Nicholas Herkimer was marching to Fort Stanwix from the east. St. Leger sent 400

---

[42] Grizzard, Jr., "General Schuyler to General Washington, 23 & 26 July, 1777," *The Papers of George Washington, Vol. 10*, 381, 431
[43] Boatner, 961
[44] Ibid.
[45] Ibid.

Fort Stanwix and Oriskany

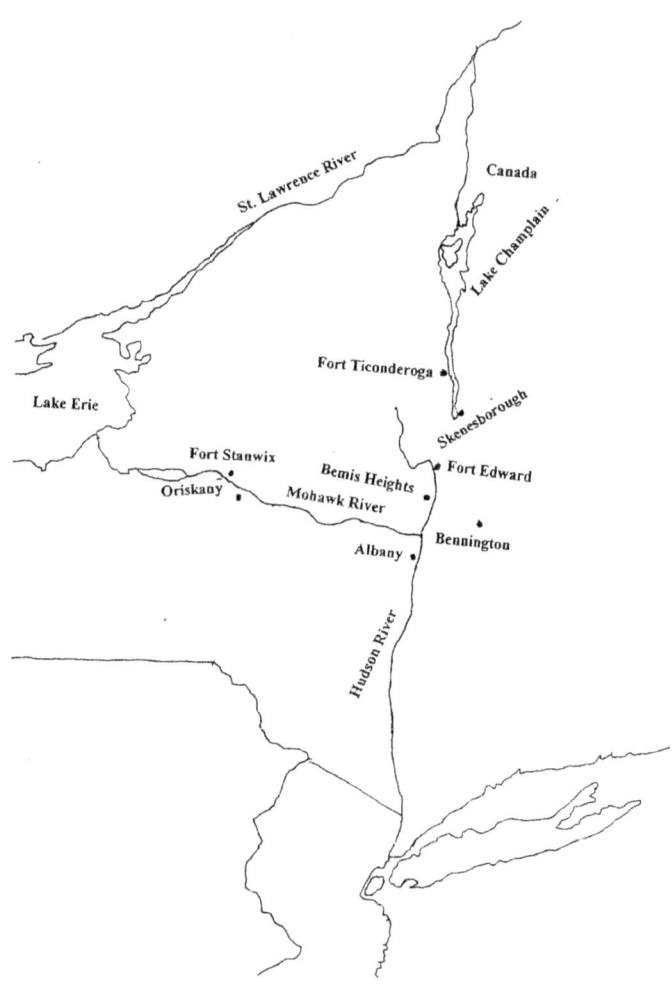

Indians under Joseph Brant, a Mohawk war chief, to ambush Herkimer. A bloody six hour battle erupted the next day that resulted in hundreds of casualties for the Americans.[46] General Herkimer was mortally wounded, and his relief force dispersed, but while the Battle of Oriskany raged a few miles east of Fort Stanwix, the Americans in the fort launched a sortie that pillaged the empty Indian camp. The loss of their personal effects and some of their comrades in the battle significantly dampened the Indians enthusiasm to continue with the expedition.

General Schuyler learned of the engagement on August 8th and dispatched two regiments from General Learned's Massachusetts brigade and a regiment of New York continentals, along with General Benedict Arnold, to relieve Fort Stanwix. When news reached St. Leger's camp that another large American force was on its way, most of the Indians abandoned the expedition. The loss of half of his force caused St. Leger to lift the siege and withdraw to Canada.

While events unfolded to the advantage of the Americans in western New York, General Schuyler struggled to find a way to stop Burgoyne's advance. Facing a force nearly twice his number, Schuyler had little choice but to withdraw in the face of Burgoyne's advance. The Americans abandoned Fort Edward and Fort George in late July and withdrew to Stillwater, a small settlement on the west bank of the Hudson River approximately 25 miles north of Albany, on August 3rd. General Schuyler reported to Washington that he was powerless to resist Burgoyne's advance in part because fear of the Indians had infected his troops:

---

[46] Boatner, 819

> *The most unaccountable panic has seized the Troops...A few shot from a small party of Indians has more than once thrown them into the greatest Confusion – The Day before Yesterday three hundred of our Men...came running in, being drove by a few Indians, certainly not more than fifty.*[47]

General Schuyler also lamented about the lack of militia support from New England:

> *We have not one Militia from the Eastern States & under forty from this – Can it therefore any longer be a matter of Surprise that we are obligated to give way and retreat before a vastly superior force daily increasing in numbers....* [48]

Burgoyne's army finished clearing the road from Fort Anne to Fort Edward in late July and reached Fort Miller on August 11th. Although General Burgoyne was closer than ever to his objective (Albany), his long supply line extended all the way to Canada and created logistical challenges for him. As a result, Burgoyne halted at Fort Miller to stockpile his supplies in preparation for a final push to Albany. In an effort to alleviate his supply problems, Burgoyne sent a detachment of 650 troops under Lieutenant Colonel Friedrich Baum towards the town of Bennington where the Americans reportedly had a supply depot.

---

[47] Grizzard Jr., "General Philip Schuyler to General George Washington, 1 August, 1777," *The Papers of George Washington, Vol.* 10, 482-483
[48] Grizzard Jr.,"General Philip Schuyler to General George Washington, 13 August, 1777," *The Papers of George Washington, Vol. 10,* 606

Battle of Bennington

Colonel Baum's detachment consisted of over 200 dismounted German dragoons, approximately 150 German infantry, over 200 loyalists and Indians, and a party of British regulars.[49] Fifteen hundred militia under General John Stark of New Hampshire gathered at Bennington to confront Baum.[50]

Advance elements of Stark's militia skirmished with Baum's detachment a few miles northwest of Bennington on August 14th. The American skirmishers withdrew to Bennington while Baum halted at the Walloomsac River and encamped. He also sent a request to General Burgoyne for reinforcements. Burgoyne received Baum's request the next morning and immediately dispatched Lieutenant Colonel Heinrich Breymann with 650 German troops and two cannon to support Baum, but heavy rain slowed Breymann's march to a crawl.[51] The same rain kept the two sides near Bennington in camp, but August 16th dawned clear, and General Stark ordered his men forward. He sent large detachments around both flanks of Baum's position and unleashed an assault that was wildly successful.

Although Colonel Baum had placed his men in strong defensive positions, they were too scattered to support each other. Most of Baum's loyalists, who had erected a redoubt on a rise of land across the river from Baum's main position, were overrun after only a few minutes of fighting. Many of Baum's dragoons put up a heroic fight atop a steep hill overlooking the Walloomsac River, but they too were eventually overwhelmed by superior numbers. Colonel Baum himself was mortally

---

[49] John Luzader, *Decision on the Hudson: The Battles of Saratoga*, (Eastern National, 2002), 28-29
[50] Ibid., 29
[51] Boatner, 72

Battle of Bennington

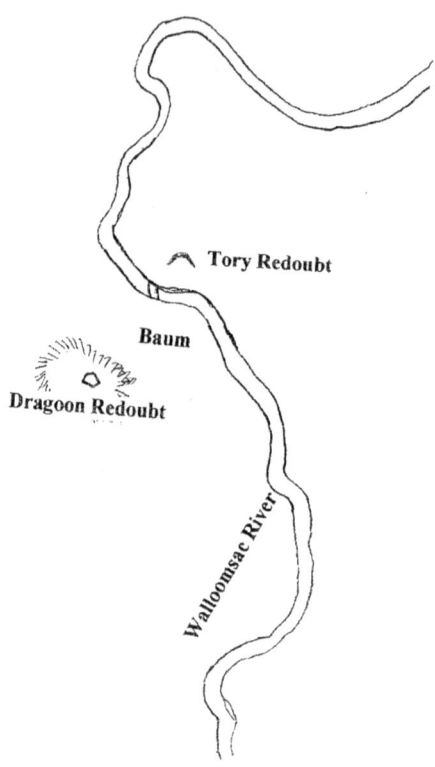

wounded in the battle, and his detachment completely routed with only a handful of men able to escape.

Colonel Breymann's relief force arrived too late to assist Baum and soon found themselves fighting for their own survival against American reinforcements under Colonel Seth Warner. Nearly a third of Breymann's force fell in the fight or were captured before Breymann was able to disengage and retreat.[52]

The Battle of Bennington was a stunning American victory, on par with Washington's victory at Trenton eight months earlier. General Burgoyne lost over 900 men (mostly captured) and was denied much needed supplies stored at Bennington.[53] More importantly, American morale soared.

The American success at Fort Stanwix and Bennington came too late to save General Schuyler's reputation with Congress. For weeks, accusations of incompetence and, in some cases, betrayal swirled around Schuyler's name; Congress responded in mid-August by relieving him of command of the northern army. General Horatio Gates assumed command of the army and noted the marked change in American morale that resulted from the victories at Fort Stanwix and Bennington:

> *Upon my leaving Philadelphia the Prospect this Way appeared most gloomy, but the severe Checks the Enemy have met at Bennington &* [Fort Stanwix] *has given a more pleasing View of public Affairs.*[54]

Morale was not the only thing growing in the American army. Reinforcements increased its size significantly in late August. Two New York regiments arrived on August 22nd followed by

---

[52] Boatner, 74
[53] Ibid., 75
[54] Philander D. Chase, ed., "General Horatio Gates to General Washington," *The Papers of George Washington, Vol. 11*, 38

the return of General Arnold with General Learned's brigade from Fort Stanwix.[55] Colonel Daniel Morgan's 400 man rifle corps also joined the army, which was posted on the south side of the Mohawk River. General Washington's orders to Morgan expressed his high regard for the colonel and his riflemen:

> *The approach of the enemy in that quarter has made a further reinforcement necessary. I know of no corps so likely to check their progress, in proportion to its number, as that under your command. I have great dependence on you, your officers and men, and I am persuaded you will do honor to yourselves, and essential services to your country.*[56]

By September, General Gates's army, which included all 15 regiments of the Massachusetts line, surpassed Burgoyne's in size, and a new sense of optimism gripped the Americans.[57] They marched north on September 8th, paused at Stillwater for a few days, and then continued on to Bemis Heights, an excellent defensive position overlooking the Hudson River. General Gates ordered his army to fortify their position and wait for Burgoyne, who had finally resumed his movement south. They would not have long to wait.

---

[55] Dearborn Journal, 103
[56] Grizzard Jr., "General Washington to Colonel Daniel Morgan, 16 August, 1777," *The Papers of George Washington*, Vol. 10, 641
[57] Charles H. Lesser, ed. "A General Return of the Continental Troops Under the Command of Major General Horatio Gates, 7 September, 1777," 49

Chapter Eight

"Both Armies Seemed to be Determined on Death or Victory" 1777

General John Burgoyne's plan to march to Albany to sever New England from the rest of the rebellious colonies had encountered significant setbacks in August 1777. A campaign that had begun with much promise in July, when the Americans abandoned Fort Ticonderoga and Mount Independence without a fight, stumbled in August at Fort Stanwix and Bennington. A whole month had passed since these setbacks during which Burgoyne stockpiled supplies at Fort Miller for a final push to Albany. Burgoyne's army resumed its march and crossed the Hudson River on September 13th. As the British drew closer to Bemis Heights, contact with the Americans increased. Burgoyne might have benefitted from the use of his Indians, but most of them abandoned the expedition by late August. Burgoyne knew that a large American force lay to his front, but he was unsure of its strength and placement. Undeterred, Burgoyne boldly advanced towards the Americans on September 19th.[1]

General Burgoyne's uncertainty about the position of the Americans caused him to divide his army into three columns. The left column, commanded by General von Riesdel, comprised approximately 1,600 men.[2] It included most of the artillery and a large baggage train protected by the 47th British regiment. The column slowly marched southward along the river road towards Bemis Heights. General Burgoyne's right

---

[1] James Baxter, ed., *The British Invasion from the North: Digby's Journal of the Campaigned of Generals Carleton and Burgoyne from Canada, 1776-1777*, (New York : De Capa Press, 1970), 267
[2] Luzader, 41

column, commanded by General Simon Fraser, was his largest detachment with 2,400 men.[3] Fraser's task was to screen the army's right flank while probing for the American left. To do this, Fraser marched nearly three miles west, away from the river, and then swung south towards Bemis Heights.

General Burgoyne marched with the center column in a diagonal direction from the river. The column totaled 1,500 men from the 9th, 20th, 21st, and 62nd British Regiments and was commanded by General James Hamilton. Four pieces of artillery were also part of this column.[4]

Battle of Freeman's Farm

Burgoyne's three columns began their march around 9:00 a.m. and were immediately spotted by American pickets. Word reached the American camp that the enemy was on the move. General Gates ordered Colonel Morgan's light corps, composed of his riflemen and 250 light infantry under Major Henry Dearborn of New Hampshire, to investigate.

Morgan's detachment, numbering around 600 men, advanced through the thick woods in two sections.[5] They marched about a mile and a half and emerged onto the edge of an abandoned farm. The clearing was dotted with trees and stumps. Two small buildings, described as cabins by many eyewitnesses, sat on a rise of ground about 300 yards away. The opposite wood line was only 150 yards beyond the cabins.

Morgan's corps arrived at the clearing just as an enemy advance guard attacked the American pickets posted in the cabins. Samuel Armstrong, a member of Major Dearborn's light infantry, described the encounter:

---

[3] Ibid.
[4] Ketchum, 357
[5] Wilkinson, Appendix E and Joseph Lee Boyle, "From Saratoga to Valley Forge: The Diary of Lt. Samuel Armstrong," *The Pennsylvania Magazine of History and Biography,* Vol. 121 No. 3 (July 1997), 245 (Henceforth referred to as Lieutenant Armstrong's Diary)

Battle of Freeman Farm

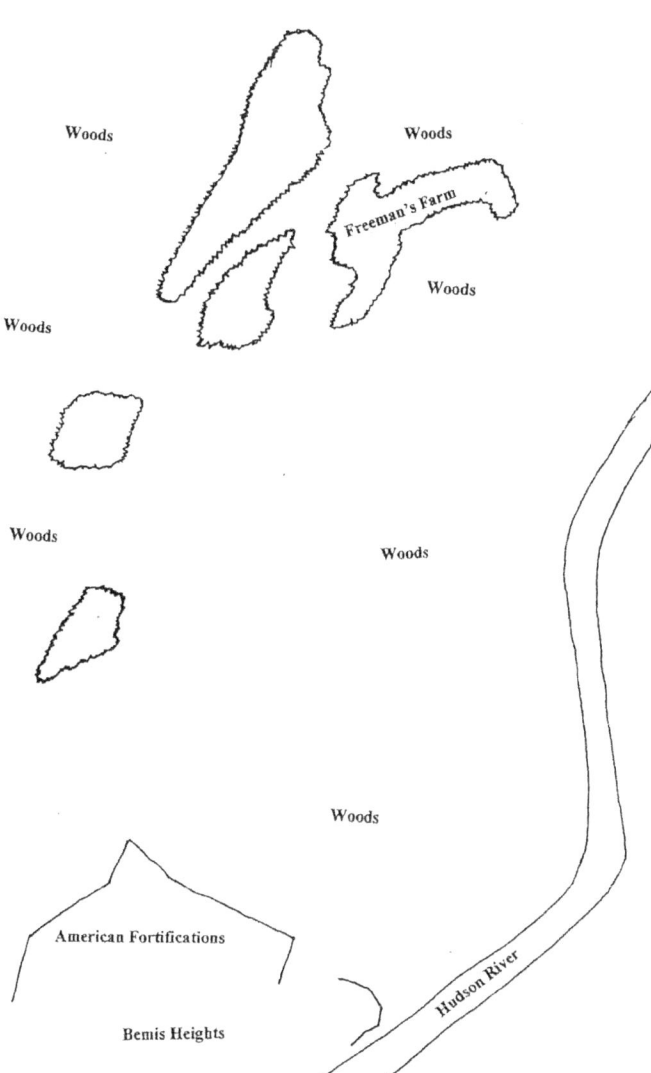

> [At] *about 12 Oclock we were Alarm'd by the firing of two or three Musketts from the Enemies Scouts, upon which the Riffle and Light Infantry Battalions were Ordered off to Scour the Woods. We* [marched] *to our Picquet Guard where we had no sooner got Sight of than we saw the Enemy surrounding them.* [6]

The American pickets quickly fled Freeman's Farm in the face of the approaching enemy.[7] As the British skirmishers pushed past the cabins and neared the southern wood line, they collided with the bulk of Morgan's light corps. British Lieutenant William Digby described what happened:

> *A little after 12 our advanced picquets came up with Colonel Morgan and engaged, but from the great superiority of fire received from him – his numbers being much greater – they were obliged to fall back, every officer being either killed or wounded except one.*[8]

The British skirmishers, outnumbered and outgunned, retreated under a deadly barrage of fire. Advance elements of Morgan's corps pursued them across the field and into the woods beyond. The pursuit abruptly ended when the Americans encountered British reinforcements. These soldiers, eager to fire on the Americans, did so without orders and before all of their comrades from the advance party had cleared their front.[9] The result was more loss for the battered British skirmishers and an end to the American pursuit.

---

[6] Lieutenant Armstrong's Diary, 245
[7] Earl of Harrington in, John Burgoyne, *A State of the Expedition from Canada*, (New York Times & Arno Press, 1969), 68
[8] Digby Journal, 272
[9] Horatio Rogers ed., *Hadden's Journal and Orderly Book: A Journal Kept in Canada and Upon Burgoyne's Campaign in 1776 and 1777*, (Boston: Gregg Press, 1972), 163
(Henceforth referred to as Hadden Journal)

Morgan's corps, which was already disorganized by the charge, disintegrated in retreat. Men ran in all directions to escape the enemy. The sudden emergence of two British companies and a cannon from General Fraser's column added urgency to their flight.[10]

Appalled by the turn of events, Colonel Morgan struggled to reorganize his shattered corps. He used an uncommon military tool to do so, a turkey whistle. As General Hamilton's main body of British troops deployed along a ridge at Freeman's Farm, Morgan reorganized his riflemen in the woods.[11] Fresh American troops from General Enoch Poor's brigade deployed on Morgan's left and extended the American line westward.

Less than a mile away a large American picket under Major William Hull of the 8th Massachusetts listened anxiously for further sounds of battle. Major Hull's picket detachment was drawn from General Learned's brigade and had been reinforced by men from two additional regiments. The men listened intently as the firing at Freeman's Farm resumed in mid-afternoon.

Suddenly, General Benedict Arnold appeared and called for 300 volunteers from the detachment to join the fray. Major Hull quickly organized the volunteers and rushed to the fight.[12]

Hull's detachment arrived just in time to plug a hole in the American line caused by the withdrawal of a militia battalion. Hull's men braced themselves for artillery fire and an enemy charge and were ordered to aim low and hold their fire. Major Hull recalled,

---

[10] Anburey, 172
[11] Rogers, ed., Hadden Journal, 164
[12] Ketchum, 363

> *Their infantry advanced...and* [kept] *up a heavy fire, which killed and wounded some of our men. When* [the enemy] *reached the centre of the field.* [I] *ordered* [the] *troops to fire. Many of the enemy fell, and their line became partially disordered. They did not retreat, but slowly advanced, still continuing an incessant fire. We returned it as rapidly as our men could load, and with such effort checked their advance and created considerable disorder in their ranks. The distance at this time between the two lines was not more than ten rods.*[13]

Up to this point, Major Hull's Massachusetts men had firmly held their position. Hull now decided that it was time to push the enemy. He ordered a bayonet charge that threw the British into a confused retreat.[14] Hull's men captured twenty British prisoners but were forced back to their original position in the American line by British cannon.[15] They fought alongside Pennsylvania and Virginia riflemen and New Hampshire, New York, and Connecticut continentals and militia.

Facing the Americans were four British regiments under General James Hamilton. The battle centered on a small ridge just beyond the Freeman house. Lieutenant James Hadden, a British artillery officer, described the action:

> *The Enemy being in possession of the wood almost immediately attacked the Corps which took post beyond two log Huts on Freemans Farm...I was advanced with two Guns to the left of the 62nd Regt and ye two left companies being formed en potence* [refused or bent to protect the flank] *I took post in the*

---

[13] Campbell, Maria Hull, *Revolutionary Services and Civil Life of General William Hull, Prepared from his manuscript,* (NY, 1848), 95
[14] Ibid.
[15] Ibid.

> *Angle...In this situation we sustained a heavy tho intermitting fire from near three hours....*[16]

The American fire, enhanced by the accuracy of the riflemen, was especially hard on the British artillerists. Lieutenant Hadden lost 19 out of 22 men and all of his horses. The 62nd regiment lost nearly half of its men.[17]

Hadden's position was not the only hot spot; the battle raged all along the line. British Lieutenant William Digby noted that he had never seen anything like it:

> *Such an explosion of fire I never had any idea of before, and the heavy artillery joining in concert like great peals of thunder, assisted by the echoes of the woods, almost deafened us with the noise.*[18]

British corporal Roger Lamb gave a similar account:

> *The conflict was dreadful; for four hours a constant blaze of fire was kept up, and both armies seemed to be determined on death or victory...Men, and particularly officers, dropped every moment on each side. Several of the Americans placed themselves in high trees, and as often as they could distinguish a British officer's uniform, took him off by deliberately aiming at his person.*[19]

The impact of American marksmanship was also noted by Colonel James Wilkinson, who observed that it repeatedly drove the British from the Freeman house hill:

---

[16] Rogers, ed., Hadden Journal, 165
[17] Ibid.
[18] Digby Journal, 237
[19] Roger Lamb, *An Original and Authentic Journal of Occurrences During the Late American War from Its Commencement to 1783*, (Dublin: Wilkinson & Courtney, 1809), 159
Reprinted by Arno Press, 1968

> *The fire of our marksmen from this wood was too deadly to be withstood by the enemy in line, and when they gave way and broke, our men rushing from their cover, pursued them to the eminence, where having their flanks protected,* they [the enemy] *rallied and charging in turn drove us back into the wood, from whence a dreadful fire would again force them to fall back; and in this manner did the battle fluctuate, like waves of a stormy sea, with alternate advantage for four hours without one moment's intermission. The British artillery fell into our possession at every charge, but we could neither turn the pieces upon the enemy, nor bring them off...The slaughter of this brigade of artillerists was remarkable, the captain and thirty-six men being killed or wounded out of forty-eight.*[20]

Even General Burgoyne acknowledged the impact of the riflemen:

> *The enemy had with their army great numbers of marksmen, armed with rifle-barrel pieces; these during an engagement, hovered upon the flanks in small detachments, and were very expert in securing themselves, and in shifting their ground. In this action many placed themselves in high trees in the rear of their own line, and there was seldom a minute's interval of smoke, in any part of our line without officers being taken off by single shot. It will naturally be supposed, that the Indians would be of great use against this mode of fighting. The example of those that remained after the great desertion*

---

[20] Wilkinson, 241

proved the contrary, for not a man of them was to be brought within the sound of a rifle shot. [21]

Late in the afternoon, reinforcements from General Learned's Massachusetts brigade and Colonel Thomas Marshall's 10th Massachusetts Regiment arrived to bolster the left side of the American line. Their involvement was mostly limited to skirmishing with General Simon Fraser's troops on the British right. The bulk of the fight raged on the right side of the American line.

As sunset approached, the British were in serious trouble. The 62nd regiment was shattered, and the other regiments were barely holding on. Suddenly, drums were heard in the woods beyond the American right flank. German reinforcements, under General Riedesel, emerged from the forest and onto the field to relieve the British. They slammed into the right flank of the startled Americans. A German artillery officer, Captain Pausch, recalled,

I had shells brought up and placed by the side of the cannon and as soon as I got the range, I fired twelve or fourteen shots in quick succession into the foe who were within good pistol shot distance. [22]

The arrival of the Germans revived British spirits, and they rallied one more time. Captain Pausch noted,

The firing from muskets was at once renewed, and assumed lively proportions, particularly the platoon fire from the left wing of Riedesel. Presently, the enemy's fire, though very lively at one time, suddenly ceased. I advanced about sixty paces sending a few

---

[21] Burgoyne, 39-40
[22] George Pausch, *Journal of Captain Pausch, Chief of the Hanau Artillery During the Burgoyne Campaign*, Translated by William L. Stone, (Albany, NY: Joel Munsell's Sons, 1886), 137-138

shells after the flying enemy, and firing from twelve to fifteen shots more into the woods into which they had retreated. Everything then became quiet; and about fifteen minutes afterwards darkness set in.... [23]

One of the most intense battles of the Revolutionary War was over, and the carnage was appalling. The field was littered with dead and wounded men who remained unattended all night. Lieutenant Digby described the scene:

During the night we remained in our ranks, and tho we heard the groans of our wounded and dying at a small distance, yet could not assist them till morning, not knowing the position of the enemy, and expecting the action would be renewed at day break. Sleep was a stranger to us...
20th. At day break we sent out parties to bring in our wounded, and lit fires as we were almost froze with cold, and our wounded who lived till the morning must have severely felt it. [24]

British ensign Thomas Anburey had the misfortune to command a burial party the next day:

The day after our late engagement, I had as unpleasant a duty as can fall to the lot of an officer, the command of the party sent out to bury the dead and bring in the wounded...They [the wounded] *had remained out all night, and from the loss of blood and want of nourishment, were upon the point of expiring with faintness; some of them begged they might lie and die, others again were insensible, some upon the least movement were put in the most horrid*

---

[23] Ibid. 138
[24] Digby, 274

> *tortures, and all had near a mile to be conveyed to the hospitals; others at their last gasp, who for want of our timely assistance must have inevitably expired. These poor creatures, perishing with cold and weltering in their blood, displayed such a scene, it must be a heart of adamant that could not be affected at it.*[25]

Although the British kept the field, it was at a heavy cost; they suffered twice as many casualties as the Americans. Some of the British, like Thomas Anburey, questioned the value of the victory:

> *Notwithstanding the glory of the day remains on our side, I am fearful the real advantage resulting from this hard fought battle will rest on that of the Americans, our army being so weakened by this engagement as not to be of sufficient strength to venture forth and improve the victory, which may, in the end, put a stop to our intended expedition; the only apparent benefit gained is that we keep possession of the ground where the engagement began.*[26]

General Burgoyne, in a letter to Lord George Germain, reached a similar conclusion about the victory:

> *It was soon found that no fruits, honour excepted, were attained by the preceding victory, the enemy working with redoubled ardour to strengthen their left, their right was already unattackable.*[27]

---

[25] Anburey, 176
[26] Ibid. 175
[27] Burgoyne, "Burgoyne to Germaine, 10 October, 1777," *A State of the Expedition*, Appendix, 88

Despite their retreat from the field, the attitude in the American camp was far from defeatist. In fact, most American accounts bragged about punishing the enemy and attributed the retreat merely to darkness. Major Dearborn's observation was typical:

> *On this Day has Been fought one of the Greatest Battles that Ever was fought in America, & I Trust we have Convinced the British Butchers that the Cowardly yankees Can & when there is a Call for it, will, fight...The Enimy Brought almost their whole force against us, together with 8 pieces of Artilery. But we who had Something more at Stake than fighting for six Pence Pr Day kept our ground til Night Closed the scene, & then Both Parties Retire'd.*[28]

Many of the British did indeed change their opinion of the Americans after the battle. Ensign Thomas Anburey's comments were typical:

> *The courage and obstinacy with which the Americans fought were the astonishment of everyone, and we now become fully convinced they are not that contemptible enemy we had hitherto imagined them, incapable of standing a regular engagement, and that they would only fight behind strong and powerful works.*[29]

An official count of American casualties listed 321 in all, with 65 killed, 218 wounded, and 38 missing.[30] General Learned's brigade accounted for about one tenth of America's

---

[28] Lloyd A. Brown and Howard H. Peckham, eds., *Revolutionary War Journals of Henry Dearborn* (NY: DaCapo, 1971),   106 (Henceforth referred to as Dearborn's Journal)
[29] Anburey, 175
[30] Wilkinson, Appendix D

losses while General Poor's brigade accounted for nearly two thirds of them.[31] Although the Americans believed they had dealt Burgoyne a significant blow, they realized that his army was still very dangerous and braced themselves for another attack. Fortunately for the Americans, who were very low on ammunition, it failed to materialize.

General Burgoyne actually planned to resume his advance on September 20th, but canceled at the last minute to rest his troops. While they rested, Burgoyne received news that General Henry Clinton was leading a British detachment northward from New York to attack the American posts in the New York Highlands in order to draw some of the Americans away from Bemis Heights. Although Clinton's force was too small to fight its way to General Burgoyne, both generals hoped that Clinton's presence would force General Gates to send some of his troops south and give Burgoyne a better chance to break through to Albany.

General Burgoyne decided to fortify his position and wait for Clinton's advance to have the desired effect. Unfortunately for Burgoyne, few Americans left Bemis Heights. In fact, during the seventeen day standoff, the American army swelled to over 10,000 men.[32]

With time on his side, the ever cautious Gates waited behind his fortified lines. Every passing day saw Burgoyne's supplies dwindle, and his situation grow more desperate. American patrols added to Burgoyne's discomfort by constantly harassing his lines and foraging parties. General Burgoyne acknowledged the impact of this constant pressure on his army in a letter:

---

[31] Ibid.
[32] Wilkinson, "A General Return of the Army of the United States, commanded by the Hon. Major-General Horatio Gates, 4 Oct. 1777," Appendix E

> *From the 20th of September to the 7th of October, the armies were so near, that not a single night passed without firing, and sometimes concerted attacks upon our advanced picquets; no foraging party could be made without great detachments to cover it; it was the plan of the enemy to harass the army by constant alarms, and their superiority of numbers enabled them to attempt it without fatigue to themselves.*[33]

The critical British supply situation finally forced General Burgoyne to act in early October. He decided to probe the American position with a large reconnaissance detachment. If the reconnaissance discovered a weakness in the American lines, he would follow with an attack the next day. If no weakness was found, the army would retreat to Fort Ticonderoga.

General Burgoyne's reconnaissance force numbered approximately 1,500 men and ten cannon.[34] Although nearly all of the army's units contributed men, the bulk came from the right wing of Burgoyne's line. Two redoubts anchored this position. One was manned by British light infantry under Lieutenant Colonel Balcarress. The other was defended by German grenadiers under Lieutenant Colonel Breymann. Since the march route of the reconnaissance detachment placed it between the Americans and the redoubts, General Burgoyne drew heavily from these fortifications and left only a skeleton force in each.[35]

Burgoyne led his troops out of camp around noon and slowly advanced toward the American left wing. His skirmishers drove off American picquets less than a mile into their march. Burgoyne halted at an open farm field and posted

---

[33] Burgoyne, 168
[34] Eric Schnitzer, "Battling for the Saratoga Landscape," *Cultural Landscape Report: Saratoga Battle, Saratoga National Park, Vol. 1* (Boston, MA: Olmsted Center for Landscape Preservation), 44
[35] Ibid.

his men in a long line facing south. The British right flank, composed of light infantry troops, rested at the base of a wooded hill. German troops, supported by artillery, held the center of the line, and the left was defended by British grenadiers and artillery.[36]

General Burgoyne tried to observe the American encampment from this position, but woods obscured his view. Ironically, as Burgoyne and his staff struggled to peer through the woods, they were observed by an American officer.

When reports of Burgoyne's advance reached American headquarters, General Gates dispatched his aide, Lieutenant Colonel Wilkinson, to investigate:

> *I perceived about half a mile from the line of our encampment, several columns of the enemy, 60 or 70 rods from me, entering a wheat field which had not been cut, and was separated from me by a small rivulet...After entering the field, they displayed, formed the line, and sat down in double ranks with their arms between their legs. Foragers then proceeded to cut the wheat or standing straw, and I soon after observed several officers, mounted on the top of a cabin, from whence their glasses they were endeavoring to reconnoitre our left, which was concealed from their view by intervening woods.*[37]

Wilkinson reported his findings to General Gates, who sent Wilkinson to Colonel Morgan with instructions to *"begin the game."*[38] Wilkinson recalled,

---

[36] Luzader, 52
[37] Wilkinson, 267
[38] Ibid. 268

> *I waited on the Colonel, whose corps was formed in front of our centre, and delivered the order... Colonel Morgan, with his usual sagacity, proposed to make a circuit with his corps by our left, and under cover of the wood to gain the height on the right of the enemy, and from thence commence his attack, so soon as our fire should be opened against their left.*[39]

General Gates approved Morgan's proposal and ordered General Enoch Poor to attack Burgoyne's left flank with his brigade of New Hampshire and New York troops. General Learned's Massachusetts brigade was also sent forward with orders to strike the center of the enemy line.

As Colonel Morgan's men hurried to gain possession of the wooded hill overlooking Burgoyne's right flank, General Poor's brigade attacked the British left flank. The intensity of the engagement caused some in Morgan's corps to worry that the Americans were losing. Major Dearborn recalled,

> *Our light troops moved on with a quick step in the course directed, and after ascending the woody hill to a small field about 500 yards to the right of the Enemies main line, we discovered a body of British light Infantry handsomely posted on a ridge 150 yards from the edge of the wood where we then were. At this time the fire of the two main armies was unusually heavy and we were apprehensive from the fire that our line was giving way.*[40]

---

[39] Ibid.
[40] Henry Dearborn, "A Narrative of the Saratoga Campaign – Major General Henry Dearborn, 1815," *The Bulletin of the Fort Ticonderoga Museum, Vol. 1, no. 5,* (January, 1929), 7 (Henceforth referred to as Dearborn Memoir)

Far from giving way, Poor's brigade overwhelmed Burgoyne's left flank, which collapsed and streamed back to the rear. As this transpired, General Learned's brigade (reinforced with a regiment of New York continentals and two regiments of New Hampshire militia) engaged the German troops holding the center of Burgoyne's line.

As this fight raged, General Benedict Arnold arrived on the field. Arnold had lost command of the left wing of the American army after a heated argument with General Gates. The sound of battle proved too seductive to Arnold, however, and he rode out of camp to join the fight. Arnold's men still recognized him as their commander and responded to his orders to advance.

While General Learned's men engaged the German troops in a fierce fight in the center of Burgoyne's line, Colonel Daniel Morgan's light corps arrived and struck Burgoyne's right flank. Captain Thomas Posey of Virginia commanded one of Morgan's rifle companies and described what happened:

> *They* [the enemy] *had repulsed* [General] *Arnold twice before Morgan made his attack, which was on the right wing of* [the] *enemy – the* [rifle] *regiment had march'd under cover of a thick wood, and a ridge, which ridge the enemy were about to take possession of as Morgan gained the summit of it, the enemy being within good rifle shot, the regiment poured in a well directed fire which brought almost every officer on horseback to the ground.*[41]

Lieutenant Colonel Wilkinson credited Morgan's riflemen (and Major Henry Dearborn's light infantry) with routing Burgoyne's right flank:

---

[41] Thomas Posey, "A Short Biography of the Life of Governor Thomas Posey," Thomas Posey Papers, (Indiana Historical Society Library)

Battle of Bemis Heights (The Wheatfield)

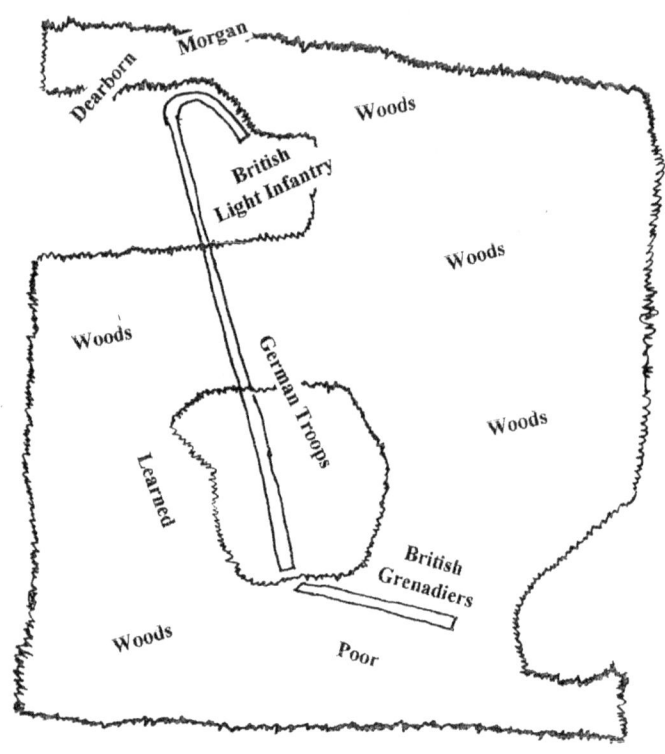

True to his purpose, Morgan at this critical moment poured down like a torrent from the hill, and attacked the right of the enemy in front and flank. Dearborn at the moment, when the enemy's light infantry were attempting to change front, [to face the riflemen] *pressed forward with ardour and delivered a close fire; then lept the fence, shouted, charged and gallantly forced them in disorder.* [42]

Despite the collapse of his flanks, Burgoyne's center continued to hold against Learned's men. The arrival of a brigade of New York militia under General Abraham Ten Broeck soon turned the tide. The pressure on the center of Burgoyne's line soon proved too great, and it joined the rest of Burgoyne's detachment in retreat. Eight British cannon and scores of men were abandoned on the field.[43] Lt. Colonel Wilkinson described the carnage:

The ground which had been occupied by the British grenadiers presented a scene of complicated horror and exultation. In the square space of twelve or fifteen yards lay eighteen grenadiers in the agonies of death, and three officers propped up against stumps of trees, two of them mortally wounded, bleeding, and almost speechless. [44]

Most of Burgoyne's detachment, including 300 German grenadiers who were drawn from Breymann's redoubt, retreated to the Balcarres redoubt. This bolstered the defenders there, but left Breymann's redoubt undermanned and vulnerable. Two fortified cabins between the redoubts were also weakly manned because of the failure of troops to return to them.

---

[42] Wilkinson, 268
[43] Luzader, 55
[44] Wilkinson, 270

The Americans initially failed to capitalize on the weakness of Burgoyne's extreme right flank and concentrated their efforts instead on the Balcarres redoubt. British Corporal Roger Lamb recalled,

> *General Arnold with a brigade of continental troops, pushed rapidly forward, for that part of the camp possessed by lord Balcarres, at the head of the British light infantry, and some of the line; here they were received by a heavy and well directed fire which moved down their ranks, and compelled them to retreat in disorder.* [45]

However, while General Arnold and his men were repulsed at the Balcarres redoubt, hundreds of American troops positioned themselves to strike the weakly defended cabins and the 150 German soldiers defending Breymann's redoubt.[46] Colonel Morgan's light corps along with General Learned's brigade of Massachusetts and New York continentals and New Hampshire militia, and troops from the 5th and 6th Massachusetts regiments of General Nixon's brigade participated in the attack.[47] Lieutenant Colonel James Wilkinson described the scene:

> *The Germans were encamped immediately behind the rail breast-work, and the ground in front of it declined in a very gentle slope for about 120 yards, when it sunk abruptly; our troops had formed a line under this declivity, and covered breast high were warmly engaged with the Germans.* [48]

---

[45] Lamb, 164
[46] Luzander, 56
[47] Ibid.
[48] Wilkinson, 272

Wilkinson recalled that General Learned acted on his recommendation to attack the two sparsely manned cabins:

> *I had particularly examined the ground between the left of the Germans and the light infantry, occupied by the provincialists, from whence I had observed a slack fire; I therefore recommended to General Learned to incline to his right, and attack at that point: he did so with great gallantry; the provincialists abandoned their position and fled; the German flank was by this means uncovered.* [49]

Learned's brigade was joined by General Benedict Arnold, who had left General Poor's brigade at the Balcarres redoubt to join the assault on Breyman's Redoubt. Colonel Wilkinson described what happened:

> [Arnold] *Dashed to the left through the fire of the two lines* [British and American] *and escaped unhurt; he then turned the right of the enemy...and collecting 15 or 20 riflemen threw himself with this party into the rear of the enemy, just as they gave way, where his leg was broke, and his horse killed under him.* [50]

Major Henry Dearborn's light infantry also participated in the assault. Dearborn noted,

> *The assault was commenced by the advance of Arnold with about 200 men through a cops of wood which covered the Enemies right, the appearance of Arnold on the right was the signal for us to advance and assault the front. The whole was executed in the*

---

[49] Ibid.
[50] Ibid.

Fall of Breymann's Redoubt

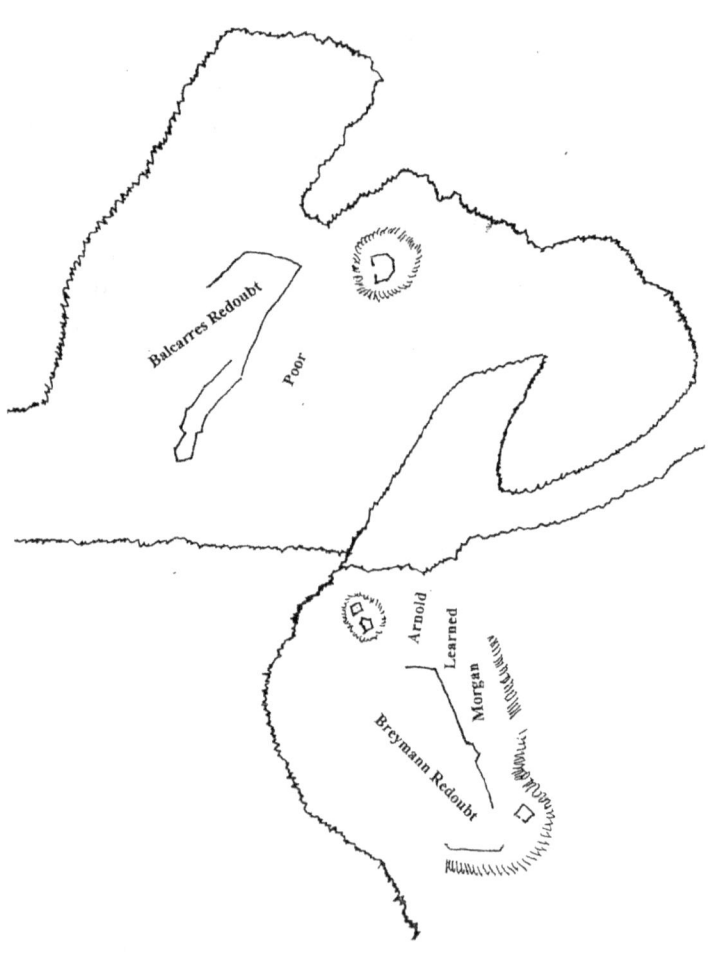

most spirited and prompted manner and as soon as the Enemy had given us one fire, he fell back from his work to his line of tents, and as we entered he gave way and retreated in confusion. [51]

Whether by design or chance, the assault on Breymann's redoubt was masterfully executed, and the Germans were quickly overwhelmed. General Burgoyne's line was breeched, and only nightfall saved the British from further disaster.

Once again, the American army had punished the enemy, inflicting far more casualties than they had suffered. This decisive American victory left General Burgoyne with only one choice, retreat. His march to Albany was over. It remained to be seen whether his retreat to Fort Ticonderoga would succeed.

Retreat and Surrender

Under cover of darkness General Burgoyne withdrew his army across a deep ravine and established a new position on a hill overlooking the Hudson River. The position was called the Great Redoubt, and its location allowed Burgoyne to consolidate his troops and protect the river transports and hospital.

When the Americans realized that Burgoyne had withdrawn across the ravine, they took possession of his old lines and commenced a steady, but ineffectual, bombardment. General Gates sent Morgan's light corps forward to reconnoiter the enemy's rear and harass them. Major Dearborn participated in this reconnaissance:

---

[51] Dearborn Memoir, 8

> *This morning [Oct. 8] the Rifle men & Light Infantry & several other Regiments march'd in the Rear of the Enimy Expecting they ware Retreeting But found they ware Not. there has Been scurmishing all Day...a Large Number of the Enimy Deserted to us to Day.*[52]

General Burgoyne realized that retreat or surrender were the only options left for his army. The former was tremendously difficult, but the latter was still unthinkable. Thus, on the evening of October 8th, Burgoyne began a retreat northward. Over 400 men too injured or sick to transport were left under a flag of truce to the care of the Americans.[53] The rest of Burgoyne's army slowly trudged towards Saratoga. After a few miles they halted to rest and wait for the boats to catch up. A heavy rain pelted the men all day and when they resumed their march the road turned to mud. They arrived at the heights of Saratoga after dark and collapsed on the ground in exhaustion. Lieutenant Digby described the scene:

> *We remained all night under constant, heavy rain without fires or any kind of shelter to guard us from the inclemency of the weather. It was impossible to sleep, even had we an inclination to do so from the cold and rain....*[54]

Ensign Anburey gave an equally distressing account of the British army's first night in Saratoga:

---

[52] Dearborn Journal, 109
[53] Luzader, 59
[54] Digby, 300

The army...arrived at Saratoga, in such a state of fatigue that the men had not strength or inclination to cut wood and make fires, but rather sought sleep in their wet clothes and on the wet ground. [55]

Despite Burgoyne's slow retreat, the Americans struggled to keep pace. The rain turned the road into a quagmire of mud, and the size of the American army, over 12,000 strong, complicated logistics. Fortunately for the Americans, Burgoyne's retreat ceased at Saratoga.

Over the next few days, as General Burgoyne grappled with his situation, American troops constantly harassed his army. A steady artillery bombardment added to their discomfort. By October 14th General Burgoyne and his army had had enough. With his officers' consent, Burgoyne asked for terms of surrender. General Gates was generous in his demands and on October 17th General Burgoyne formally surrendered his army.

The most decisive battle of the Revolutionary War to date was over and hundreds of Massachusetts and Maine men played an important role in the victory. News of the American victory helped convince France to form an alliance with the United States. The war had reached a turning point, but it would be months before the Americans learned of the alliance. In the meantime, they had to deal with the loss of Philadelphia to General Howe. And for those living along the Maine coast, the threat of attack from the British navy remained a real concern despite the successful defense of Machias in August 1777.

---

[55] Anburey, 190

British Raid on Machias

While most of America's attention in the summer of 1777 focused on events in New York and the whereabouts of General William Howe's army, a British flotilla under Captain Sir George Collier sailed along the Maine coast in August to attack Machias. Ever since Jonathan Eddy's attack on Fort Cumberland in 1776, the British viewed Machias as a threat to Nova Scotia. On August 13th, 1777, Collier's flotilla, which included a ship of 44 guns, another of 28, one of 16 and one of 14 guns entered Machias Bay to neutralize this threat.[56]

Approximately 120 British Marines formed a landing party and were loaded upon the brig *Hope* (whose shallow draft allowed it to navigate upriver).[57] Long boats towed the brig upriver until it was stopped by a boom stretched across the river. Captain Collier reported that the rebels had built "*a trifling Fortification,*" at the boom and "*kept up a pretty brisk Fire of Musketry upon,*" the brig and long boats, but they did little damage.[58] Colonel Jonathan Eddy commanded the American defenders and provided a more detailed account from the American perspective:

> *The Hope stood immediately up the River attended by a Sloop and twelve Boats, till they came opposite to a small Battery we had about 2 miles below the Falls, mann'd with about Twenty men with small Arms and one 2 pounder. The enemy attempted to land there with six Boats and a Number of Men, but were repuls'd by our People with some Loss.*[59]

---

[56] Clark, "Colonel Jonathan Eddy to the Massachusetts Council, 17 August, 1777," *Naval Documents of the American Revolution, Vol. 9*, 758

[57] Clark, Captain Sir George Collier to Philip Stephens, 16 August, 1777," *Naval Documents of the American Revolution, Vol. 9*, 750

[58] Ibid.

[59] Clark, "Colonel Jonathan Eddy to the Massachusetts Council, 17 August, 1777," *Naval Documents of the American Revolution, Vol. 9*, 758

Early the next morning, the British Marines landed under cover of fog near the American battery and easily captured it. Captain Collier reported that stocks of flour, rice, leather hides, shoes, and ammunition were discovered nearby and destroyed as well as several vessels, a corn mill and a large quantity of corn.[60] The Marines re-boarded the *Hope* which passed the boom and continued towards the town, two miles upstream. Captain Collier reported,

> *The Rebels, however, accumulated fast on the adjacent Heights, & kept up a constant Fire of Musketry upon* [the Hope], *which did no Damage as she was well barricaded: She got almost as high up as the Saw-Mills in the Town, but finding Breast Works of fell'd Trees, & a number of arm'd Rebels to the amount of about 400 (including 40 or 50 Indians)...Capt. Dawson with great Propriety* [returned] *satisfy'd with the Damage already done the Rebels.*[61]

Colonel Jonathan Eddy attributed the British withdrawal more to the strong presence of the Americans in town than any satisfaction the British gained with the damage they had inflicted on Machias. According to Eddy,

---

[60] Clark, Captain Sir George Collier to Philip Stephens, 16 August, 1777," *Naval Documents of the American Revolution, Vol. 9,* 750-51
[61] Ibid., 751

Machias 1777

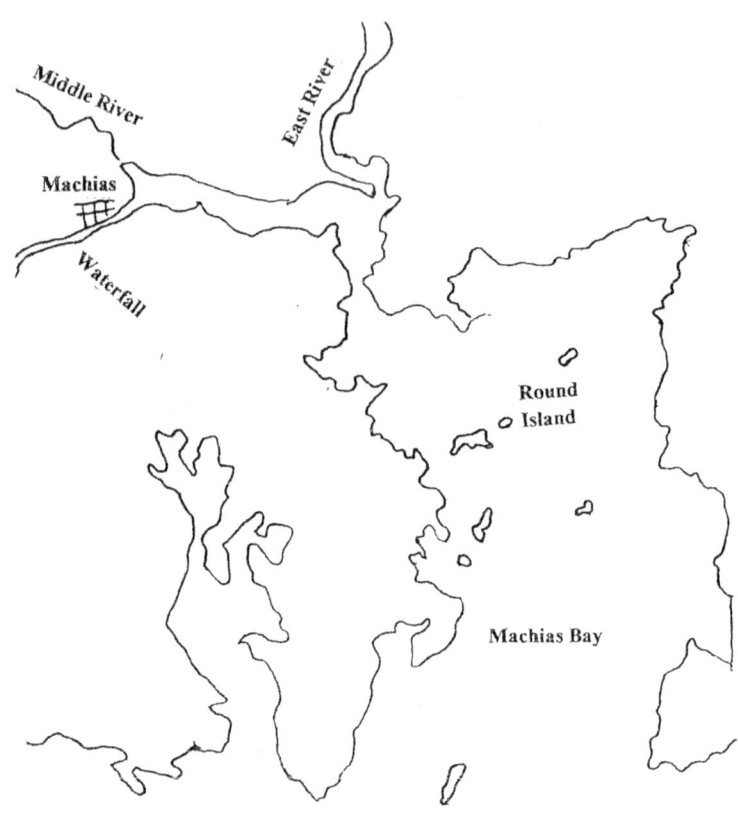

> [The British brig] *came...within good Shot of the Falls, not expecting to meet with any Resistance, but seeing Continental Colours flying, and two Breastworks fill'd with Men, one of them having two 2 pounders, the other, one 2 pounder and six swivels, they began to think of retreating and accordingly got the Boats ahead to Tow the Brig down* [river].[62]

As the *Hope* started downriver, Colonel Eddy sent men in pursuit. It was their turn to inflict some damage on the British:

> *I instantly detach'd Major* [George] *Stillman with thirty Men to attack the Boats & harass the Enemy in their Retreat; The Major proceeded by Land till he got abreast of the Brig and Boats about a Mile and a half below the Falls and began a heavy Fire, which was warmly return'd for some Time from the Brig with Cannon and small Arms.*[63]

The fight subsided in the evening, but resumed just as fierce the next day when the brig ran aground. Colonel Eddy noted, "*Our People got one of the 2 pounders down & began to play upon her in this Position, and Hull'd her several times.*"[64] The American cannon was too small to do much damage, however, and the *Hope* was able to extricate itself at high tide. It rejoined the rest of the British flotilla, which then departed Machias Bay.

Both sides appear to have viewed the outcome of the engagement at Machias in favorable terms. Captain Collier highlighted the destruction of supplies his force inflicted

---

[62] Clark, "Colonel Jonathan Eddy to the Massachusetts Council, 17 August, 1777," *Naval Documents of the American Revolution, Vol. 9*, 759
[63] Ibid.
[64] Ibid.

(which he argued disrupted the settlement's ability to attack Nova Scotia) while Colonel Eddy highlighted the conduct of his men and the fact that the British were repulsed with what he considered significant losses.

Chapter Nine

"Never Did Men Behave With So Much Courage" 1778-79

While much of America celebrated the victory at Saratoga in the fall of 1777, General Washington's army sat outside Philadelphia discouraged by the loss of the American capital to General Howe and his army. Washington's troops had lost two pitched battles in a three week period (Brandywine and Germantown) and placed their hope of regaining Philadelphia on two river forts they still held below the city and the arrival of reinforcements from the northern army. General Howe's hold on Philadelphia was tenuous as long as Washington was able to block navigation of the Delaware River. The Americans bravely resisted British and Hessian attacks on the forts, but the garrisons fell in mid-November and the British navy was able to re-supply Howe's army in Philadelphia. The American capital was securely under British control.

Although the loss of the river forts was another blow to American morale, the arrival of reinforcements from the northern army, including the Massachusetts brigades of Generals Paterson, Learned, and Glover, eased the disappointment and caused General Washington to consider an attack on Philadelphia; however, he reluctantly concluded that the likelihood of success was slim and decided to maintain his position outside of the city. A large British force probed Washington's lines at White Marsh in December, but after a sharp skirmish, they returned to Philadelphia and settled in for the winter.

Valley Forge

The onset of winter required better shelter than the thin tents Washington's men had used all fall. Lieutenant John Marshall of Virginia, a veteran of the Philadelphia campaign and future Chief Justice of the Supreme Court, recalled that by mid-December

> *The cold was now becoming so intense that it was impossible for an army, neither well clothed, nor sufficiently supplied with blankets, to keep the field in tents.*[1]

Washington decided to establish winter quarters at Valley Forge, about 25 miles northwest of Philadelphia. This was far enough from Philadelphia to hinder a surprise British attack, but close enough for American detachments to harass British foraging parties.

The army marched into Valley Forge on December 19th, 1777 and immediately began building huts. The men were placed in twelve man squads, and a twelve dollar reward was offered to the squad from each regiment who completed their hut first. The dimensions of the huts were specified:

> *The Soldier's huts are to be of the following dimensions, viz: fourteen by sixteen each, sides, ends and roofs made with logs, and the roof made tight with split slabs, or in some other way; the sides made tight with clay, fire-place made of wood and secured with clay on the inside eighteen inches thick, this*

---

[1] John Marshall, *The Life of George Washington, Vol. 2*, (Fredericksburg, VA: The Citizens Guild of Washington's Boyhood Home, 1926), 354

> *fireplace to be in the rear of the hut; the door to be in the end next the street; the doors to be made of split oak-slabs, unless boards can be procured. Side-walls to be six and a half feet high. The officers huts to form a line in the rear of the troops, one hut to be allowed to each General Officer...one to the commissioned officers of two companies, and one to every twelve non-commissioned officers and soldiers.*[2]

The men also constructed a series of earthworks and redoubts. An outer defense line was extended along a ridge from the Schuylkill River to the foot of Mount Joy. An inner defense line was established near the summit of Mount Joy.

Provisions and supplies quickly became a problem for the troops. On December 22nd, General James Varnum of Rhode Island reported to General Washington that for

> *Three Days successively, we have been destitute of Bread. Two Days we have been intirely without Meat. – It is not to be had from Commissaries. – Whenever we procure Beef, it is of such a vile Quality, as to render it a poor Succedanium for Food. The Men must be supplied, or they cannot be commanded.*[3]

General Washington passed the bad news on to Congress:

---

[2] Frank E. Gizzard, Jr. and David R. Hoth, eds. "General Orders for 18 December, 1777,"*The Papers of George Washington Vol. 12*, 627-628

[3] Joseph Lee Boyle, *Writings from the Valley Forge Encampment of the Continental Army Vol. 1*, (Bowie MD: Heritage Books Inc., 2000), 2

Valley Forge

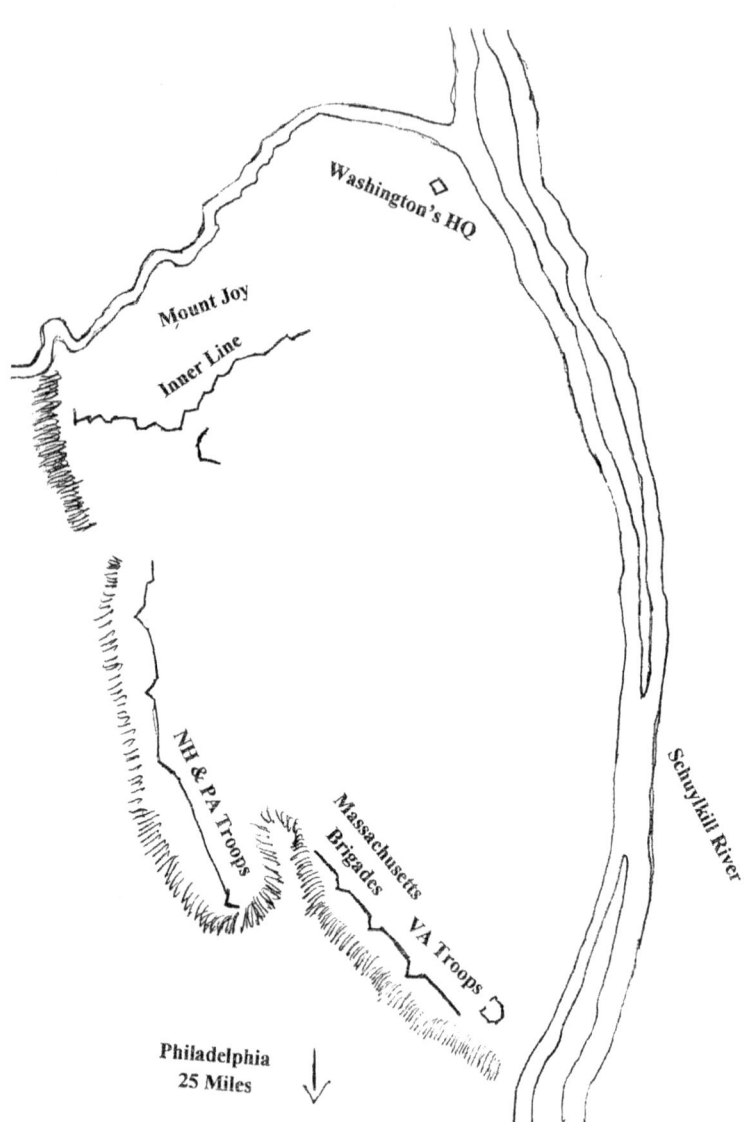

> *I do not know from what cause this alarming deficiency, or rather total failure of Supplies arises: But unless more vigorous exertions and better regulations take place in that line and immediately, This Army must dissolve.*[4]

The lack of clothing was another significant problem for the army. Lieutenant Colonel John Brooks of the 8th Massachusetts Regiment noted in early January:

> *Ever since our march from Albany our men have been suffering all the Inconveniences of an inclement Season, & a want of cloathing. For a Week past we have had Snow, & as cold weather as I almost ever knew at Home. To see our poor brave Fellows living in Tents, bare footed, bare leg'd, bare breech'd, in Snow, in Rain, on marches, in Camp, & on Duty without being able to supply their wants is really distressing.*[5]

The lack of clothing and supplies contributed to a startling drop in the number of men fit for duty. The Massachusetts continental line, which included over 500 men from Maine in three brigades, was a mere shadow of itself.[6] Of the 1,265 men listed on the January roll of General Paterson's brigade, only 374 were fit for duty.[7] The other continental brigades at Valley Forge had similar numbers. Although some of the

---

[4] Gizzard Jr. and Hoth, eds. "General Washington to Henry Laurens, 22 December, 1777," *The Papers of George Washington, Vol. 12*, 667
[5] Boyle, 16
[6] "Maine at Valley Forge", 9
[7] Charles H. Lesser, ed. *The Sinews of Independence: Monthly Strength Reports of the Continental Army*, 58

missing men were on detached service, half were sick or unfit for service due to inadequate clothing.[8] The Massachusetts brigades shrank further in February as hundreds of men succumbed to illness. On February 1st, Lieutenant Archelaus Lewis of the 1st Massachusetts Regiment lamented to a friend on the condition of the army at Valley Forge:

> *We have had a Successful Campaign, but I am almost discouraged and am sometimes ready to think our case is almost desperate; Really America is in a deplorable condition. The United States has but a handful of Men engaged in the Service in these parts, and they are naked, barefooted and destitute of Money to help themselves.... There is Two thirds of our Regt. barefooted and bare back'd not a second Shirt to put on nor Breeches to cover their nakedness, and Really my dear friend this is the case with the greatest part of our Army.*[9]

General John Paterson confirmed Lewis's observations in a letter to one of his officers on furlough in Massachusetts:

> *Pray Use your Influence with the Council to get our Soldiers clothed, they are ten Times worse now than they were when you left the Camp, they are Naked from the Crown of their Heads to the Soles of their Feet; I have the Returns now before me, and find that out of Seven Hundred and fifty Six Rank and file present, exclusive of those on Command and in the*

---

[8] Ibid.
[9] Boyle, 39

Hospital, I have four hundred and fifty returned unfit for Duty for want of Shoes and other clothing.[10]

General Paterson's men, along with their comrades in General Glover's and Learned's brigades, endured the worst part of Valley Forge. The supply system, which barely functioned in January, completely failed in February. Major Alexander Scammell of New Hampshire described the crisis:

A moments Opportunity presents of telling you our Distress in Camp has been infinite....In all the Scenes since I have been in the army, want of provisions these ten Days past, has been the most distressing; [a] great part of our Troops 7 Days with only half a pound of Pork during the whole time – Our poor brave Soldiers living upon bread & water & naked exhibited a Sight exceedingly affecting to the Officers. [11]

William Weeks, the paymaster of the 3rd New Hampshire Regiment, expressed similar concerns:

The first thing I must enter upon is the Scarcity of Provision here. Death seem'd to stare the poor Soldiers in the Face; for this five Days the Soldiers have not drawn [a] Tenth Part of their Allowance.[12]

---

[10] Boyle, 67
[11] Joseph Lee Boyle, *Writings from the Valley Forge Encampment of the Continental Army Vol. 2*, (Bowie MD: Heritage Books Inc., 2001), 50
[12] Boyle, *Writings from the Valley Forge Encampment of the Continental Army Vol. 1*, 55

Even General Washington noted the hardship, writing to George Clinton of New York for assistance:

> *For some days past, there has been little less, than a famine in camp. A part of the army has been a week, without any kind of flesh, and the rest three or four days. Naked and starving as they are, we cannot enough admire the incomparable patience and fidelity of the soldiery, that they have not been ere this excited by their sufferings, to a general mutiny and dispersion. Strong symptoms, however, of discontent have appeared in particular instances; and nothing but the most active efforts every where can long avert so shocking a catastrophe.*[13]

Thankfully, the crisis passed when more provisions found their way to camp.

With the approach of spring, the camp routine changed. Work on the entrenchments continued, as did guard and fatigue duty, but the arrival of Baron von Steuben, an experienced officer from the Prussian army, meant that the men soon learned a new military drill.

Steuben arrived in Valley Forge in late February and immediately impressed General Washington with his military knowledge and humility.[14] Washington asked the Baron to evaluate the American troops.[15] Steuben's observations led to significant reforms for the American army:

---

[13] Edward G. Lengel, ed., "General Washington to George Clinton, 16 February, 1778," *The Papers of George Washington Vol. 13*, 552-553

[14] John W. Jackson, *Valley Forge, Pinnacle of Courage*, (Gettysburg: PA, Thomas Publications, 1992), 124

[15] Ibid. 126

> *I directed my attention to the condition of the troops,* [recalled Steuben years later] *and found ample field, where disorder and confusion were supreme...the words company, regiment, brigade, and division, were so vague that they did not convey any idea upon which to form a calculation...I have seen a regiment consisting of thirty men, and a company of one corporal!* [16]

Steuben was particularly critical of the haphazard system of drill the army employed:

> *Each colonel had a system of his own, the one according to the English, the other according to the Prussian or French style.* [17]

Steuben's keen observations prompted General Washington to ask him to oversee the implementation of reforms. Steuben immediately went to work. He drafted instructions for a new military drill in the evening and supervised their implementation during the day. Gradually, through Steuben's tireless efforts, a uniform system of drill emerged in the American army. Lieutenant John Marshall witnessed Steuben's efforts and summarized the Prussian volunteer's impact on the troops at Valley Forge:

---

[16] Friedrich Kapp, *The Life of Frederick William von Steuben*, (NY: Corner House Historical Publications, 1999), 115 (Originally published in 1859)
[17] Ibid. 118

> *This gentleman was a real service to the American troops. He established one uniform system of field exercise; and, by his skill and persevering industry, effected important improvements through all ranks of the army during its continuance at Valley Forge.*[18]

The advent of spring brought a surge of troops to the American army. The arrival of much needed clothing allowed over 550 Massachusetts troops to return to duty in April, and hundreds more recovered from illness or returned from duty outside of Valley Forge.[19] The situation was similar for the rest of the army and by May, Washington's ranks swelled to over 10,000 effective men.[20]

As summer approached, rumors circulated throughout Valley Forge that the British planned to evacuate Philadelphia. The city's capture months earlier did not convince America to surrender or sue for peace as the British expected. In fact, in June 1778, Congress, emboldened by its alliance with France, spurned British peace overtures that effectively gave America everything it demanded before 1776.[21]

The lack of a resolution to the conflict cost General William Howe his command. He returned to Britain in May and was replaced by General Henry Clinton, who was immediately confronted with a new strategic problem, France's entry into the conflict.

---

[18] Marshall, 439
[19] Lesser, Continental Army Troop Returns from March to April, 1778, 60-65
[20] Ibid., 68-69
[21] William Stryker, *The Battle of Monmouth*, (Princeton: Princeton University Press, 1927), 35

News of the American alliance with France bolstered American spirits and caused the British to re-think their strategy. Britain could no longer depend on its dominance of the sea. In addition, Britain's other global possessions were at risk to French attack and had to be protected. This stretched British resources and drew much needed men and supplies away from America.

The British, concerned that their forces were overextended, decided to consolidate around New York. Preparations for Philadelphia's evacuation began in May. By mid-June, the British army, along with thousands of loyalist civilians, was on the move. A portion of the army and most of the loyalists departed Philadelphia by ship. The remainder, numbering over 10,000 men, marched into New Jersey with an immense baggage train.[22]

General Washington, with nearly 13,000 men, cautiously pursued the British into New Jersey.[23] On June 22nd, Washington formed the first of several picked detachments (comprised of men from nearly every brigade) and ordered it forward to harass the British rearguard. This force of approximately 1,400 men was commanded by General Charles Scott of Virginia. A few days later, a similar detachment of 1,000 select men was formed under General Anthony Wayne. The bulk of the Massachusetts and Maine troops who saw combat at Monmouth likely served in these two detachments

---

[22] Mark M. Boatner III, *Encyclopedia of the American Revolution, 3rd. Ed.* (Stackpole Books, 1994), 716 (Originally published in 1966)

[23] Edward G. Lengel, "Council of War, 24 June, 1778 ," *The Papers of George Washington, Vol. 15,* 520

or a smaller, 200 man battalion that was also sent forward under Colonel Henry Jackson of Massachusetts.[24]

By June 27th, the eve of the battle of Monmouth, the number of American troops attached to advance attachments numbered approximately 5,000.[25] Command of this large force fell to General Charles Lee. Lee had returned to the American army in April after sixteen months of captivity in New York and, despite his opposition to an aggressive pursuit of the British, General Washington placed Lee in command of the advance corps. Washington was determined to risk an engagement with the British and ordered General Lee to attack the British rearguard as soon as an opportunity presented itself.[26]

The Battle of Monmouth

June 28th dawned hot and humid and signaled another stifling day for the troops on both sides. General Clinton sent his baggage train northeastward before dawn under a strong guard. Clinton's main body, commanded by General Charles Cornwallis, followed and was trailed by a rear guard of dragoons, light infantry, and the Queens Rangers near Monmouth Courthouse.[27]

A few miles to the west, General Lee's troops, divested of their baggage and coats, marched towards the British. Lee spotted General Clinton's rearguard around 9:30 a.m. and ordered part of his detachment to attack it while he sent General LaFayette with three battalions to the right to strike

---

[24] Stryker, 277
[25] Ibid., 80
[26] Ibid., 106
[27] Boatner, 721

Battle of Monmouth

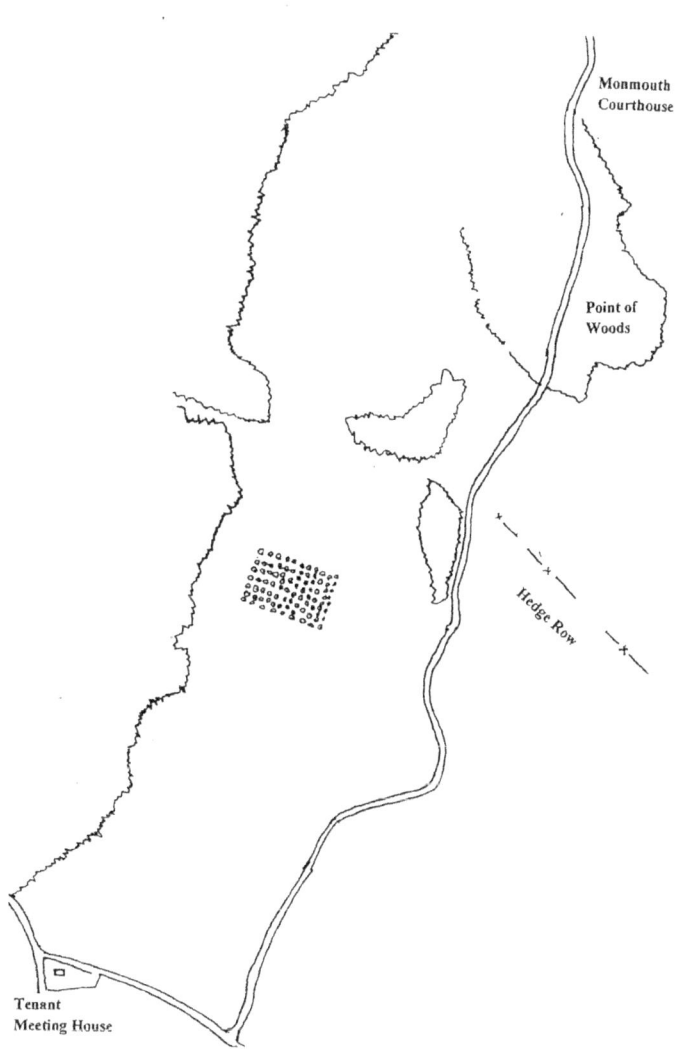

the British left flank and rear. LaFayette's men came under British artillery fire, which wounded Colonel James Wesson of the 9th Massachusetts Regiment, and were shocked to discover thousands of British troops from Lord Cornwallis's division approaching them. Cornwallis had not marched far with the main British body when he was ordered by General Clinton to return and reinforce the rearguard. This meant that instead of confronting an enemy that was only a quarter of the size of his force, General Lee's troops were outnumbered.

Lee ordered LaFayette to withdraw to the courthouse, and then to a patch of woods. It appears that General Lee hoped to find a good position to make a stand, but he failed to inform his commanders of this, and the American situation soon descended into chaos and confusion. General Scott and General Maxwell, whose detachments were to the left of General Lee and LaFayette, observed the arrival of British reinforcements and LaFayette's withdrawal on the right and decided to pull their troops back to a more defensible position. When General Lee was unable to locate General Scott and General Maxwell in their new position, he assumed that they had retired to the rear. Meanwhile, another part of Lee's detachment, posted to the left of Scott's original position, found themselves nearly encircled by the British. They were anxious for some direction from General Lee, but it never came. As a result, Colonels William Grayson, Richard Butler, and Henry Jackson led their detachments to the rear.[28]

The situation had quickly spun out of control for General Lee, and soon his entire force was streaming backwards. It was this scene that General Washington encountered when he rode out ahead of the main body of the army to investigate.

---

[28] Stryker, 150, 154

Washington, who started the day five miles behind Lee's advance corps, heard the fighting and expected to find his advance troops pressing the enemy. Instead, he found them retreating. General Washington confronted General Lee and sent him rearward to reform his troops. Washington then ordered General Anthony Wayne to post troops in a patch of woods and delay the enemy's advance while Washington's main body formed for battle in the rear. Wayne's stand at the Point of Woods involved men from Massachusetts, Maryland, Pennsylvania, and Virginia in a desperate fight to delay the British.[29] General Wayne described what happened:

> *His Excellency... Ordered me to keep post where he met us with Stewart &* [Wesson's] *Regiments and a Virginia Regt...then under my Command with two pieces of Artillery and to keep* [the Enemy] *in play until he had an* [opportunity] *of forming the Remainder of the Army and Restoring order – we had but just taken post when the Enemy began their attack with Horse, foot, & Artillery, the fire of their whole united force Obliged us after a Severe Conflict to give way....*[30]

A British account of the engagement in the Point of Woods noted that the advancing British

---

[29] Note: The composition of the American troops in the Point of Woods is difficult to determine with certainty as most of the men were from General Wayne's picked detachment of a 1,000 men. Thus, it is possible that troops from more than the four states mentioned above fought at this location.

[30] Charles Lee, "Anthony Wayne to his wife, 1 July, 1778," *Lee Papers, Vol. 2*, (New York Historical Society, 1871), 448-449

> *Received a Fire on the Right from the Wood, of 300 of the Enemy posted in Ambush. Orders were now given to face to the Right, and Charge through the Wood. This Order was executed with such Alacrity; that the Rebels were forced with Bayonets through a deep Morass, a Wood hardly penetrable, during a very hot Fire, cross a Plain and Ravine, to the Edge of a second Wood;*[31]

The American stand at the Point of Woods was determined but brief. The outnumbered continentals were overwhelmed in a matter of minutes. Many of the men withdrew towards the main body. Others joined a second American line along a hedge row fence. This line was also formed to delay the British advance and included hundreds of troops from New England. Colonel John Laurens, an aide to General Washington, described the engagement at the hedge line:

> *Two regiments were formed behind a* [hedge] *fence...The enemy's horse advanced in full charge with admirable bravery to the distance of forty paces, when a general discharge from these regiments did great execution among them, and made them fly with the greatest precipitation.*[32]

The unsuccessful British cavalry attack was followed by a frontal assault by British grenadiers. This was also repulsed, and the grenadier commander, Colonel Henry Monckton, died

---

[31] John Rees, *"What is this you have been about to day?" : The New Jersey Brigade at the Battle of Monmouth* (2003) (Accessed via http://www.revwar75.com in the Complete Works of John U. Rees / New Jersey Brigade)

[32] Charles Lee, "John Laurens to Henry Laurens, 30 June, 1778," *Lee Papers, Vol. 2*, (New York Historical Society, 1871), 431-434

in the charge. Colonel Laurens reported, *"In this spot the action was the hottest and there was considerable slaughter of the British Grenadiers."*[33] Although the grenadiers were repulsed, they reformed their lines and attacked again. The pressure on the Americans at the hedgerow became too great, so they retreated across a ravine to the main American line.

Over the next few hours one of the most intense artillery duels of the war occurred as both sides pounded the other with cannon fire. It was during this phase of the battle, in stifling 100 degree heat, that Mary Ludwig Hays (Molly Pitcher) was observed assisting with one of the American cannon. She had spent much of the battle bringing water to the men, but stepped forward to replace her husband William on a cannon crew when he was wounded. Joseph Martin of Connecticut recalled a very close call for Mrs. Hays:

> *While in the act of reaching a cartridge and having one of her feet as far before the other as she could step, a cannon shot from the enemy passed directly between her legs without doing any other damage than carrying away all the lower part of her petticoat.*[34]

As the day wore on, General Washington sent troops and cannon against Clinton's flanks. General William Woodford's brigade of Virginians, with four cannon, gained possession of a hill overlooking the British left flank and delivered a devastating enfilade fire on the British line while Colonel Joseph Cilley of New Hampshire led 300 men against the

---

[33] Ibid.
[34] Joseph Plum Martin, 132

British right flank in an orchard. Private Joseph Martin participated in this attack and recalled,

> *We...marched towards the enemy's right wing, which was in the orchard, and kept concealed from them as long as possible by keeping behind the bushes. When we could no longer keep ourselves concealed, we marched into the open field and formed our line. The British immediately formed and began to retreat to the main body of their army. Colonel Cilly, finding that we were not likely to overtake the enemy...on account of fences and other obstructions, ordered three or four platoons from the right of our corps to pursue and attack them, and thus keep them in play till the rest of the detachment could come up. I was in this party; we pursued without order. As I passed through the orchard I saw a number of the enemy lying under the trees, killed by our* [cannon]. *We overtook the enemy just as they were entering upon the meadow, which was rather bushy.... I could distinguish everything about them. They were retreating in line, though in some disorder.*[35]

Martin recalled taking deliberate aim at a fleeing British soldier at close range but not knowing whether he hit the man or not. "*I took as deliberate aim at him as ever I did at any game in my life*", recalled Martin, "*but after all, I hope I did not kill him, although I intended to at the time.*"[36] The British troops turned and made a brief stand at the edge of a patch of

---

[35] Martin, 129-130
[36] Ibid.

wood and then continued their retreat to the main British body. The British withdrawal encouraged General Washington to send more troops forward, and General Wayne led three regiments of Pennsylvanians towards the center of the position vacated by the enemy. This caused the British to halt their retreat and counterattack. According to General Wayne,

> *The Enemy began to Advance again in a heavy* [column], *against which I...advanced with some of my* [troops] *to meet them –the Action was Exceedingly warm and well Maintained on each side for a Considerable time.*[37]

Eventually, both sides disengaged and withdrew, leaving the ground littered with more bodies.

The Battle of Monmouth thus ended in stalemate, with each side suffering about 350 casualties.[38] Massachusetts troops paid a heavy toll in the battle, accounting for nearly 25% of the 70 plus American deaths.[39] Scores of men died not from combat wounds, but from heat stroke, and both sides were thoroughly exhausted. The two armies remained on the field into the evening convinced that they had prevailed. The British believed they fought a successful rear guard action that repulsed the Americans and protected their baggage train. The Americans countered that they had repulsed the British counterattack and inflicted heavy losses on the British. Furthermore, the late night withdrawal of the British left the

---

[37] Lee, "Anthony Wayne to his wife, 1 July, 1778," *Lee Papers, Vol. 2*, 448- 449
[38] Boatner, III 725
[39] Stryker, Appendix 5

Americans in sole possession of the field at sunrise. This development infused the American army with pride. General Washington expressed his pleasure with the army's conduct in the following day's general orders:

> *The Commander in Chief congratulates the Army on the Victory obtained over the Arms of his Britanick Majesty yesterday and thanks most sincerely the gallant officers and men who distinguished themselves upon the occasion and such others as by their good order and coolness gave the happiest presages of what might have been expected had they come to Action.*[40]

The Battle of Monmouth marked a new milestone for General Washington's army. They fought the British army to a standstill in the longest sustained engagement of the war. The Americans successfully endured near 100 degree heat and held the battlefield at nightfall, while the enemy scampered off to New York under cover of darkness. Roles had reversed and it was now the British army that was on the defensive, at least temporarily.

---

[40] Fitzpatrick, "General Orders, 29 June, 1778," *The Writings of Washington*, Vol. 12, 130.

Battle of Rhode Island

While General Clinton considered his options in New York, General Washington moved to take advantage of the support of America's new ally, France. A powerful French fleet under Admiral Count d'Estaing arrived off the coast of New Jersey in July and Washington sought to organize a joint attack on the British in New York.[41] When it became clear that some of d' Estaing's larger ships could not cross the sand bar at Sandy Hook to enter New York Harbor, Washington and d' Estaing directed their focus to Rhode Island.

General John Sullivan, with 1,700 troops (mostly Rhode Island state troops) had been posted at Providence since the spring to keep watch on a large British garrison at Newport.[42] The British had seized control of Newport in 1776. The town was situated on the southwest end of a large island (Rhode Island) in Narragansett Bay and provided an excellent harbor for the British navy. Approximately 6,000 British troops under General Robert Pigot were entrenched in the town and a small squadron of British warships guarded the garrison's access to the sea.[43]

The arrival of Admiral d'Estaing's powerful French fleet in July presented the French and American allies with an opportunity to trap General Pigot's garrison in Newport. Washington and d'Estaing agreed that the French fleet would sail to Rhode Island, neutralize the small British squadron there, and blockade the British garrison while General Washington assembled a large land force (supplemented by 4,000 French soldiers who were with d'Estaing), to attack Newport. Washington sent two continental brigades (Glover's

---

[41] David R. Hoth, ed., "Loose thoughts upon an Attack of N. York," Note 3, *The Papers of George Washington, Vol. 16*, 69
[42] Hoth, ed.,"General Greene to General Washington, 16 July, 1778," *The Papers of George Washington, Vol. 16*, 83
[43] Boatner, 788

Battle of Rhode Island

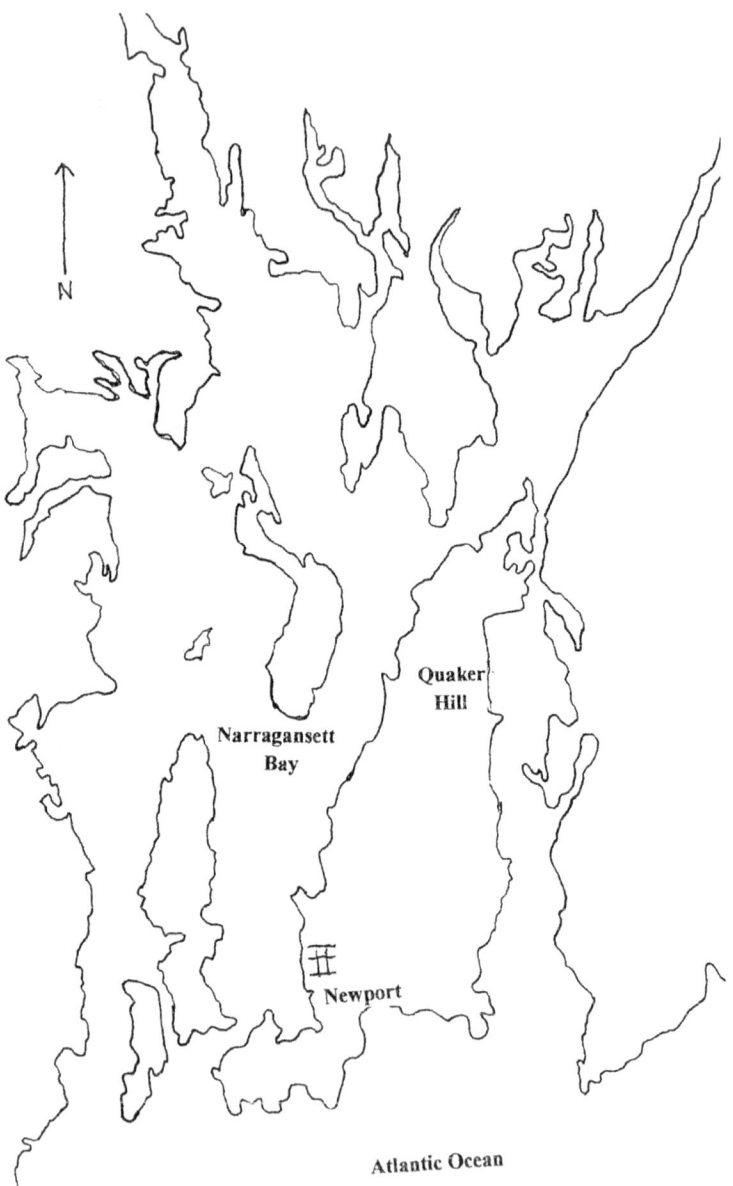

and Varnum's) to Rhode Island and ordered General Sullivan to summon 5,000 militia troops from the New England states.[44]

Men from all three Maine counties served in the Massachusetts militia units that marched to Rhode Island. Scores of Maine men also served in General Glover's continental brigade.[45] The continental troops and militia joined General Sullivan in Providence in early August and swelled Sullivan's army to nearly 10,000 men.[46] General Washington instructed Sullivan to split his force into two divisions by distributing the militia between the two continental brigades.[47] General LaFayette commanded one division and General Nathanael Greene the other. With Admiral d'Estaing's French fleet blocking British access to the sea, Greene confidently predicted success for his commander, General Sullivan:

You are the most happy man in the World. What a child of fortune. The expedition going on against Newport I think cannot fail of success. You are the first General that has ever had an opportunity of cooperating with the French forces.... I wish you success with all my Soul....[48]

---

[44] Hoth, ed., "General Washington to General LaFayette, 22 July, 1778," *The Papers of George Washington, Vol. 16,* 127
[45] "Maine at Valley Forge", 9
[46] Hoth, ed., "Lieutenant Colonel John Laurens to General Washington, 4 August, 1778, *The Papers of George Washington, Vol. 16,* 249
[47] Hoth, ed., "Lieutenant Colonel John Laurens to General Washington, 27 July, 1778," *The Papers of George Washington, Vol. 16,* 187
[48] Richard Showman, ed., "General Greene to General John Sullivan, 23 July, 1778," *The Papers of General Nathanael Greene, Vol. 2,* (Chapel Hill: The University of North Carolina Press, 1980), 466

Although General Greene would play an important role in Rhode Island, it was the French fleet that ultimately decided the outcome of American efforts there. The situation initially looked promising for the allies as the handful of British ships trapped at Newport by the French were burned by their crews to prevent their capture. General Sullivan and Admiral d' Estaing conferred and agreed to a joint attack on the British garrison. The plan called for simultaneous allied landings upon Rhode Island on the morning of August 10th. Approximately 9,000 Americans would cross onto the northern end of Rhode Island from the mainland while 4,000 French troops landed on the western shore of the island.[49] These landings would place the British troops stationed on the northern end of Rhode Island between two strong armies and force them to either flee or surrender to avoid their complete destruction. Once the northern half of the island was secured, the Americans and French would converge on Newport and overwhelm the British defenses there.

When General Sullivan learned on August 9th that the British had abandoned their entrenchments on the northern end of the island and had withdrawn to Newport, he ignored his arrangements with Admiral d' Estaing and landed his troops early. The French began to disembark their troops the next day, but as they did so, reports of a strong British naval force off the coast disrupted the operation and caused Admiral d' Estaing to recall his troops and sail out to sea to meet the British threat.[50] General Sullivan decided to postpone any attack upon Newport until the French fleet returned. His army encamped outside the town and endured a terrible storm. Sullivan described the storm's effect on his men:

---

[49] Hoth, ed., "General Greene to General Washington, 28 August, 1778," 397 and Christopher Ward, *The War of the Revolution, Vol. 2*, (New York: The Macmillan Co., 1952), 591
[50] Ward, 590-91

> *A storm so violent* [occurred]...*that it last night blew down tore, and almost irreparably ruined the few tents my troops had in their possession. The arms of course were rendered unfit for immediate use and almost the whole of the ammunition damaged. My men have suffered much, the greater part of them have had no kind of covering, nor would tents (if they had them) prove a sufficient security against the severity of the storm. Our communication with the* [mainland] *is intirely cut off by the violence of the winds which will scarcely permit the passage of a whale boat. Should the enemy move out to take advantage of our situation, our dependence must rest on the superiority of our numbers and the length of our Bayonets. How our Militia would behave on such an occasion I am unable to determine – they may be desperate when they find it impossible to retreat, and that their only alternative is to conquer or die. Several men have perished with the Severity of the weather & I Expect more will as I See no probability of the Storm Ceasing. I despair of deriving any immediate advantage from our allies, as they must have been driven to a distance...if not entirely from our coasts.*[51]

Sullivan was correct about the storm's impact on the French fleet. Although the violent gale prevented the British and French navies from engaging on the high seas, it significantly damaged and dispersed both fleets. The British limped back to New York while the French headed back to Newport. It took Admiral d'Estaing days to reach Rhode Island.

General Sullivan, unaware of the condition of the French navy and anxious for its return, decided to offer battle to the

---

[51] Hoth, ed., "General Sullivan to General Washington, 13 August, 1778," *The Papers of George Washington, Vol. 16*, 307-308

British before Admiral d'Estaing returned. He informed General Washington on August 17th,

> *I halted the army in full sight of and within long shot of the enemy (in hopes) that they would be thereby tempted to meet us in the plain and become an easy conquest.*[52]

General Pigot refused to leave his earthworks so Sullivan laid siege to the town. General Sullivan boasted to General Washington:

> *I began my approaches (under cover of night) within two hundred and fifty yards of their lines. This days fog favors my operations, and I promise your Excellency that by to-morrow noon, I shall be able to keep up so warm a fire upon them as to render the properties of a salamander essentially necessary to their existence.... I shall have it shortly in my power either to force them to an action, upon disadvantageous destructive principles, or reduce them to honourable terms of capitulation.*[53]

Sullivan's confidence lasted a few more days until Admiral d'Estaing returned with devastating news. The French fleet was so damaged by the storm that the admiral had decided to sail to Boston for repairs. General Sullivan and his staff tried to convince Admiral d'Estaing to remain at Newport or at least leave his 4,000 troops, but the d'Estaing refused. The American officers realized that without d'Estaing's soldiers or the presence of the French navy to screen the Americans from the British navy, their chances for success at Newport were

---

[52] Hoth, ed., "General Sullivan to General Washington, 17 August, 1778," *The Papers of George Washington, Vol. 16*, 324
[53] Ibid., 324-325

slim. General Sullivan lamented the consequences of d'Estaing's departure to General Washington:

> The Enemy have twice attempted to Relieve [Newport] by Reinforcements the Last Fleet had 4000 Troops on Board. Should they make another attempt They must Succeed. They will then have Near Ten thousand Troops on the Island & the Command of the water of Every Side of us.[54]

General Sullivan attempted to maintain the siege, but the withdrawal of the French significantly depressed morale among his troops, especially the militia. General Nathanael Greene informed General Washington that

> The departure of the Count de Estaing with his fleet...struck such a panic among the Militia and Volunteers that they began to desert by shoals. The fleet no sooner set sail than they began to be alarm'd for their safety. This misfortune damp'd the hopes of our Army and gave new Spirits to that of the Enemy.... Our strength is now reduced from 9000 to between 4 and 5000.[55]

General Sullivan conferred with his officers on August 26th and they agreed that the expedition against Newport was lost. Sullivan's new objective was to withdraw the American army from Rhode Island with as little loss as possible. The Americans retreated northward under cover of darkness on August 28th. The British pursued in two columns at daybreak

---

[54] Hoth, ed., "General Sullivan to General Washington, 23 August, 1778," *The Papers of George Washington, Vol. 16,* 359
[55] Showman, "General Greene to General Washington, August 28/31, 1778," *The Papers of General Nathanael Greene, Vol. 2,*, 499

and caught up with Sullivan's rearguard. General Nathanael Greene described what happened:

> *Our Light Troops commanded by Col. Livingston and Col. Laurens attacked the head of the* [enemy] *columns about seven oClock in the morning but were beat back. They were reinforced with a Regiment upon each road. The Enemy still proved too strong. General Sullivan form'd the army in order to battle... and sent orders to the Light troops to fall back. The Enemy came up and formd upon Quaker Hill...about* [1¼] *miles from our Line. We were well Posted with strong works in our rear and a strong redoubt in front.... In this position a warm Cannonade commenced and lasted for several hours with continual Skirmishes.... About two oClock the Enemy began to advance in force upon our right as if they intended to dislodge us.... I had command of the Right Wing. After advancing four Regts and finding the enemy still gaining ground I advanced with two more Regiments of regular Troops and a Brigade of Militia and at the same time Gen Sullivan ordered Col Livingston with the Light Troops under his command to advance. We soon put the Enemy to the rout and I had the pleasure to see them run in worse disorder than they did at the battle of Monmouth. Our Troops behavd with great spirit and the brigade of militia, under the command of General Lovel advanced with great resolution and in good order and stood the fire of the Enemy with great firmness.*[56]

Greene reported that the day concluded with a steady cannonade from both sides and much skirmish fire. The following day was relatively peaceful with only sporadic

---

[56] Ibid., 501-502

cannon fire between the two sides. Late in the evening, the Americans withdrew from the island and returned to the mainland.

Although the Americans were disappointed with the outcome of the expedition and in the support their French ally provided, the withdrawal of Sullivan's army from a dire situation ended the affair on a somewhat positive note for them. Both sides suffered over 200 casualties in killed, wounded, and missing men and the British navy lost a number of ships, but the British still held Newport, so little had changed.[57]

Bloodshed on the Frontier

In the fall of 1778, attention shifted to the New York and Pennsylvania frontier where bloodshed on a wide scale had erupted. Disturbing reports of Tory and Indian raids on the frontier had reached General Washington soon after Monmouth. The inhabitants of that region were largely dependent upon the local militia for protection, but attacks on Cobleskill New York and in the Wyoming Valley of Pennsylvania (where a large militia detachment was defeated and massacred) highlighted the militia's inability to defend the exposed settlements and spurred appeals for help. General Washington responded in late July by sending reinforcements to the frontier. He informed Congress of his decision:

The accounts from the Western frontiers of Tyron County are distressing. The spirit of the Savages seems to be roused, and they appear determined on mischief and havoc, in every Quarter...I have detached the 4th Pennsylvania Regiment and the remains of Morgans [rifle] corps [all] under Lt. Colo. [William]

---

[57] Boatner, 793

New York Frontier

Butler… to co-operate with the Militia and check the Indians if possible. [58]

Lieutenant Colonel Butler established his headquarters at Fort Defiance in the Schoharie Valley. Butler was eager to launch an offensive against the Indians, but a number of obstacles delayed his march until the fall. Butler finally set off in early October on a two week expedition with the 4th Pennsylvania Regiment, a detachment of riflemen, and some local militia to destroy the Indian towns of Onoquaga and Unadilla.[59] The Americans arrived at Onoquaga on October 8th and destroyed the town and crops with little resistance. They moved on to Unadilla, which met a similar fate, and returned to Scholarie in mid-October. Although little blood was shed (largely because most of the Indian warriors were away), Butler believed he had dealt a severe blow to the Indians and confidently informed Governor Clinton,

I am well convinced that [the expedition] *has sufficiently secured these Frontiers from any further disturbances from the Savages at least this Winter; and it will ever, hereafter,* [be] *difficult for them to distress these parts, By reason of their having no Settlements near.*[60]

Although the destruction of Onoquoga and Unadilla did create significant hardship for the Indians in the area, it did not end the fighting. In November, Joseph Brant, a Mohawk chief, led hundreds of Indians into Cherry Valley, New York to retaliate. Brant was joined by Captain Walter Butler's Tory

---

[58] Fitzpatrick, "General Washington to Congress, 22 July, 1778," *The Writings of George Washington, Vol. 12*, 214
[59] "Extracts from Lt. Col. Butler's Journal," *Public Papers of George Clinton, Vol. 4*, 224
[60] "Willim Butler to George Clinton, 28 October, 1778," *Public Papers of George Clinton, Vol. 4*, 223

rangers. Responsibility for the defense of Cherry Valley fell to Colonel Ichabod Alden of Massachusetts. Alden's regiment of Massachusetts continentals had been posted in Cherry Valley since July and included many men from Maine.[61]

The unit found itself in a unique situation compared to the rest of the Massachusetts continental line because it was the only Massachusetts regiment posted on the New York frontier. While the other Massachusetts regiments spent the winter of 1777-78 at Valley Forge and in the New York Highlands, Alden's regiment had wintered in Albany. The unit was chosen in the spring of 1778 to participate in an invasion of Canada, but the plan was scrapped, so the regiment remained in Albany.

When reports arrived in the spring of 1778 of possible Indian raids to the west, Colonel Alden sent out patrols to support the militia. One of those patrols was ambushed by a large party of Indians and Tories in late May. Captain William Patrick and approximately ten of his men were killed, and the small settlement of Cobleskill was destroyed in the engagement.[62]

About six weeks later, reports that Fort Stanwix was threatened by a large enemy force prompted Colonel Alden's regiment to march westward as a reinforcement. Two days after their arrival, with the situation at Fort Stanwix under control, Alden's regiment was ordered back east to Cherry Valley to defend that area from possible raids. The 250

---

[61] Boatner, 223, and William McKendry, "Journal of William McKendry," *Collections of the Massachusetts Historical Society*, (May 1880), 445-446 and a survey of *Massachusetts Soldiers and Sailors of the Revolutionary War*, 17 volumes, (1896-1908)

[62] Glenn F. Williams, *Year of the Hangman: George Washington's Campaign Against the Iroquois*, (Yardley: Westholme, 2005), 88 and Mark Bradford Richardson, *The Virtues of Continental Soldiers With a History of Colonel Ichabod Alden's Regiment and the Seventh Massachusetts Regiment During the American Revolution*, (1993, Unpublished), 77

continentals under Alden were greeted by the inhabitants of the Cherry Valley as heroes and took post inside a crude wooden fort.[63]

As weeks of relative calm passed and autumn began to give way to winter, Colonel Alden and his regiment grew more at ease. Although several patrols had encountered small parties of Indians on the outskirts of Cherry Valley and rumors of Indian retaliation for Colonel Butler's October raid on Onoquaga and Unadilla circulated throughout the valley, most of Alden's senior officers, including the colonel himself, had grown comfortable enough to quarter themselves in a private residence hundreds of yards from the fort.[64]

Early on the morning of November 11th, however, the officers were shocked to find themselves under attack. Colonel Alden was killed, and his lieutenant colonel was captured, so command of the regiment fell to Major Whiting, who scrambled to the fort with a handful of men. While the Massachusetts troops in the fort held off the enemy, the unfortunate civilians outside the fort suffered at the hands of hundreds of Indians and Tories. Scores of settlers were killed, many others were captured, and virtually every dwelling in Cherry Valley was plundered and burned to the ground.[65] It was too late in the season to launch a retaliatory strike against the enemy, so the Massachusetts continentals hunkered down for a long, bleak winter.

Harsh winters were a common occurrence for the settlers of Maine, and they had become especially harsh because of the shortage of provisions caused by the economic disruptions of the war. Unlike the settlers of the New York and Pennsylvania frontiers, Maine's settlers had maintained good

---

[63] Boatner, 223
[64] Williams, 177
[65] Max M. Mintz, *Seeds of Empire: The American Revolutionary Conquest of the Iroquois*, (New York: New York University Press, 1999), 73

relations with the native population thanks largely to the efforts of John Allan of Nova Scotia. Allan was a strong proponent of the American cause and arrived in Machias in 1776 to offer his support. He travelled to Philadelphia in 1777 in search of Congressional support for another invasion of Nova Scotia. Allan's efforts received only luke warm support from Congress and Massachusetts and resulted in a failed attempt to occupy the Saint John's River Valley in the summer of 1777.[66] Allan's small force returned to Machias in time to help repulse Captain Collier's raid in August.

Although Allan's plans for Nova Scotia were a failure, he did succeed in earning a commission as colonel in the continental army and superintendent for the eastern Indians. Allan was also successful (despite the lack of provisions and trade goods used to purchase Indian goodwill) in keeping the Penobscot, Micmac, Malecites, and Passamaqquoddy Indians from joining the British camp. France's alliance with America and the affinity of the Indians towards France also helped keep the Indians from joining Britain's side.

Such was not the case on the western frontier of America. On the New York and Pennsylvania frontiers, bloodshed between American settlers and the British, and their Indian and Tory allies, took a high toll on soldiers and civilians alike. In 1779, General Washington hoped to severely curtail Indian raids on the frontier by sending a large expedition westward to chastise the Indians. The expedition was led by General John Sullivan of New Hampshire and included a large number of mid-Atlantic and New England continentals.

---

[66] Leamon, 91

Sullivan's Expedition

General Washington's instructions to General John Sullivan, the commander of the American expedition against the Indians in 1779, were explicit:

> *The expedition you are appointed to command is to be directed against the hostile tribes of the six nations of Indians...The immediate objects are the total destruction and devastation of their settlements and the capture of as many prisoners of every age and sex as possible...Parties should be detached to lay waste on all the settlements around...that the country may not be merely overrun but destroyed...You will not by any means, listen to any overture of peace before the total ruin of their settlements is effected. It is likely enough their fears if they are unable to oppose us, will compel them to offers of peace, or policy may lead them to endeavour to amuse us in this way to gain time and succour for more effectual opposition. Our future security will be in their inability to injure us; [the distance to wch. they are driven] and in the terror with which the severity of the chastisement they receive will inspire them. Peace without this would be fallacious and temporary.*[67]

General Sullivan was to destroy the ability of the natives to wage war and in doing so, pacify the long troubled frontier.

Sullivan's expedition began as two different detachments. General James Clinton led 1,500 men, including Alden's 7th Massachusetts Regiment, southwestward from Conojoharie, New York, to unite with General Sullivan's 2,500 continental

---

[67] Fitzpatrick, "General Washington to General John Sullivan, 31 May, 1778," *The Writings of George Washington, Vol. 15,* 189

troops.[68] Sullivan began his march from Easton, Pennsylvania and proceeded through the Wyoming Valley to rendezvous with Clinton at Tioga, near the New York – Pennsylvania border. From there the expedition would continue into the heart of Iroquois County and spread as much destruction as possible.[69]

General Clinton began his march in June and slowly led his column southwest. Clinton's advance was hampered by an abundance of supplies. The transport of these supplies delayed his rendezvous with General Sullivan until August. When the two detachments finally united, General Sullivan assumed overall command. The combined force marched deeper into Indian territory. In late August General Sullivan's advance troops discovered a large enemy force laying in ambush near New Town, New York. It was Joseph Brant with approximately 800 Indians and John Butler with another 250 Tories.[70]

The discovery saved Sullivan's army from a trap and allowed General Sullivan to stage a surprise of his own. He hoped to hold the enemy in place with his artillery and General Edward Hand's advance troops, while other units moved around Brant's flanks and encircled the enemy. General James Clinton described the attempt to his brother after the battle:

About ten O' clock a scattering Fire commenced between some of their Scouts and a few of our Rifle men & Volunteers when the former gave way, and the latter proceeded until they plainly discouvered their Works which were very extensive, tho' not impregnable. As our design was not to drive them, but to surround or bring them to a fair open

---

[68] Boatner, 1072
[69] Fitzpatrick, "General Washington to General John Sullivan, 31 May, 1778," *The Writings of George Washington, Vol. 15,* 189
[70] Boatner, 794

action...it was concluded that the artillery supported by Genl. Hand with the Infantry and Rifle Corps shoud commence the action...allowing sufficient time for General Poor's and my brigade to gain their right Flank, while Maxwell's and the covering party under Col. Ogden might gain their left.[71]

Unfortunately for the Americans, the flanking parties were delayed by difficult terrain. As time passed with no major American push, Brant and Butler grew suspicious and withdrew from their barricade. General James Clinton noted,

About one O' clock Col. Proctor commenced a very warm Cannonade upon their Works, which continued near two hours...The Enemy finding their Situation in their Lines rather uncomfortable and finding we did not intend to storm them, abandoned them...[72]

Lieutenant Erkuries Beatty of the 4th Pennsylvania, provided a more detailed account of the battle in his journal:

We found the Enemy strongly Entrenched with Logs, Dirt brush &ct the firing Imidiately begun in front with the Rifle Corps & the Indians made great halooing, orders were given then for the troops to form in line of battle which was done. Genl. Hands brigade in front but none of the troops advanced as we discovered the main body of the Enemy was here and had their front secured by a large Morass & brook, their right by the River & on their left partly in the rear was a very large hill, their lines extended upwards of a Mile the firing was kept up very briskly by the Rifle men & a company who was sent to

---

[71] "James Clinton to His Brother, 30 August, 1779," *Papers of George Clinton, Vol. 5*, 225-226
[72] Ibid.

> reinforce them, likewise the Indians returned the fire very brisk with many shouts for about 2 hours while a disposition was made to attack them.
>
> Genl. Clintons & Poors brigades were sent off round their left flank to take possession of the hill in the Enemys rear and extend their line intirely round them if possible. After they had gone about half an hour Genl. Hands brigade advanced in a line of battle with all our Artillery in the Centre within about 300 Yards of the Enemys works but in full View of them a very heavy cannonade began & throwing of Shells the enemy returned the fire very briskly for about half an hour when the Enemy retreated up the hill in a great Disorder & as they got near the top received a very heavy fire from Genl. Poor's brigade: the enemy then took around Genl. Poors right flank by the river which Genl. Poors had not guarded as he had not the time to, therefore they made their Escape leaving a number of their dead behind them. As soon as the Enemy left their works Genl. Hands brigade pursued them up the hill as far as where Genl. Poor was when we make a halt, the rifle men pursued them about one Mile farther....[73]

The withdrawal of Brant and Butler (whose demoralized men scattered into the frontier) exposed the region to Sullivan's wrath. Over the next month, forty Indian towns were burned and thousands of bushels of food destroyed.[74] The region was severely chastised but not permanently pacified, and hundreds of Indian warriors and Tory rangers would retaliate in 1780.

---

[73] Frederick Cook, ed., "Journal of Lieut. Erkuries Beatty," *Journals of the Military Expedition of Major General John Sullivan Against the Six Nations of Indians in 1779*, (Freeport, NY: Books for Library Press, 1887), 26-27

[74] Boatner, 1076

Penobscot Expedition

About the same time General Sullivan and his expedition was closing in on Newtown, another American expedition along the Maine coast was meeting with disaster. The 1779 Penobscot Expedition was an entirely Massachusetts operation organized in late June in response to the British fortification of Bagaduce Peninsula (Castine) in Penobscot Bay. General Francis McLean and 700 British troops, along with a handful of British warships and transports, had been sent to Penobscot Bay to protect local loyalists and harass local rebels.[75] General McLean's post was to be the start of a new British province, New Ireland, carved out of Lincoln County, Massachusetts and extending from the Penobscot River eastward to the St. Croix River. British leaders believed that the presence of a strong British force in Penobscot Bay would help hasten the establishment of New Ireland, neutralize the settlement of Machias, and deter further American attacks on Nova Scotia.

McLean's force reached Bagaduce in mid-June and immediately began constructing a fort upon a hill overlooking Penobscot Bay and the mouth of Bagaduce River, which flowed south and east of the peninsula. Much of the peninsula was heavily wooded and the western shore, which overlooked the bay, rose steeply over a hundred feet above the sea making an attack from that direction very difficult. Three British warships under Captain Henry Mowat (of Falmouth fame) blocked the entrance of Bagaduce River and protected the southern and eastern approaches to the British fort (dubbed Fort George by General McLean) while the northern approach, which bordered a marsh, was covered by the fort's guns.

---

[75] George E. Buker, *The Penobscot Expedition: Commodore Saltonstall and the Massachusetts Conspiracy of 1779*, (Annapolis, MD: Naval Institute Press, 2002), 7, 11

Penobscot Bay

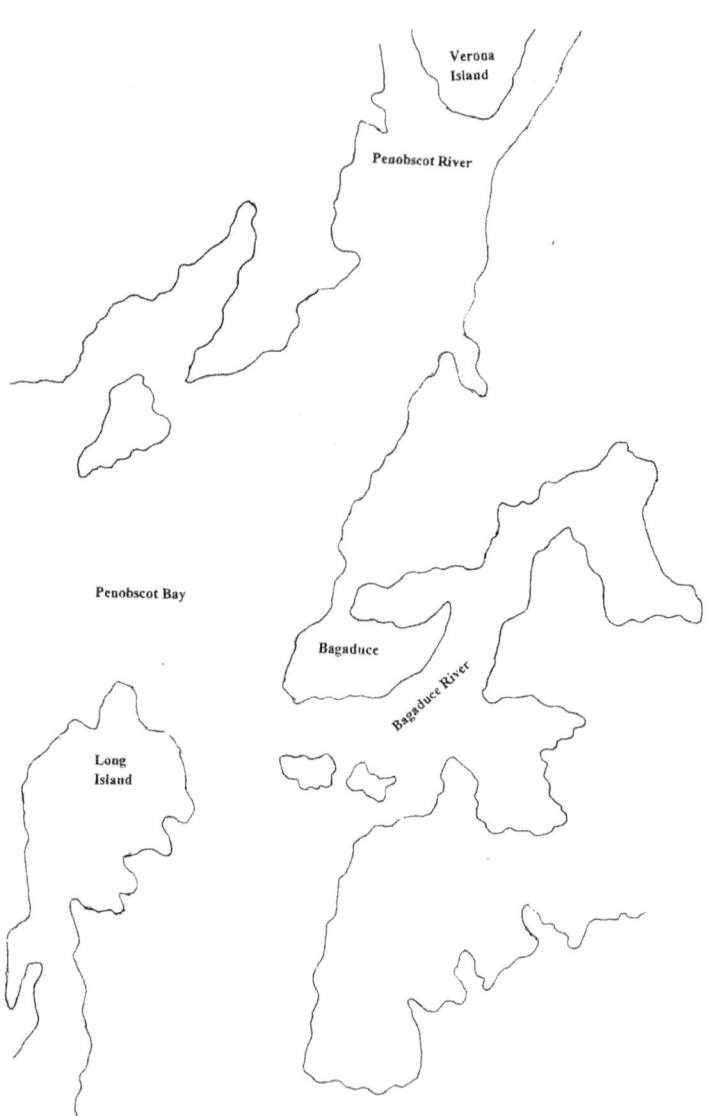

News of the British arrival at Bagaduce reached Boston within a week and the state government reacted decisively by authorizing a military expedition to drive the enemy from Penobscot Bay. Fifteen hundred troops from the counties of York (300 men), Cumberland (600 men), and Lincoln (600 men), were summoned, and a large fleet of ships, including the 32 gun continental frigate *Warren*, was organized into an expeditionary force.[76] Command of the ground forces went to General Solomon Lovell of Weymouth. Lovell, whose military experience stretched back to the French and Indian War, had led a brigade of Massachusetts militia at Rhode Island in 1778. Lovell's second in command, General Peleg Wadsworth, had also seen action in Rhode Island.

The expedition's ground troops were divided into three militia regiments. Unfortunately, all three regiments failed to recruit its allotted quota so the expedition began almost 500 men short of its goal.[77] Furthermore, the quality of the recruits was questionable. One observer noted that "*One fourth part of the Troops...appear'd to be Small Boys & old men, & unfit for the service.*"[78] Regardless of these concerns, the expedition's leaders pushed forward and prepared to sail to Penobscot Bay. Colonel Samuel McCobb commanded the militia troops from Lincoln County while Colonel Jonathan Mitchell led the Cumberland County troops and Major Daniel Littlefield did the same for the York County troops. About one hundred artillerists under Lieutenant Colonel Paul Revere and over two hundred marines onboard the continental and Massachusetts state warships rounded out the available ground troops which amounted to approximately 1150 men.[79]

---

[76] Nathan Goold, "Colonel Jonathan Mitchell's Cumberland County Regiment, Bagaduce Expedition, 1779," *Collections of the Maine Historical Society*, ser. 2, vol. 10, 54

[77] Ibid.

[78] Buker, 26

[79] Ibid., 41

The troops were transported and protected by a large fleet of 21 transport ships and 18 warships.[80] The warships included continental and Massachusetts state naval vessels as well as a number of privateers outfitted for combat. Commodore Dudley Saltonstall of the continental navy commanded the fleet. The total number of cannon distributed among his 18 warships numbered nearly 300 and ranged from a few 18 and 12 pound guns aboard the *Warren* to numerous 4, 6, and 9 pound guns aboard the rest of the warships.[81]

The ships and men of the expedition rendezvoused at Boothbay Harbor in mid-July and set sail for Penobscot Bay on July 24th. Saltonstall's fleet entered the bay the next day, and a few of his ships traded cannon fire with Captain Mowat's ships, but the exchange had little effect on either side.

General Lovell attempted to land some of his troops near Dice's Point, along the high bluffs on the west side of the peninsula, but recalled his men before they landed because of poor weather conditions. A second attempt to land troops early the next morning was repulsed by a small British force atop the bluffs. The Americans redirected their attention to Nautilus Island, directly across from Bagaduce, where a British artillery battery helped Captain Mowat cover the mouth of the Bagaduce River. The British battery was manned by 40 British sailors who fled in the face of a large detachment of American marines. The captured British cannon were repositioned by a detachment of Lieutenant Colonel Paul Revere's artillerists, so that they could fire on Captain Mowat's ships. This forced Mowat to withdraw his ships further up the Bagaduce River and made it impossible for Mowat to cover the western shore of Bagaduce with his cannon.[82]

While all of this occurred, General Lovell's militia made a third attempt to land on the western shore, but the death of

---

[80] Ibid., 29-31
[81] Ibid., 29
[82] Ibid., 39-40

Major Littlefield of York County ended this effort. Littlefield and two of his men drowned in the assault when a British cannonball sunk their boat before it reached the shore. Thirty-six hours later, early in the morning of July 28th, Lovell launched a fourth and final assault on Dice's Point. General Peleg Wadsworth recounted the dawn landing years later:

> *The morning was quite still but somewhat Foggy. The Vessels of War were drawn up in a Line just out of reach of Musket Shot & 400 Men (viz. 200 of Militia & 200 Marines) were in Boats along side ready to push for the Shore on Signals. The highest Clift was preferred by the commander of the Party, knowing that his men would make the best shift in rough ground. The fire of the Enemy opened upon us from the top of the Bank or Clift, just as the boats reached the Shore. We step'd out & the boats immediately sent back. There was now a stream of fire over our heads from the Fleet & a shower of Musketry in our faces from the Top of the Cliff. We soon found the Clift unsurmountable even without Opponents. The party therefore, was divided into three parts, one sent to the right, another to the left till they should find the Clift practicable & the Center keeping up their fire to amuse the Enemy. Both parties succeeded & gained the Height, but closing in upon the Enemy in the Rear rather too soon gave them opportunity to escape, which they did, leaving 30 kill'd, wounded & prisoners. The conflict was short, but sharp, for we left 100, out of 400, on the shore & bank. The marines suffer'd most, by forcing*

Bagaduce

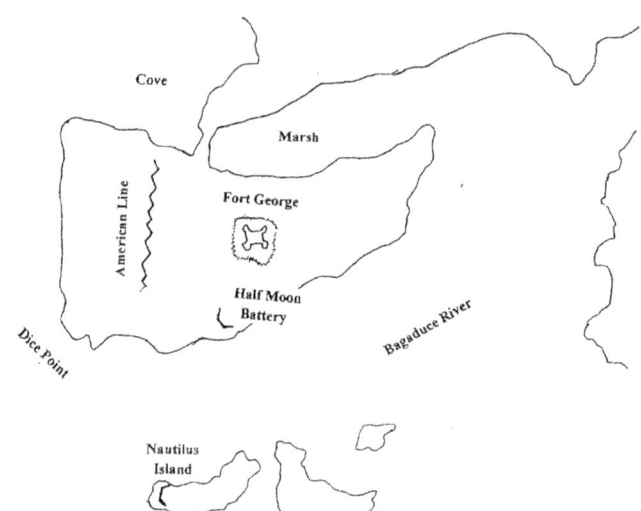

their way up a foot Path leading up the Clift. This Action lasted but 20 Minutes....[83]

Captain John Welsh commanded the marines who scaled the cliff one shrub or branch at a time. He was fatally wounded in the assault, but his marines reached the top. Another account of the assault from an unknown American participant proudly boasted of the courage displayed by the troops:

> *Landed our troops under a shower of cannon and musquet balls, some loss on both sides – never did men behave with so much courage – They jumped ashore, stood three fires from* [the enemy] *then drove them into their fort.*[84]

General Lovell was also proud of his men and recorded the following in his diary:

> *When I returned to the Shore it struck me with admiration to see what a Precipice we had ascended, not being able to take so scrutinous a view of it in time of Battle, it is at least where we landed three hundred feet high,* [actually closer to 100 feet] *and almost perpendicular & the men were obliged to pull themselves up by the twigs & trees.*[85]

British resistance to the assault was surprisingly weak in part because General McLean never believed that the main American attack would come from the west. McLean assumed that all of the previous American activity along the

---

[83] "General Peleg Wadsworth to William D. Williamson," *Collections of the Maine Historical Society, Series 2, Vol. 2,* 157-158
[84] Buker, 44
[85] C.B. Kevitt, "Gen. Lovell, July 28, 1779," *General Solomon Lovell and the Penobscot Expedition: 1779,* (Weymouth, MA: 1976), 35

western shore (which he considered impossible to ascend) was really a feint to distract the British from the main assault somewhere else on the peninsula. As a result, he posted only a small picket guard of about 80 men along the bluff. Lieutenant John Moore commanded part of this picket guard and described the American attack:

> *After a very sharp cannonade from the shipping upon the wood, to the great surprise of General M'Lean and the garrison, they effected a landing. I happened to be upon picket that morning, under command of a captain of the 74th regiment, who, after giving them one fire, instead of encouraging his men (who naturally had been a little startled by the cannonade) to do their duty, ordered them to retreat, leaving me and about twenty men to shift for ourselves. After standing for some time I was obliged to retreat to the fort, having five or six of my own men killed and several wounded. I was lucky to escape untouched.*[86]

Moore and his surviving men joined the rest of the British picket force in a hasty retreat to Fort George and the garrison braced for a full scale assault. Based on the size of the American fleet, General McLean believed the Americans vastly outnumbered him and reportedly commented,

> *I was in no situation to defend myself, I only meant to give* [the Americans] *one or two guns, so as not to be called a coward, and then have struck my colors, which I stood for some time to do, as I did not wish to throw away the lives of my men for nothing.*[87]

---

[86] Joseph Williamson, "Lieutenant Moore to his father, Sir John Moore at Castine During the Revolution," *Collections of the Maine Historical Society, series 2, Vol. 2*, 408

[87] Buker, 45

McLean avoided the humiliation of surrender when the expected American attack never materialized. After the successful landing onshore, General Lovell became cautious and entrenched his army about 600 yards from Fort George. Lovell informed the Massachusetts Council of his actions soon after the landing:

> This morning I have made my landing good on the S.W. head of the Peninsula which is one hundred feet high and almost perpendicular very thickly covered with Brush & trees, the men ascended the Precipice with alacrity and after a very smart conflict we put them to the rout, they left in the Woods a number killed & wounded & we took a few Prisoners. Our loss is about thirty kill'd & wounded, we are within 100 Rod of the Enemy's main fort on a Commanding piece of Ground, & hope soon to have the Satisfaction of informing you of Capturing the whole Army....[88]

While General Lovell and the Massachusetts ground forces settled into a siege of Fort George, Commodore Saltonstall displayed some aggressiveness by leading three of his warships, including the thirty-two gun continental frigate *Warren*, against Captain Mowat's ships. As they entered the mouth of the Bagaduce River, Saltonstall's vessels were pounded by British cannon in the fort and along the shore, and by Mowat's ships. The American ships inflicted only minimal damage on Mowat's vessels and withdrew badly battered.[89] Despite this setback, Commodore Saltonstall remained determined to capture or destroy Captain Mowat's ships and moved to neutralize one of the British shore batteries on the peninsula that had damaged his ships. The Half Moon battery

---

[88] Kevitt, "General Lovell to Jeremiah Powell, 28 July, 1779," 80-81
[89] Buker, 46-47

was a strong British outpost on the southwestern shore of the peninsula. Its purpose was to help Captain Mowat defend the mouth of the Bagaduce River and prevent the Americans from sailing into the river to attack Fort George from the south and east.

A detachment of Saltonstall's marines and sailors, supported by some of Colonel Samuel McCobb's militia, attacked the battery early in the morning of August 1st. The militia performed poorly and fled in the face of British resistance, but the marines and sailors overwhelmed the garrison and seized the position before daybreak. Unfortunately for the Americans, a British counterattack at dawn dislodged the marines and sailors and returned the Half Moon battery to British hands. Commodore Saltonstall, discouraged by this setback, changed tactics and began a siege upon Mowat's ships by placing naval cannon on the mainland to bombard the British ships.

An uneasy stalemate ensued over the next two weeks as the Americans slowly extended their trench line and batteries closer to Fort George and the British ships. General Wadsworth recalled,

> *We were employed daily, or rather Nightly in advancing upon their Fort by Zigzag intrenchments till within a fair gunshot of their Fort so that a man seldom shew his Head above their Works.*[90]

By August 13th, anxiety among the American commanders about the possible arrival of a British relief force finally convinced General Lovell and Commodore Saltonstall to launch a joint attack on the British fort and ships. The

---

[90] Nathan Goold, "Peleg Wadsworth to William D. Williamson, January 1, 1828" Colonel Jonathan Mitchell's Cumberland County Regiment: Bagaduce Expedition, 1779," *Collections of the Maine Historical Society, Vol. 10*, 71

Americans were about to proceed with a direct assault on both when several large vessels were sighted off in the distance entering Penobscot Bay. The American commanders feared that the approaching vessels were British warships with reinforcements and cancelled their attack. When their fears were confirmed, General Lovell and Commodore Saltonstall ended the siege and evacuated Bagaduce. Lovell's troops and almost all of their gear and supplies were quietly loaded aboard transport ships under cover of darkness.[91] By morning the American transport ships were struggling to sail upriver, away from the British threat.

Commodore Saltonstall's warships followed Lovell's transports and were pursued by the British. To the shock of General Lovell and his men on the transports, instead of standing to fight the British navy and protect the transports, Saltonstall's warships sailed past them. It was now every American ship for itself. Many of the transport captains panicked and guided their slow ships towards the western shore of the Penobscot River. One by one they beached and burned their vessels rather than let the troops and sailors fall into British hands. Most of the transports were aground and on fire before nightfall, scattered along the western shore of the Penobscot River below present day Bucksport.[92] The Americans aboard the doomed ships scrambled ashore, leaving most of their gear and supplies behind. Fortunately for these men, the British were more interested in the armed American ships and continued their pursuit upriver. The stranded Americans on the western shore of the Penobscot River were left to make their way westward through the Maine wilderness to the Kennebec River. Behind them burned the wreckage of over half the American fleet. The American ships still afloat struggled further up the Penobscot River.

---

[91] Buker, 77
[92] Ibid., 84-85

Destruction of the American Fleet

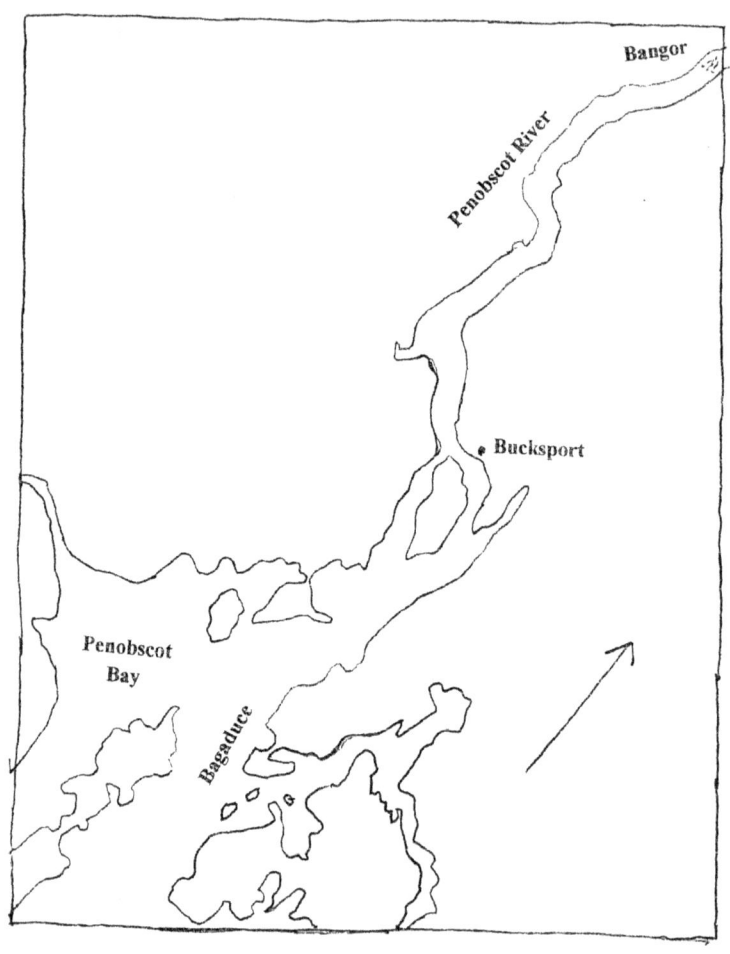

Some made it to the falls of Bangor where General Lovell proposed that a fortified position along the shore be built to protect them, but the captains and crews disagreed and chose to burn their vessels and flee westward.[93]

The demise of the Penobscot Expedition was a significant military and financial blow to Massachusetts. Hundreds of men were lost and the state was nearly bankrupted by the cost.[94] The reputations of Paul Revere, Dudley Saltonstall, and Solomon Lovell, along with all of the troops associated with the expedition, were tarnished. Criticism of the sailors and troops, especially the marines, was largely undeserved. The men of the Penobscot Expedition were hastily assembled and poorly led, any yet they had nearly defeated a well entrenched force of British regulars. Had Commodore Saltonstall and General Lovell been more decisive in their actions, the entire affair may have ended differently. Alas, bad luck and bad leadership caused the expedition to end disastrously.

Although the outcome of the Penobscot Expedition was devastating to Massachusetts, the success of American arms elsewhere helped soften the blow. General Sullivan's victory at Newtown and the destruction his force wrought on scores of Indian settlements temporarily pacified the New York / Pennsylvania frontier and boosted American morale as did General Anthony Wayne's stunning victory at Stony Point a month before the Penobscot Expedition in mid-July.

---

[93] Ibid.
[94] Boatner, 852

Stony Point

The first half of 1779 had been relatively quiet for General Washington and the main American army. Washington's troops were concentrated near West Point and the New York Highlands. The Americans were too weak to attack New York City, but were determined to confront the British whenever they ventured too far into the countryside. To do this, and protect an important Hudson River crossing called King's Ferry, General Washington established fortified posts twelve miles below West Point, at Stony Point and Verplanks.

These posts were seized by the British in early June and significantly strengthened. The British garrison at Stony Point numbered over 600 men and was built on a rocky promontory rising 150 feet above the river.[95] It was surrounded by water on three sides and connected to land by a swampy morass that was often submerged at high tide. Two lines of earthworks with abbatis, which were sharp sticks and logs that protruded toward the enemy and acted as barbed wire, were constructed by the British. Several redoubts with cannon were also erected, and the post was protected by British ships in the Hudson.

At first glance, Stony Point looked impregnable, but General Washington was determined to re-take it. On July 1st, he ordered General Wayne to conduct a detailed reconnaissance of the fort to determine the feasibility of an attack. Wayne reported his findings to Washington on July 3rd. A week later, Washington recommended the following plan of attack to General Wayne:

---

[95] Don Loprieno, *The Enterprise in Contemplation: The Midnight Assault of Stony Point*, (Westminster, MD: Heritage Books, 2004), 6-7

Attack on Stony Point

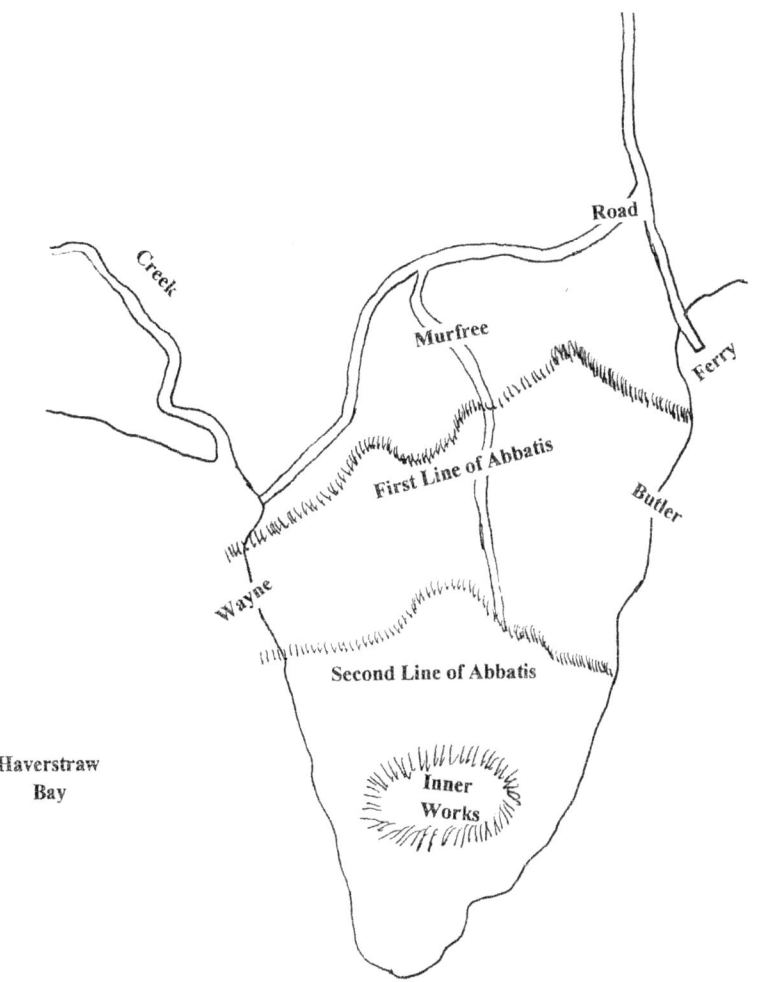

My ideas of the enterprize in contemplation are these. That it should be attempted by the light Infantry only, which should march under cover of Night and with the utmost secrecy to the enemys lines, securing every person they find to prevent discovery...the approach should be along the Water on the South side crossing the Beach and entering at the abbatis. This party is to be preceded by a van-guard of prudent and determined men, well commanded who are to remove obstructions, secure the Sentries, and drive in the Guards. They are to advance (the whole of them) with fixed Bayonets and Muskets unloaded...These parties should be followed by the main body at a small distance for the purpose of support and making good the advantages which may be gained, or to bring them off in case of repulse and disappointment; other parties may advance to the Works...by the way of the causeway and River on the North...for the purpose of distracting the enemy in their defence as to cut off their retreat. These Parties may be small unless the access and approaches should be very easy and safe. A white feather or Cockade, or some other visible badge of distinction for the night should be worn by our Troops and a watch word agreed on to distinguish friends from foes.[96]

Washington added that General Wayne was free to alter the plan as he saw fit.

On July 15th, the Light Infantry corps, composed of four regiments totaling about 1200 men and commanded by General Wayne, assembled for inspection at Fort Montgomery, eleven miles north of Stony Point. They were

---

[96] Fitzpatrick, "General Washington to General Wayne, 10 July, 1779," *The Writings of George Washington, Vol. 15*, 396-397

the cream of the American army, chosen men all and unaware that they were about to be severely tested.

Instead of returning to camp like they usually did after such inspections, the light corps marched west and then south, along a heavily wooded and mountainous path. Great lengths were taken to preserve the secrecy of the march. Parties of dragoons patrolled the march route and detained anyone they found for fear that word would reach the enemy of the American advance. This same fear caused General Wayne to keep the destination of the march from his officers.

The Americans finally halted around sunset at Springsteel's Farm, about a mile and a half west of Stony Point. The men rested and refreshed themselves and waited for further orders. Scouts reported to General Wayne that nothing was out of the ordinary in the enemy camp.[97] The British appeared to be unaware of the impending attack.

General Wayne decided to attack at midnight and ordered

> *Every Officer and Soldier...to fix a Piece of White paper in the most Conspicuous part of his Hat or Cap as an Insignia to be distinguished from the Enemy.*[98]

Wayne's plan called for three detachments to simultaneously attack the fort from three directions. The smallest detachment consisted of two companies of North Carolina troops under Major Hardy Murfree. They were the only troops allowed to load their muskets and were ordered to "*keep up a perpetual and Galling fire*" on the center of the enemy's line only after

---

[97] Henry Commager and Richard Morris, ed., "Journal of Captain Allen McLane, 15 July, 1779," *The Spirit of 'Seventy-Six: The Story of the American Revolution as Told by Participants*, (NY: Castle Books, 1967), 732

[98] Charles Stille, "General Wayne's Order of Battle, 15 July, 1779," *Major-General Anthony Wayne ad the Pennsylvania Line in the Continental Army*, (Port Washington, NY: Kenniket Press, Inc., 1968), 402 (First published in 1893)

the British pickets became alarmed by the other detachments.[99] General Wayne hoped that Major Murfree's fire would draw the enemy's attention to the center of their line and away from their flanks.

Lieutenant Colonel Richard Butler, with 300 Maryland and Pennsylvania troops, would assault the northern side of the fort with only bayonets and swords. A twenty man advance party, called a forlorn hope, led the column. Its task was to remove the abbatis and other obstructions for the troops behind them. At the same time, Colonel Christian Febiger and General Wayne would lead the main American force of 700 men against the southern side of the fort. They planned to wade into Haverstraw Bay to avoid the outer line of abbatis and then charge up the hill to attack the inner works by bayonet. This force also included a twenty man forlorn hope commanded by Lieutenant George Knox. A battalion of Massachusetts continentals under Major William Hull made up part of Wayne's main force. Many of the Massachusetts troops hailed from Maine. If all went as planned, Wayne's light corps would overwhelm the enemy from two directions.[100]

The American attack began at 12:20 a.m., twenty minutes behind schedule due to high water in the bay.[101] As the Americans approached the fort, British sentries grew alarmed. Although they could not see the Americans, they heard them and fired in their direction. Lieutenant John Ross, the commander of the British picket guard, initially believed that his men were trigger happy and had fired at the wind. A visiting officer asked him what all the commotion was about, and Lieutenant Ross replied,

---

[99] Ibid.
[100] Ibid., and Loprieno, 22
[101] Henry Johnson, "General Wayne to General Washington, 17 July, 1779," *The Storming of Stony Point on the Hudson, Midnight, July 15, 1779: Its Importance in the Light of Unpublished Documents,* (New York: James T. White, 1900), 209

> *I told [the officer] that I saw No Enemy the Night being extremely dark and very Windy, made me suppose that what the Men reported to me to have heard, was occasioned by the Wind rustling amongst the Bushes....* [102]

British sentries on the left side of the line, however, alarmed by the firing of their comrades, soon noticed movement in Haverstraw Bay. It was the main American column approaching from the south. Simon Davis of the British 17th Regiment noted that he heard,

> *A Noise in the Water on my left which appeared...to have been Occasioned by a large body of Men wading through it....* [103]

The British pickets fired and withdrew to the outer earthworks and braced for an attack. On the left of their line, a twelve pound cannon illuminated the night. Lieutenant William Horndon of the Royal Artillery recalled,

> *By the light occasioned by the flash of the Gun I could perceive a Body of them [the Americans] coming thro' the Water; upon the left... I attempted to bring the Gun to bear upon them, but could not effect it, the Embrazure being too confined.* [104]

The main American column ignored the activity above them and waded through waist deep water to pass around the enemy's outer abbatis. Major William Hull described the advance:

---

[102] Laprieno, 25
[103] Ibid., 26
[104] Ibid., 176

> *The beach was more than two feet deep with water, and before the right column reached it we were fired upon by the out-guards which gave the alarm to the garrison. We were now directly under the fort, and closing in a solid column ascended the hill, which was almost perpendicular. When about half way up our course was impeded by two strong rows of abatis, which the fornlorn hope had not been able entirely to remove. The column proceeded silently on, clearing away the abatis, passed to the breastwork, cut and tore away the pickets, cleared the cheveaux de frise at the sally port, mounted the parapet and entered the fort at the point of the bayonet. All this was done under a heavy fire of artillery and musketry, and as strong a resistance as could be made by the British bayonet.*[105]

While the main American column scaled the hill and approached the inner works, Major Murfree's small, diversionary, center column engaged the center of the enemy. Murfree successfully occupied a large portion of the British troops. They were unaware of the American flank attacks and believed that the main attack was directed at the center of the line.

On the American left, Lieutenant Colonel Richard Butler's column successfully swept around the outer abbatis, but it encountered stiff resistance near the inner works. The twenty man forlorn hope party suffered seventeen casualties and the whole column was temporarily pinned down.[106]

On the right, the main American column overcame a brief delay of its own and stormed into the inner works. British Lieutenant John Roberts of the Royal Artillery described this part of the assault from the British perspective:

---

[105] Johnson, 191
[106] Johnson, "General Wayne to General Washington, 17 July, 1779," 210

> *I heard a Body of them* [the Americans] *Approaching, and I then concluded that the Enemy were in Possession of the Howitzer Battery,* [in front of the inner line] *and were pushing for the Upper Work, upon which I also bent my steps that way, but fell over a Log of Wood, and several People fell over me before I recovered myself, and I have great reason to believe that the Enemy entered the upper Work at the Barrier.*[107]

Lieutenant Roberts heard cries of "throw down your arms!" and discovered that the Americans had also got into the rear of the fort. Convinced that the garrison was lost, he scampered down the hill to Haverstraw Bay and swam to a British ship. Roberts was one of only two British officers to escape.[108]

Victory belonged to the Americans, and an exhausted General Wayne dashed off a quick report to General Washington announcing their success:

> *It was about twenty minutes after twelve before the assault began – previous to which I placed myself at the Head of Febiger's Regiment or Right Column & gave the troops the most pointed Orders not to attempt to fire, but put their whole dependence on the Bayonet – which was faithfully & Literally Observed,-- neither the deep Morass, the formidable & double rows of abbatis or the high & strong works in front & flank could damp the ardor of the troops – who in the face of a most tremendous and Incessant fire of Musketry & from Artillery loaded with shells & Grape-shot forced their way at the point of the Bayonet thro' every Obstacle, -- both Columns meeting in the Center of the Enemy's works nearly at*

---

[107] Loprieno, 207
[108] Ibid., 208-209

the same Instant." Too much praise cannot be given to Lieut. Colonel Fleury (who struck the enemy's standard with his own hand) & to Major Steward who Commanded the Advance parties, for their brave & prudent Conduct; Colonels Butler, Meigs & Febiger conducted themselves with that coolness, bravery & perseverance that ever will ensure success.[109]

A few weeks later, responding to complaints from some of the light infantry officers who felt that they had not received the recognition they deserved, General Wayne sent a second report to Congress:

I feel very hurt that I did not in my letter to [General Washington] of the 17th July, mention (among other brave and worthy officers), the names of Lieut. Col. SHERMAN, Majors HULL, MURPHY and POSEY, whose good conduct and intrepidity justly entitled them to that attention...Permit me, therefore, thro your Excellency, to do them that justice now which the state of my wound diverted me from in the first instance....[110]

Regardless of who deserved the credit, the American attack on Stony Point was a stunning success. The American light infantry corps, which consisted of numerous troops from Maine, defeated a heavily fortified garrison of nearly 600 men, at the cost of 15 killed and 83 wounded.[111] The British reported approximately 100 men killed or wounded and over

---

[109] Johnson, 209
[110] Stille, "Wayne's Supplementary Report to the President of Congress, 26 August, 1779," 403-404
[111] Boatner, 1066

450 captured.[112] This decisive American victory boosted morale throughout the army in the summer of 1779 and reminded the British that the Americans were still a dangerous adversary.

---

[112] Ibid.

Chapter Ten

"Our Public Affairs Never Looked in so Dubious & Precarious a Situation" 1780-81

In the two years following Valley Forge, American forces experienced mixed results on the battlefield. Defeats at Rhode Island, Savannah (twice), Penobscot, and on the New York frontier were offset by victories at Monmouth, Vincennes (George Rogers Clark), Newtown, and Stony Point. As 1780 approached, American resolve (especially in eastern Maine and the South) was once again put to the test.

The economic disruption caused by five years of war struck the residents of Maine particularly hard because many of them relied on imported food to survive. Wartime correspondence between Maine communities and the Massachusetts government frequently included pleas for relief from impending famine.[1]

The Massachusetts government was largely powerless to alleviate the suffering of downeast Maine, especially after the disaster of the Penobscot expedition. With a strong British force firmly in control of Penobscot Bay, the residents of Lincoln County were at the mercy of the British. As a result, some residents accepted a British offer of amnesty while others proclaimed their neutrality in the hope that they be allowed to trade and import food again.[2]

General Peleg Wadsworth commanded the local militia forces in Lincoln County, but there were few troops to actually command. The service of hundreds of Lincoln men in the continental army and the desperation of many families just to

---

[1] Leamon, 135-138
[2] Ibid.

feed themselves, left few men available for local military service. In an effort to curtail trade among the county residents and the British at Bagaduce, General Wadsworth declared martial law in April 1780. The decree, which banned trade with the British, had little effect on residents who were desperate to feed their families, and it was suspended after six months.[3] In February 1781, resistance to the British suffered another blow when General Wadsworth was captured by a British raiding party in Thomaston. Wadsworth was wounded in the incident and managed to escape from Fort George a few months later, but his capture only highlighted the inability of local forces to defend eastern Maine from the British.[4]

The inhabitants of Georgia and South Carolina could empathize with the residents of eastern Maine. British troops occupied Savannah and Augusta, Georgia and seized control of Charlestown, South Carolina in May 1780. General Washington sent what little help he could to South Carolina in the form of Maryland and Delaware continentals, but they were too few to turn the tide and were poorly led by General Horatio Gates at Camden.

In New York, General Washington's army, composed of continental troops from New England and the mid-Atlantic states, remained north of Manhattan Island. The Massachusetts continentals, which included hundreds of Maine men, saw little action in 1780 and spent the first half of the year guarding the New York Highlands.[5] They redeployed to New Jersey in August and were there when the shocking news of Benedict Arnold's betrayal became known. Arnold, disgruntled at his treatment by Congress and lured by a British offer of wealth and rank, attempted to smuggle West Point's defensive plans to the British. Arnold's British contact, Major John Andre' was apprehended by the

---

[3] Ibid., 123-126
[4] Ibid., 128-129
[5] Lesser, "Troop Strength Reports for January to July 1780," 148-172

Americans with the plans and consequently executed, but Arnold escaped to the British. General Washington and his fellow countrymen were stunned by Arnold's treason. Considered by many to be the best field commander in the American army, Arnold's betrayal capped a series of setbacks in 1780 that seriously weakened American morale.

American spirits rose in October, however, on the news that American riflemen had defeated a large loyalist force under Major Patrick Ferguson at Kings Mountain in South Carolina. Ferguson and many of his men were killed, and the rest of his 1,000 man force were wounded and captured. Three months later, General Daniel Morgan won an equally significant victory over the British at Cowpens, South Carolina.

Satisfaction at General Morgan's victory in January 1781 was tempered in Virginia by the arrival of General Benedict Arnold and a strong detachment of British, Hessian, and loyalist troops. Arnold's force sailed up the James River to Richmond in early January and plundered the new capital. They returned back down the river a few days later and encamped in Portsmouth, shadowed by a weak contingent of Virginia militia.

In New York, General Washington's ability to assist Virginia (and possibly capture Arnold) was limited. The departure of thousands of veteran troops (whose enlistments expired in December 1780) had significantly reduced the size of Washington's army in 1781. The Massachusetts line shrank from fifteen regiments to ten (all under strength), and similar reductions occurred throughout the army.[6] Despite his limited numbers, General Washington ordered all the regiments in the army to bring their light infantry companies (of which each regiment had one) to full strength (50 men) in

---

[6] Fitzpatrick, "General Orders, 1 January, 1781," *Writings of George Washington, Vol. 21,* 45

February.[7] He then detached the light companies from their regiments and formed a 1200 man corps of light infantry under General Marquis de LaFayette.[8]

LaFayette had joined the American army in 1777 as a nineteen year old French volunteer and quickly endeared himself to General Washington. In 1781 Washington entrusted LaFayette with his best troops and sent the young Frenchman south to counter British moves in Virginia. LaFayette's detachment left camp in late February and, after long delays at Head of Elk and Annapolis, Maryland (caused by the presence of British warships in Chesapeake Bay and British reinforcements under General William Phillips in Virginia) marched on to Virginia.[9] His troops were mostly New Englanders. Ten of LaFayette's twenty-four companies were Massachusetts men that included scores of troops from Maine.[10] Colonel Joseph Vose commanded one of the three light battalions of LaFayette's corps; it consisted of eight companies from Massachusetts. Companies from Connecticut, Massachusetts, and Rhode Island formed LaFayette's second light battalion under Lieutenant Colonel Jean-Joseph de Gimat, another French volunteer. LaFayette's last battalion was commanded by Lieutenant Colonel Francis Barber of New Jersey. Barber's battalion comprised New Jersey and New Hampshire troops and a company of Canadian troops from Colonel Moses Hazen's regiment.[11]

Although LaFayette commanded many of Washington's most experienced troops, they were not necessarily the best

---

[7] Fitzpatrick, "General Orders, 15 February, 1781," *Writings of George Washington, Vol. 21*, 228
[8] Fitzpatrick, "General Washington to General LaFayette, 20 February, 1781," *The Writings of George Washington, Vol. 21*, 253-256
[9] John E. Selby, *The Revolution in Virginia: 1775-1781*, (Charlottesville, VA: University of Virginia Press, 1988), 265, 270, 273
[10] Fitzpatrick, "General Washington to General Heath, 17 February, 1781," *Writings of George Washington, Vol. 21*,
[11] Ibid.

equipped for the journey south. LaFayette described the formation of his detachment and some of the challenges it faced in letters to General Nathanael Greene and the Chevalier de La Luzerne. LaFayette wrote,

> *When this Detachment was ordered Every Individual in it thought they were Going on a tour of duty of two or three days And Provided Accordingly. The Light [Companies] of Every Regiment (New York Excepted) which Consisted of 25 men were By Common Drafts from the Regiments Increased to 50...Thus Circumstanced, our officers Had No Money, No Baggage of Any Sort, No Summer Cloathes and Hardly a Shirt to Shift. To these Common Miseries the Soldiers Added their Shocking Nakedness and a want of Shoes etc.*[12]

> *Our officers and soldiers are not too happy about it. We have no money, clothing, shoes, nor shirts, and in a few days we shall be making our meals on green peaches; our feet are torn for lack of shoes and our hands itchy for lack of linens* [scabies].[13]

When LaFayette's appeals for clothing went unfulfilled, he used his personal credit to obtain $2,000 worth of clothing and shoes from the merchants of Baltimore.[14]

Most of LaFayette's men strongly objected to the march south but grudgingly followed orders. Scores deserted along the march, however, which prompted LaFayette to express his concern to General Greene in mid-April:

---

[12] Stanley J. Idzerda, ed., "General LaFayette to General Greene, April 17, 1781," *LaFayette in the Age of the American Revolution, Vol. 4*, 37

[13] Idzerda, "General LaFayette to the Chevalier de La Luzerne, April 10, 1781," 22

[14] Idzerda, "General LaFayette to General Washington, 18 April, 1781," 43

> *The Men, Whose discipline does not Give them the Idea of Complaining Began to Desert in Great Numbers.... The New England troops Have taken An idea that Southern Climates Are Very Unwholesome and that of Carolina Mortal to them. Every officer Assured me that our detachment Would Soon Be Reduced to five or Six Hundred Men* [out of originally 1,200 men].[15]

When LaFayette's corps reached Richmond on April 29th, desertion, fatigue, and illness had reduced it to 800 men.[16] A Massachusetts officer with LaFayette glumly observed,

> *Our publick affairs never looked in so Dubious and precarious a situation as they do in this Quarter at this time.... Philips and Arnold have taken all the principle towns in Virginia and have ben 500 Miles into the Country and no force sufficient to oppose them neither will their be unless the New England states furnish Troops and send them here, for the Carolinias are little or no better than this state and Georgia is wholly Conquered and have raised troops to fight against us.*[17]

Despite the pessimism of this officer, the presence of General LaFayette's light corps and hundreds of militia in Richmond convinced General Phillips (who had assumed command of all British troops in Virginia in April) to lead his troops from the outskirts of Richmond to Petersburg and await additional reinforcements.

---

[15] Idzerda, "General LaFayette to General Greene, 17 April, 1781," 38

[16] Idzerda, "General LaFayette to General Greene, 3 May, 1781," 79

[17] John Shy ed., "Gilbert to his Father, 5 May, 1781," *Winding Down: The Revolutionary War Letters of Lieutenant Colonel Benjamin Gilbert of Massachusetts, 1780-83*, (University of Michigan, Press: William L. Clements Library, 1989), 43

Virginia Campaign of 1781

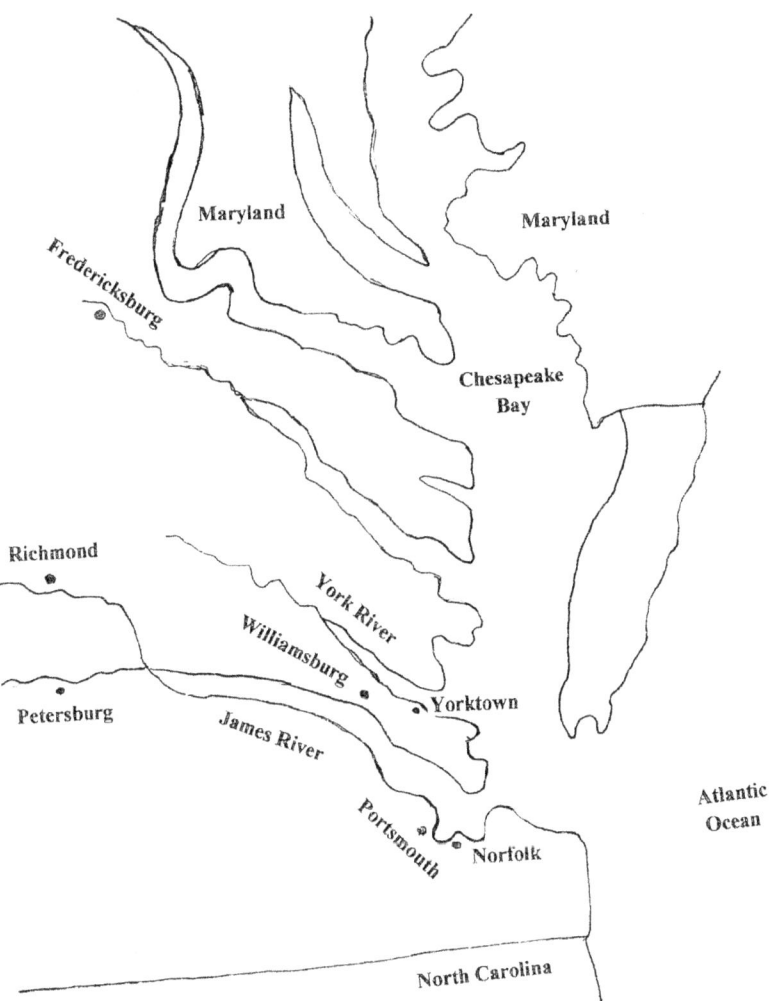

General Phillips had arrived in Virginia in April with approximately 2500 troops and had already defeated the Virginia militia at Petersburg and the Virginia State Navy at Osborne Landing. He returned to Petersburg in May to rendezvous with another British force -- General Charles Cornwallis's battered army of 1500 men from the Carolinas. Cornwallis had spent the last five months in pursuit of General Nathanael Greene's resilient southern army and had won an expensive victory in mid-March (at the cost of over 500 men) in North Carolina at Guilford Courthouse. Although Cornwallis had won the battle, General Greene's army remained intact and elusive, and a frustrated General Cornwallis opted to lead his weakened force to Virginia to unite with British forces operating there. Cornwallis hoped that a successful campaign in Virginia would halt the state's ability to support General Greene in the Carolinas.

General Cornwallis arrived in Petersburg on May 20th and assumed command of all British troops in Virginia (which included a recent reinforcement from New York). This brought the total British force in the state to over 7,000 men.[18] General Cornwallis was deprived, however, of a key subordinate and friend. A few days before Cornwallis arrived in Petersburg, General Phillips succumbed to an illness and died.

Cornwallis vs. LaFayette

The arrival of General Cornwallis, as well as additional reinforcements from New York, created a very powerful British presence in Virginia, one that General LaFayette, the ranking American commander in the state, wished to avoid. LaFayette anxiously waited for his own reinforcements, 800 Pennsylvania continentals under General Anthony Wayne.

---

[18] Selby, 275

Transport, supply, and morale problems, however, delayed Wayne's march south and prompted an anxious LaFayette to give a bleak assessment of his situation in late May:

> *We are still alive...and so far our little corps has not received the terrible visit. Lord Cornwallis is in Petersburg and peacefully crossed North Carolina. He may well pay a toll to cross Virginia, but we cannot hope to offer great resistance. The proportion of their regular infantry to ours is between four and five to one and their cavalry ten to one; there are a few Tories, with whom I hardly bother. Our militia is not very numerous on paper, and it is even less so in the field. We lack arms, we haven't a hundred riflemen, and if we are beaten, that is to say if we are caught, we shall all be routed.... For the love of God, let me know what had become of the Pennsylvanians. They were to have crossed the Potomac ahead of me, and if we had remained en route as long as they have the British would be in possession of all of Virginia. Their junction with us would make our little army a bit more respectable. We would be beaten but at least we would be decently beaten.*[19]

A few days later, LaFayette updated Governor Jefferson. He summed up his problem in one sentence:

> *No Riflemen, no Cavalry, no arms, and few Militia coming.*[20]

---

[19] Idzerda, "LaFayette to Chevalier de La Luzerne, 22 May, 1781," 120
[20] Idzerda, "General LaFayette to Governor Jefferson, 28 May, 1781," 137

Wayne's continued absence caused LaFayette to retreat northward when Cornwallis crossed to the north side of the James River on May 24th. Cornwallis pursued LaFayette, but the French general wanted no part of an engagement until he was reinforced, so he retreated further north.

Cornwallis eventually grew frustrated at his inability to bring LaFayette to battle and ended his pursuit at Hanover Courthouse.[21] He redirected his attention westward with raids on Charlottesville, where the Virginia government was gathered, and Point of Fork, where a continental supply depot was located. Both raids were successful and further weakened Virginia's ability to resist the British presence in the state.[22]

In mid-June, General Cornwallis marched his troops to Williamsburg, the old colonial capital. General LaFayette, finally reinforced on June 10th by General Anthony Wayne's 800 Pennsylvanian continentals, followed Cornwallis south looking for a chance to strike. An opportunity emerged in late June on the outskirts of Williamsburg when an American detachment of cavalry, riflemen, and Pennsylvanian continentals surprised a British detachment near Spencer's Ordinary. The skirmish that ensued ended in a draw and highlighted General LaFayette's new found determination to press Cornwallis when an opportunity arrived. That determination nearly cost LaFayette dearly a few days later along the James River.

---

[21] Ward, 195
[22] Banastre Tarleton, *A History of the Campaigns of 1780 and 1781 in the Southern Provinces of North America,* (North Stratford, NH: Ayer Co., Reprinted, 1999, 297 (Over 1000 weapons a many barrels of gunpowder were destroyed)

Battle of Green Spring

The British occupied Williamsburg for over a week while the Americans hovered nearby at New Kent Court House. On July 4th, Cornwallis broke camp and marched to Jamestown to cross the James River. Cornwallis's destination was Portsmouth; however, he set a trap for General LaFayette before crossing the river. On July 6th, he sent his baggage across the James River but hid the bulk of his army along the shoreline. Cornwallis hoped to induce LaFayette to attack by convincing him that only a weak British rearguard remained north of the river. British pickets were posted along the road to Jamestown with instructions to draw the Americans towards the British trap.

General Wayne took the bait and marched his 500 man advance guard towards Jamestown. His force included militia horsemen, Virginia riflemen, Pennsylvania continentals, and a detachment of light infantry under Major Galvan. The Americans skirmished with British pickets and slowly advanced along a wooded causeway towards the river. General Wayne recalled,

At three o' clock the riflemen, supported by a few regulars, began and kept up a galling fire upon the enemy, which continued until five....[23]

---

[23] Jared Sparks, ed. " Brigadier-General Wayne to General Washington, 8 July, 1781," *Correspondence of the American Revolution Being Letters of Eminent Men to George Washington,* (Boston: Little, Brown, and Co., 1853), 348
(Henceforth referred to as Wayne)

Lieutenant Colonel James Mercer commanded about 150 Virginia riflemen on the right flank of the American line. After a long running skirmish his riflemen encountered a strong British detachment posted at a house. Mercer recalled,

> *The* [enemy] *Picket was speedily driven* [from a house] *with loss, & possession gain'd of the house. To support them & regain the house,* [a second British detachment] *advanc'd with spirit, but they were unable to stand the deadly fire of the Riflemen, and were driven back with...loss.... The Riflemen embolden'd by this success, were with difficulty restrain'd from advancing...and a number of them crowded into the house and began to fire to the left on the main body of the British army now plainly discover'd at a distance of about 300 yards.*[24]

In the American center, General Wayne was startled by the sudden appearance of five British columns in his front. It was Cornwallis's main force, emerging from the shoreline. General Wayne *"Thought proper to order Major Galvan, at the head of the advanced guard, to meet and attack their front...."*[25] Galvan's 150 light infantrymen conducted a *"spirited though unequal"* fight and withdrew after only a few minutes.[26]

Colonel Mercer witnessed Galvan's brave stand but was soon occupied with his own front. British artillery killed his

---

[24] Gillard Hunt, ed., "Colonel John Francis Mercer," *Eyewitness Accounts of the American Revolution: Fragments of Revolutionary History*, (NY Times & Arno Press, Reprint, 1971), 48 (Originally printed in 1892 and henceforth referred to as Mercer)
[25] Sparks, 348
[26] Ibid.

horse and panicked his riflemen. Mercer recalled that as the riflemen scurried to the rear *"The whole front line of the enemy was advancing with shouts."*[27] The situation was equally desperate on the American left, which quickly collapsed.

In the center, General Wayne struggled to make a stand. He was reinforced by two battalions of Pennsylvania continentals and a battalion of light infantry, but his 800 man line was still greatly outnumbered.[28] With the enemy pressing his flanks and threatening his rear, Wayne made a bold decision:

> *It was determined among a choice of difficulties, to advance and charge them. This was done with such vivacity as to produce the desired effect, that is, checking them in their advance, and diverting them from their [attempted encirclement].*[29]

Lieutenant William Feltman, a Pennsylvania continental, described the advance:

> *We...displayed to the right and left, the 3rd battalion on our right, and the 2nd on our left, being then formed, [we] brought on a general engagement, our advance [was] regular at a charge till we got within eighty yards of their whole army, they being regularly formed, standing one yard distance from each other...We advanced under a heavy fire of*

---

[27] Mercer, 49
[28] Rankin, 55
[29] Sparks, 348

> *grape-shot at which distance we opened our musketry.*[30]

British Lieutenant Colonel Banastre Tarleton was impressed by the intensity of the fight:

> *The conflict in this quarter was severe and well contested. The artillery and infantry of each army...were for some minutes warmly engaged not fifty yards asunder...on the left of the British, the action was for some time gallantly maintained by the continental infantry.*[31]

General Wayne's aggressiveness surprised the British and disrupted their attack. This allowed the Americans to withdraw, albeit rather disorderly, and escape disaster.

Although the battle was a clear British victory, American losses, which totaled approximately 140 men, could have been far worse.[32] In that sense, the battle of Green Spring was a missed opportunity for the British, one that General Cornwallis would soon regret.

Cornwallis moved his army to Portsmouth and stayed there through July. LaFayette remained on the northern bank of the James River and waited. In early August General Cornwallis moved his army (minus Benedict Arnold who sailed to New York) from Portsmouth to Yorktown. When they arrived, Cornwallis's men immediately began to fortify the town. General Clinton and the British naval command in New York

---

[30] Peter Decher, ed., *Journal of Lt. William Feltman of the First Pennsylvania Regiment, 1781-1782*, (Samen, NH: Ayer Co, 1969),
[31] Tarleton, 354
[32] Henry P. Johnson, *The Yorktown Campaign and the Surrender of Cornwallis:* 1781, (Eastern National, 1997), 190 (Originally printed in 1881)

desired a safe winter port, and Yorktown was to be the site. Fate, however, had other plans for this small coastal Virginian town. News of Cornwallis's move to Yorktown reached General Washington in New York on the heels of a report that a large French naval squadron planned to sail to Chesapeake Bay and remain there until October. Washington had long desired to attack New York but coordinating the assault with the French proved difficult. Developments in Virginia now presented the Americans and French with an ideal opportunity to work together. If the French navy could seize control of Chesapeake Bay and sever Cornwallis' supply line to New York, and if the allies could assemble enough troops at Yorktown to prevent Cornwallis' escape by land, they might capture Cornwallis' entire army. General Washington acted quickly and ordered part of the American army southward on August 24th.[33]

Continental regiments from Rhode Island, New York, New Jersey, and Maryland trekked south. They were joined by a large detachment of light infantry under Colonel Alexander Scammell of New Hampshire. Scammell's light corps was formed in May to replace LaFayette's corps and included five companies of Massachusetts men. These soldiers, along with the Massachusetts light troops with LaFayette and those attached to specialized units like the miners and sappers and the artillery, represented Massachusetts's (and Maine's) presence at Yorktown. The majority of Massachusetts continentals remained in the New York Highlands with fellow

---

[33] Fitzpatrick, "General Washington to General Benjamin Lincoln, 24 August, 1781," *The Writings of George Washington, Vol. 23*, 41-43

Connecticut and New Hampshire troops to defend against a possible British push north from New York City.

The American and French troops which had been ordered south, marched rapidly through New Jersey, Pennsylvania, and Maryland in late August. When they reached the head of Chesapeake Bay, the soldiers boarded ships and completed the journey by water. They disembarked in the James River, west of Williamsburg, in mid-September and joined General LaFayette's troops in the old capital.

General Washington and General Jean Bapiste Rochambeau, commander of the French land forces, traveled overland with the cavalry. They stopped at Mount Vernon for three days and arrived in Williamsburg on September 14th.

Fortune had shined on General Washington's plan up to this point. General Henry Clinton, the commander of British forces in America, misinterpreted Washington's troop movements in late August as preparations for an attack on New York and was shocked to discover that General Cornwallis was Washington's real target. General Clinton was even more shocked to learn about the defeat of a British naval squadron off the Virginia coast in early September. With the Chesapeake Bay blockaded by the French, water transport of British supplies and men to and from Yorktown was no longer possible. Despite this dangerous new development, General Cornwallis chose to remain in Yorktown with his 7,500 men and hold the town until a new British naval force arrived to break the French blockade.[34]

The last of the French and American troops from the north landed near Williamsburg in late September, swelling the

---

[34] Rankin, 66

allied army to nearly 16,000 men.[35] On the morning of September 28th they marched to the outskirts of Yorktown and spent the night under arms. The last great battle of the Revolutionary War was about to begin.

The Siege of Yorktown

American and French troops moved closer to Yorktown on September 29th. They formed a rough semi-circle around the British fortifications and blocked all land access to and from the town. General Cornwallis appeared unconcerned by the allied presence. He was confident that his men, behind their strong earthworks, could defend Yorktown until the British navy ended the French blockade and relieved him. As a precaution, Cornwallis fortified Gloucester Point, which was directly across the York River from Yorktown, with one thousand men. This force protected Cornwallis's rear from bombardment and maintained a possible escape route to the north if necessary.[36]

To prevent the French fleet from sailing up the York River to shell Yorktown, Cornwallis scuttled a number of boats and prepared a few fire ships. Three of these fire ships were unsuccessfully sent amongst a portion of the French fleet a week before Washington and Rochembeau arrived at Yorktown, and the possibility of a second attack kept Admiral De Grasse and his fleet at a safe distance.[37] General Cornwallis also built a few outworks half a mile in front of his main fortifications to hamper the approach of the enemy. These redoubts were the allies' first target.

---

[35] Ibid.
[36] Boatner III, 1242
[37] Ewald, 328

General Washington and his officers spent September 29th reconnoitering the British outworks. The allies awoke the next morning to a pleasant surprise. The British had abandoned their outworks during the night and withdrew to Yorktown because General Cornwallis received word that a relief force from New York would arrive soon.[38] Cornwallis decided to spare his troops in the vulnerable outworks from unnecessary sacrifice and concentrate his troops behind his main fortifications at Yorktown and Gloucester Point. The allies promptly occupied the abandoned outworks and converted them into their own fortifications.

The allied gains were marred by the loss of Colonel Alexander Scammell who was surprised by enemy dragoons while reconnoitering their lines. The battle tested veteran of numerous engagements was captured and mortally wounded in the incident.

The next few days were relatively uneventful as both armies concentrated on preparations for the siege. The hundreds of Massachusetts light troops at Yorktown joined thousands of fellow soldiers in picket and fatigue duty and constructed gabions and fascines for the first parallel.[39] General Washington, aware of the importance of resting his men, was careful to rotate their duties so no single unit was overworked or overextended. While some units rested, some worked on the earthworks and implements of the siege, and others protected the work parties from a sudden enemy attack.

---

[38] Tarleton, 373
[39] Fitzpatrick, "General Orders, 30 September, 1781," 155

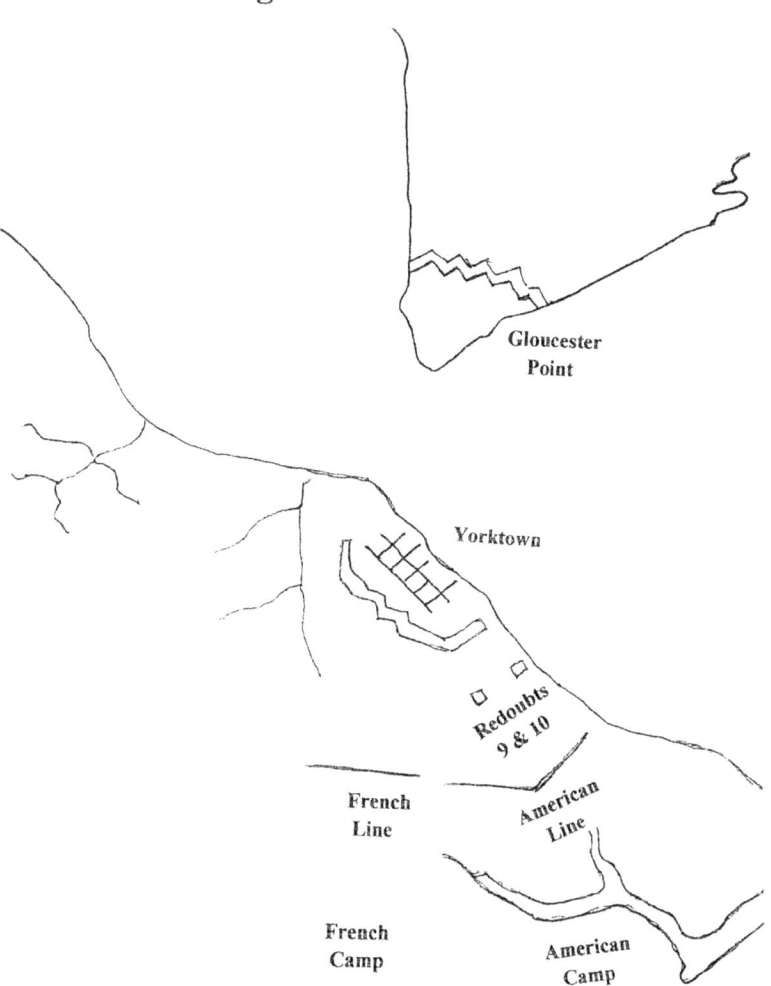

Across the York River in Gloucester County a combined force of Virginia militia and French dragoons and marines clashed with a large British foraging party under Lieutenant Colonel Banastre Tarleton. The Battle of Gloucester Point began when a party of mounted Virginia militia stumbled upon the rear guard of Tarleton's foraging party a few miles north of Gloucester Point.[40] The British easily dispersed the militia horsemen but were soon confronted by French hussars (cavalry). A confused melee ensued as dragoons from both sides attempted to sweep the field of the enemy. Just as the British appeared to be getting the upper hand, 160 Virginia militia under Lieutenant Colonel James Mercer arrived. Mercer recalled that his men *"were at first somewhat startled to find the French horse retreating so rapidly..."*[41] The Virginians recovered their nerve and deployed to meet the oncoming British. Mercer proudly recalled,

> [My men formed] *with great celerity & good order, & commenced firing, one half on the cavalry on the right, & the other half on the infantry advancing rapidly thro' the wood. The horse of the enemy had approach'd within 250 yards & the infantry were not at more than 150 yards distance when the firing began. No regular troops cou'd behave with more zeal & alacrity than this corps of Militia; their spirits had been rais'd by running them up, and being hurried into action without time to reflect on their danger, they discovered as much gallantry & order as any regular corps that I ever saw in action. Fortunately Tarleton did not like the reception prepared for him & at a critical moment sounded a*

---

[40] Tarleton, 376
[41] Hunt, "Colonel John Francis Mercer," 58

retreat, when not 100 cartridges remain'd unexpended in the regiment....[42]

Tarleton disengaged from the battle once he determined that the British foragers had safely withdrawn towards Gloucester Point.

Across the river, Washington applauded the outcome of the skirmish and prepared to open the first parallel (siege trench). He informed Edward Rutledge of South Carolina,

We have been hitherto employed in constructing some necessary advanced Works, in preparing fascines, Gabions etc. and bringing our heavy Artillery and Stores from the landing place on James River. This last has been carried on slowly till within a few days past, when our Waggons arrived from the Northward. The Engineers now think we have a sufficient stock to commence serious operations, and we open Trenches this Evening.[43]

Opening the Trenches

On October 6th, General Washington's army crept forward under cover of night and began to dig the first parallel about six to eight hundred yards from the British works. Colonel Richard Butler of Pennsylvania described the process:

---

[42] Ibid., 59
[43] Fitzpatrick, "General Washington to Edward Rutledge, 6 October, 1781," 186

> *The first parallel and other works being laid out by the engineer; a body of troops [were] ordered...to break ground and form works, the materials being got ready and brought previously to the spot. The enemy kept up a severe cannonade all night.*[44]

Sergeant Joseph Plum Martin, of Connecticut, recalled that General Washington ceremoniously started the trench with a pick ax:

> *The troops of the line were there ready with entrenching tools and began to entrench, after General Washington had struck a few blows with a pickax, a mere ceremony....The ground was sandy and soft, and the men employed that night* [were not idle], *so that by daylight they had covered themselves from danger from the enemy's shot ....*[45]

Surgeon James Thacher observed the opening of the parallel:

> *This business was conducted with great silence and secrecy, and we were favored by Providence with a night of extreme darkness, and were not discovered before day-light. The working party carried on their shoulders fascines and intrenching tools, while a large part of the detachment was armed with the implements of death. Horses, drawing cannon and ordinance, and wagons loaded with bags filled with*

---

[44] Commager and Morris, "Journal of Colonel Richard Butler, 6 October, 1781," 1229
[45] Joseph Plum Martin, *Private Yankee Doodle*, (Eastern Acorn Press, 1962), 232
(Originally published in 1830)

sand for constructing breastworks, flowed in the rear.[46]

At sunrise, the British discovered the new allied works and unleashed an intense bombardment, but to little effect. Over the course of the day, American and French work parties labored to improve the trench under a steady, but ineffectual, British bombardment.

By October 9th, the allies completed construction of their first artillery batteries and responded to the British bombardment with one of their own. The French were first to fire, directing their artillery on an isolated redoubt on the right flank of the British works and on British ships in the river.[47] General Washington reportedly began the American bombardment two hours later.[48] The barrage smashed through buildings and fortifications and killed a few British officers and men.[49] Over the next two days, additional allied batteries joined the bombardment, and soon over fifty artillery pieces hurled their ordinance into Yorktown.[50] Captain Johann Ewald described the impact on the town:

> *Since yesterday the besiegers have fired bombshells incessantly…. The greater part of the town lies in ashes, and two [of our] batteries have already been completely dismantled.*[51]

---

[46] James Thacher, *Military Journal of the American Revolution*, Gansevoort, NY: Corner House Historical Publications, 1998, 281-282 (Originally published in 1862)
[47] Nell Moore Lee, *Patriot Above Profit: A Portrait of Thomas Nelson Jr. Who Supported the American Revolution With His Purse and Sword*, (Nashville, TN: Rutledge Hill Press, 1988), 470
[48] Thacher, 283
[49] Ewald, 334 and Nell Moore Lee, 471
[50] Selby, 306
[51] Ewald, 334

Stephan Popp, another German soldier, noted,

> *The heavy fire forced us to throw our tents in the ditches.... We could find no refuge in or out of town. The people fled to the waterside and hid in hastily contrived shelters on the banks, but many of them were killed by bursting bombs.*[52]

General Washington also noted the effect of the allied bombardment. He informed the Governor of Maryland,

> *Our Shells have done considerable damage to the Town, and our fire from the Cannon have been so heavy and well directed against the embrasures* [openings in the British works which their cannon fire through] *that they have been obliged, during the day, to withdraw their Cannon and place them behind their* [earthworks].[53]

On the evening of October 11th, the allies advanced to within 300 yards of Yorktown and constructed a second parallel. Lieutenant William Feltman of Pennsylvania recorded:

> *Just at dusk we advanced within gun-shot of the enemy, then began our work. In one hour's time we had ourselves completely covered, so we disregarded their cannonading; they discharged a number of pieces at our party, but they had but little effect and only wounded one of our men.*[54]

---

[52] Nell Moore Lee, 471
[53] Fitzpatrick, "General Washington to Governor Thomas Sim Lee, 12 October, 1781," 210
[54] Feltman, 19

Feltman and his fellow soldiers were actually more endangered from errant allied cannon fire than fire from the British lines:

> We were in the center of two fires, from the enemy and our own, but the latter was very dangerous; we had two men killed and one badly wounded from the French batteries, also a number of shells burst in the air above our heads, which was very dangerous to us. We dug the ditch three and a half feet deep and seven feet in width.[55]

The allies' second parallel allowed the French and Americans to pound the British fortifications with greater accuracy. Dr. James Thacher recalled,

> From the 10th to the 15th, a tremendous and incessant firing from the American and French batteries is kept up, and the enemy return the fire, but with little effect.... We have now made further approaches to the town, by throwing up a second parallel line, and batteries within about three hundred yards; this was effected in the night, and at day-light the enemy roused to the greatest exertions; the engines of war have raged with redoubled fury and destruction on both sides, no cessation day or night...The siege is daily becoming more and more formidable and alarming, and his lordship must view his situation as extremely critical, if not desperate.[56]

Dr. Thacher was fascinated by the aerial display of the siege:

---

[55] Ibid.
[56] Thacher, 283-284

> *Being in the trenches every other night and day, I have a fine opportunity of witnessing the sublime and stupendous scene which is continually exhibiting. The bomb-shells from the besiegers and the besieged are incessantly crossing each other's path in the air. They are clearly visible in the form of a black ball in the day, but in the night, they appear like a fiery meteor with a blazing tail, most beautifully brilliant, ascending majestically from the mortar to a certain altitude, and gradually descending to the spot where they are destined to execute their work of destruction.... When a shell falls, it whirls round, burrows and excavates the earth to a considerable extent, and bursting, makes dreadful havoc around. I have more than once witnessed fragments of the mangled bodies and limbs of the British soldiers thrown into the air by the bursting of our shells....*[57]

Although the British suffered extensive damage in the exchange, they were able to inflict some loss on the allies. On October 13th, a French observer noted,

> *The day was spent in cannonading and firing bombs at each other in such profusion that we did one another much damage. The enemy seemed to have been saving up their ammunition for the second parallel. It was of very small caliber and very effective, being fired at short range. That night we had six men killed and twenty-eight wounded.*[58]

---

[57] Ibid., 284
[58] Howard Rice and Anne Brown, "Clermont, Crevecoeur Journal," *The American Campaigns of Rochambeu's Army, Vol. 1*, (Princeton, NJ: Princeton University Press, 1972), 59

Storming Redoubts 9 and 10

Work on the American section of the second parallel was delayed by the presence of two British redoubts in advance of Cornwallis's main line. These fortifications, situated about 300 yards in advance of the main British works, protected Cornwallis's left flank. The Americans had to capture these redoubts in order to complete the second parallel. On the night of October 14th, two 400 man detachments, one American and the other French, moved against these redoubts. The American force was made up of light infantry troops under Colonel Alexander Hamilton and was assigned the redoubt closest to the river, which was defended by approximately 70 British soldiers.[59] The French, under Colonel de Deux-Ponts, assaulted the other redoubt, which sat about 150 yards to the left of the river redoubt. This post was defended by over 120 German soldiers.[60] Both redoubts were protected by earthen walls, a ditch, and extensive abatis, all of which the allies had to overcome before they reached the enemy.

The American and French detachments approached the redoubts around 8:00 p.m. with unloaded muskets to prevent an accidental discharge. Their bayonets would decide the struggle. One French attacker recalled,

---

[59] Nell Moore Lee, 476
[60] Ibid.

> *The enemy discovered the column early and opened a very lively musket fire upon it. We found their abatis in far better condition than we had anticipated, since much of our artillery had been battering the redoubt for several days. Ignoring the enemy fire and slashing those that resisted with their axes, our pioneers had opened passages for us....*[61]

The French swarmed upon the fort's defenders and engaged in brutal hand to hand combat. One hundred and fifty yards away, a similar scene unfolded for the Americans. Joseph Plum Martin recalled,

> *We...moved silently on toward the redoubt we were to attack, with unloaded muskets. Just as we arrived at the abatis, the enemy discovered us and directly opened a sharp fire upon us.... Our people began to cry, "The fort's our own!" and "Rush on boys!" The Sappers and Miners soon cleared a passage for the infantry, who entered it rapidly.... While passing, [through the abatis] a man at my side received a ball in his head and fell under my feet, crying out bitterly. While crossing the trench, the enemy threw hand grenades into it. As I mounted the breastwork, I met an old associate hitching himself down into the trench. I knew him by the light of the enemy's musketry, it was so vivid.*[62]

---

[61] Howard Rice and Anne Brown, "Verger Journal" *The American Campaigns of Rochambeu's Army, Vol. 1*, 142
[62] Martin, 235-236

The small British garrison was soon overwhelmed by the Americans and the redoubt fell in ten minutes.[63] The French had a more difficult time but were also victorious. American work parties followed the assault and quickly incorporated the redoubts into the second parallel.

General Cornwallis responded to the loss of the redoubts with a furious bombardment of the allied lines. Lieutenant William Feltman of Pennsylvania noted that *"the enemy threw a number of shells this day and wounded a great number of men, especially militia."*[64] Feltman had little sympathy for the wounded militia:

> *Several were wounded this day in their sleep, such is the carelessness of those stupid wretches who are not acquainted with the life of a soldier.*[65]

In addition to the intensified bombardment of the allied lines, General Cornwallis also sent his first sortie against the allies. In the early morning hours of October 16th, Lieutenant Colonel Robert Abercrombie led 350 soldiers into the French and American trenches.[66] They overwhelmed two artillery batteries and spiked a number of cannon before withdrawing in the face of a French counterattack. The assault, although brave, was largely ineffectual as most of the cannon were repaired and put back in service by that afternoon. The allies concentrated over a hundred artillery pieces on the British lines and pounded Yorktown from point blank range. Dr. James Thacher noted,

---

[63] Nell Moore Lee, 477
[64] Feltman, 20
[65] Ibid.
[66] Tarleton, 386

> *Not less than one hundred pieces of heavy ordinance have been in continual operation during the last twenty-four hours. The whole peninsula trembles under the incessant thunderings of our infernal machines; we have leveled some of their works in ruins and silenced their guns; they have almost ceased firing.*[67]

With his ordinance and provisions nearly exhausted, and his force reduced by death, injury, and illness, General Cornwallis made one last attempt to forestall disaster. During the evening of October 16th, he ferried part of his army across the river to Gloucester Point. He hoped to gather all those who could march and try to break through the allied line at Gloucester. His plan was foiled when a violent storm scattered many of his boats. It was now impossible to complete the movement before daylight, so Cornwallis cancelled the attempt and recalled the troops to Yorktown.

Captain Johann Ewald grimly assessed the British situation on October 17th:

> *All the batteries were dismantled, the works destroyed, munitions and provisions wanting, the wounded and sick lying helpless without medicine, and the army melted away from 7,000 to 3,200, among whom not a thousand men could be called healthy....*[68]

---

[67] Thacher, 286
[68] Ewald, 336

The time had arrived for General Cornwallis to do the unthinkable.

At 10:00 a.m. on October 17, 1781, General Cornwallis ordered a British drummer to beat a parley upon the parapet of the British earthworks. Beside the drummer stood a British officer with a white handkerchief. The American gunners opposite the scene could not hear the drummer over the noise of the shelling, but they recognized the meaning of a white flag and ceased their bombardment. A flurry of messages passed between the lines, followed by two days of negotiations that resulted in the capitulation of General Cornwallis and his army at Yorktown.

The official surrender ceremony occurred on October 19th. The British received the same surrender terms as the Americans at Charleston, which meant that most of the troops were held as prisoners of war until they were exchanged for American prisoners. The British and German prisoners were marched to Winchester under militia escort. General Cornwallis and a few of his fellow officers avoided this humiliation. They were granted their parole and allowed to return to New York unescorted.

Just days after the victory at Yorktown, General Washington returned north with most of the American continental troops to rejoin the rest of the American army outside of New York. Most of the French army remained in Williamsburg for the winter, much to the pleasure of local Virginians who enjoyed their commerce and company.

Although Washington's victory at Yorktown broke Britain's will to continue the war, peace negotiations stretched into 1782 and then 1783. While the negotiators haggled over the terms of a peace settlement, the occupation of eastern

Maine continued. Throughout the continent, British, German, French, and American troops waited for the diplomats to finalize a decision that had already been settled at Yorktown in 1781.

Treaty of Paris: 1783

Benjamin Franklin opened peace talks with the British in April 1782, weeks after the British Parliament reached the painful decision to end the war. A preliminary agreement was signed in late November 1782, and, a month later, the British evacuated Charleston, South Carolina, their last post in the South. In early 1783, the French reached a peace agreement with Britain. This paved the way for America and Britain to finalize their own peace accord on September 3, 1783. Three months later, British troops departed New York and a month after that, on January 15th, 1784, the last British troops on the east coast of the United States – the garrison at Bagaduce (Castine) in Penobscot Bay – sailed for Nova Scotia.

Twenty years after the American colonists first expressed their concerns about British policies, the long dispute with Britain was over. The Treaty of Paris recognized the former colonies of Great Britain as a sovereign nation whose border stretched to the Mississippi River. Few Americans envisioned or desired this prior to 1776, yet the determination to protect cherished political rights prompted thousands of Americans to endure enormous hardship in a noble struggle, a struggle in which thousands of Maine men played a crucial role.

Bibliography

Ahlin, John Howard. *Maine Rubicon: Downeast Settlers during the American Revolution*. Camden, ME: Picton Press, 1966.

Anburey, Thomas. *With Burgoyne from Quebec: An Account of the Life at Quebec and of the Famous Battle at Saratoga*. Toronto: Macmillan, 1963.

Ballagh, James C. ed., *Letters of Richard Henry Lee, Vol. 1*. New York : Macmillan Co., 1911.

Baxter, James, ed., *The British Invasion from the North: Digby's Journal of the Campaigned of Generals Carleton and Burgoyne from Canada, 1776-1777*. New York : De Capa Press, 1970.

Baxter, James Phinney, ed. *Documentary History of the State of Maine*. Portland: LaFavor-Tower Co. 1910.

Boatner III, Mark M. *Encyclopedia of the American Revolution*. 3rd ed., Stanpole Books, 1994.

Bodle, Wayne. *The Valley Forge Winter: Civilians and Soldiers in War*. PA: Pennsylvania State University Press, 2002.

Boyd, Julian. ed. *The Papers of Thomas Jefferson*, Vol. 3-6. Princeton, NJ: Princeton University Press, 1951.

Boyle, Joseph Lee. *Writings from the Valley Forge Encampment of the Continental Army.* Vol. 1-5 Bowie: Heritage Books Inc., 2000.

Brown, Lloyd A. & Howard H. Peckman ed. *Revolutionary War Journals of Henry Dearborn: 1775-1783.* Freeport, NY: Books for Libraries Press, 1939.

Buchanan, John. *The Road to Guilford Courthouse: The American Revolution in the Carolinas.* NY: John Wiley & Sons, Inc., 1997.

Buker, George E. *The Penobscot Expedition: Commodore Saltonstall and the Massachusetts Conspiracy of 1779.* Annapolis, MD: Naval Institute Press, 2002.

Burgoyne, John. *A State of the Expedition from Canada.* New York Times & Arno Press, 1969.

Campbell, Maria Hull, *Revolutionary Services and Civil Life of General William Hull, Prepared from his manuscript,* NY, 1848.

Carrington, Henry B. *Battles of the American Revolution.* New York: A. S. Barnes & Co., 1877.

Cecere, Michael. *An Officer of Very Extraordinary Merit: Charles Porterfield and the American War for Independence, 1775-1780.* Westminster, MD: Heritage Books, 2004.

Cecere, Michael. *Captain Thomas Posey and the 7th Virginia Regiment*. Westminster, MD: Heritage Books, 2005.

Cecere, Michael. *Great Things Are Expected From the Virginians: Virginia in the American Revolution*. Westminster, MD: Heritage Books, 2008.

Cecere, Michael. *They Are Indeed a Very Useful Corps: American Riflemen in the Revolutionary War*. Westminster, MD: Heritage Books, 2006.

Cecere, Michael. *They Behaved Like Soldiers: Captain John Chilton and the Third Virginia Regiment*. Westminster, MD: Heritage Books, 2004.

Chase, Philander D., et al., eds. *The Papers of George Washington: Revolutionary War Series*. Vols. 1-16. Charlottesville: University Press of Virginia, 1985-2008.

Clark, William., et al., eds. *Naval Documents of the American Revolution*, Vol. 1-9. Washington: 1970.

Commager, Henry Steele. *Documents of American History*, New York: Appleton-Century-Crofts, 1963.

Commager, Henry and Richard Morris, ed. *The Spirit of 'Seventy-Six: The Story of the American Revolution as Told by Participants*. NY: Castle Books, 1967.

Cook, Frederick ed. *Journals of the Military Expedition of Major General John Sullivan Against the Six Nations of Indians in 1779*. Freeport, NY: Books for Library Press, 1887.

Cresswell, Nicholas. *The Journal of Nicholas Cresswell; 1774-1777.* New York: The Dial Press, 1924.

Cushing, Harry A. ed.. *The Writings of Samuel Adams, Vol. 1.* NY:G.P. Putnam's Sons, 1904.

Dandridge, Danske."Henry Bedinger to --- Findley," *Historic Shepherdstown.* Charlottesville, VA: Michie Co., 1910.

Dann, John C. *The Revolution Remembered: Eyewitness Accounts of the War Independence.* Chicago: University of Chicago Press, 1980.

Davies, K.G. ed. *Documents of the American Revolution: 1770-1783,* Vol. 9. Irish University Press, 1975.

Davis, Robert. *The Revolutionary War: The Battle of Petersburg.* E. & R. Davis, 2002.

De Chastellux, Marquis. *Travels in North America in the Years 1780, 1781, and 1782,* Volume 2. The New York Times and Arno Press, 1968.

Decher, Peter. ed., *Journal of Lt. William Feltman of the First Pennsylvania Regiment, 1781-1782.* Samen, NH: Ayer Co, 1969.

Desjardin, Thomas A. *Through A Howling Wilderness: Benedict Arnold's March to Quebec, 1775.* New York: St. Martin's Press, 2006.

Dorman, John Frederick. *Virginia Revolutionary Pension Applications,* Volumes 1-52. Washington D.C., 1958-1995.

Dwyer, William M. *This Day is Ours! An Inside View of the Battles of Trenton and Princeton: November 1776-January 1777.* New Brunswick, NJ: Rutgers University Press, 1983.

Ewald, Captain Johann. *Diary of the American War: A Hessian Journal.* New Haven: Yale Univ. Press, 1979. Translated & edited by Joseph Tustin.

Fischer, David Hackett. *Paul Revere's Ride.* New York: Oxford University Press, 1994.

Fischer, David Hackett. *Washington's Crossing.* Oxford University Press, 2004.

Fitzpatrick, John C. *The Writings of George Washington from the Original Manuscripts, 1745-1799.* Washington: U.S. Govt. Printing Office, 1931.

Fletcher, Ebenezer. *Narrative of the Captivity & Sufferings of Ebenezer Fletcher of New Ipswich.* New Ipswich, NH: S. Wilder, 1827.

Force, Peter. ed., *American Archives:* 5th Series. Washington D.C.: U.S. Congress, 1848-1853.

Graham, James. *The Life of General Daniel Morgan.*
Bloomingburg, NY: Zebrowski Historical Services,
1993. Press of Virginia, 1965.

Greenwood, John. *The Wartime Services of John Greenwood:
A Young Patriot in the American Revolution, 1775-
1783.* Westvaco, 1981.

Hall, Henry. *Battle of Hubbardton.* (1877) Vermont Historical
Society, John Williams Papers, MS 149.

Hamilton, Stanislaus M. ed. *Letters to Washington &
Accompanying Papers,* Vol. 5. Boston & New York:
Houghton, Mifflin, Co., 1902.

Hatch, Robert M. *Thrust for Canada: The American Attempt
on Quebec in 1775-76.* Boston: Houghton Mifflin Co.,
1979.

Heath, William. *Memoirs of Major General William Heath.*
NY: William Abbatt, 1901.

Heckert, C.W. *A German-American Diary: Notes of Related
Historical Interest, Including Translated Excerpts
from the Wiederholdt Diary.* Parsons, WV : McClain
Printing Co., 1980.

Hume, Ivor Noel. *1775: Another Part of the Field.*
New York: Alfred A. Knopf, 1966.

Hunt, Gillard ed., *Eyewitness Accounts of the American
Revolution: Fragments of Revolutionary History.* NY
Times & Arno Press, Reprint, 1971.

Hunt, Gaillard. ed., *The Writings of James Madison, Vol. 1.* NY: G.P. Putnam's Sons, 1900.

Idzerda, Stanley J. ed. *LaFayette in the Age of the American Revolution,* Vol. 4. Cornell University Press, 1983.

Jackman, Sydney ed. *With Burgoyne from Quebec: An Account of the Life at Quebec and of the Famous Battle at Saratoga.* Toronto: Macmillan of Canada, 1963.

Jackson, John W. *Valley Forge: Pinnacle of Courage.* Gettysburg, PA: Thomas Publications, 1992.

Johnson, Henry P. *The Campaign of 1776 Around New York and Brooklyn.* New York: Da Capa Press, 1971.

Johnson, Henry P. *The Storming of Stony Point on the Hudson, Midnight, July 15, 1779: Its Importance in the Light of Unpublished Documents.* New York: James T. White, 1900.

Johnson, Henry P. *The Yorktown Campaign and the Surrender of Cornwallis: 1781.* Eastern National, 1997. Originally printed in 1881.

Kapp, Friedrich. *The Life of Frederick William von Steuben.* NY: Corner House Historical Publications, 1999. (Originally published in 1859)

Ketchum, Richard. *Decisive Day: The Battle for Bunker Hill.* New York: Henry Holt and Co., 1962.

Ketchum, Richard M. *Saratoga,: Turning Point of America's Revolutionary War*. NY: Holt & Co., 1997.

Ketchum, Richard M. *The Winter Soldiers.: The Battles For Trenton and Princeton*. New York: Henry Holt Co., 1973.

Kevitt, C.B. "Gen. Lovell, July 28, 1779," *General Solomon Lovell and the Penobscot Expedition: 1779*. Weymouth, MA: 1976.

LaCrosse Jr., Richard B. *Revolutionary Rangers: Daniel Morgan's Riflemen and Their Role on the Northern Frontier*. Bowie, MD: Heritage Books, 2002.

Lamb, Roger. *An Original and Authentic Journal of Occurrences During the Late American War from Its Commencement to 1783*. Dublin: Wilkinson & Courtney, 1809.

Leamon, James S. *Revolution Downeast: The War for American Independence in Maine*. Amherst: University of Massachusetts Press, 1993.

Lee, Charles. *The Lee Papers,* Vol. 1. Collections of the New York Historical Society, 1871.

Lee, Henry. *The Revolutionary War Memoirs of General Henry Lee*. New York: Da Capo Press, 1998. Originally Published in 1812.

Lee, Nell Moore. *Patriot Above Profit: A Portrait of Thomas Nelson Jr., Who Supported the American Revolution With His Purse and Sword*. Nashville, TN: Rutledge Hill Press, 1988.

Lefkowitz, Arthur S. *Benedict Arnold's Army: The 1775 American Invasion of Canada During the Revolutionary War*. NY & CA: Savas Beatie, 2008.

Lesser, Charles H. ed. *The Sinews of Independence: Monthly Strength Reports of the Continental Army*. Chicago: The University of Chicago Press, 1976.

Loprieno, Don. *The Enterprise in Contemplation: The Midnight Assault of Stony Point*. Westminster, MD: Heritage Books, 2004.

Lowell, Edward J. *Letters and Memoirs Relating to the War of American Independence and the Capture of the German Troops at Saratoga*. Williamstown, MA: Corner House Publishers, 1975.

Lumpkin, Henry. *From Savannah to Yorktown: The American Revolution in the South*. New York: toExcel, 1987.

Lundeberg, Philip K. *The Gunboat Philadelphia And the Defense of Lake Champlain in 1776*. Lake Champlain Museum, 1995.

Luzader, John. *Decision on the Hudson: The Battles of Saratoga*. Eastern National, 2002.

Marshall, John. *The Life of George Washington, Vol. 2.* Fredericksburg, VA: The Citizens Guild of Washington's Boyhood Home, 1926.

Martin, Joseph Plum. *Private Yankee Doolittle: Being a Narrative of Some of the Adventures, Dangers and Sufferings of a Revolutionary Soldier.* Eastern Acorn Press, 1962. (First published in 1840)

Mays, David John, ed., *The Letters and Papers of Edmund Pendleton,* Vol. 1. Charlottesville: University Press of Virginia, 1967.

Mintz, Max M. *Seeds of Empire: The American Revolutionary Conquest of the Iroquois.* New York: New York University Press, 1999.

Moore, Frank. *Diary of the American Revolution, from Newspapers and Original Documents.* 2 vols. New York: Charles Schibner, 1860. Reprint. New York: New York Times & Arno Press, 1969.

Morgan, Edmund S. *Prologue to Revolution: Sources and Documents on the Stamp Act Crisis, 1764-1766.* Chapel Hill, NC: University of North Carolina Press, 1959.

Morgan, Edmund and Helen, *The Stamp Act Crisis: Prologue to Revolution.* Chapel Hill, NC: Univ. of NC Press, 1953.

Morrissey, Brendan. *Saratoga 1777: Turning Point of the Revolution.* Osprey Publishing, 2000.

Morrissey, Brendan. *Quebec 1775: The American invasion of Canada.* Osprey Publishing Ltd., 2003.

Nelson, James. *Benedict Arnold's Navy.* McGraw Hill, 2006.

Otis, James. *The Rights of the British Colonies Asserted and Proved,* 1763.

Palmer, William. *Calendar of Virginia State Papers,* Vol. 1- 2. Richmond: James E. Goode, 1881.

Pausch, George. *Journal of Captain Pausch, Chief of the Hanau Artillery During the Burgoyne Campaign.* Translated by William L. Stone. Albany, NY: Joel Munsell's Sons, 1886.

Posey, John Thornton. *General Thomas Posey: Son of the American Revolution.* East Lansing: Michigan State Univ. Press, 1992.

Rankin, Hugh F. *The War of the Revolution in Virginia.* Williamsburg, VA: Virginia Independence Bicentennial Commission, 1979.

Read, Parker McCobb. *History of Bath and Environs, Sagadahoc County, Maine 1677-1894.* Portland, ME: Lakeside Press, 1894.

Reed, John F. *Campaign to Valley Forge: July 1, 1777 – December 19, 1777.* Pioneer Press, 1980.

Rice, Howard C. and Anne S. K. Brown, translated and edited. *The American Campaigns of Rochambeau's Army:* 1780-1783 Vol. 1-2. Princeton, NJ : Princeton University Press, 1972.

Riedesel, Madam. *Letters and Memoirs Relating to the War of American Independence and the Capture of the German Troops at Saratoga.* New York: G. & C. Carvill, 1827.

Roberts, John M. ed., *Autobiography of a Revolutionary Soldier.* New York : Arno Press, 1979

Roberts, Kenneth. *March to Quebec: Journals of the Members of Arnold's Expedition.* New York: Country Life Press, 1938.

Rodney, Caesar. *The Diary of Captain Thomas Rodney, 1776-1777.* Wilmington: The Historical Society of Delaware, 1888.

Rogers, Horatio ed. *Hadden's Journal and Orderly Book: A Journal Kept in Canada and Upon Burgoyne's Campaign in 1776 and 1777.* Boston: Gregg Press, 1972.

Rowland, Kate Mason. *The Life and Correspondence of George Mason,* Vol. 1. New York: Russell & Russell, 1964.

Rutland, Robert A. ed., *The Papers of George Mason, Vol. 1.* University of North Carolina Press, 1970.

Ryan, Dennis P. *A Salute to Courage: The American Revolution as Seen Through Wartime Writings of Officers of the Continental Army and Navy.* NY: Columbia University Press, 1979.

Saffell, W.T.R. *Records of the Revolutionary War*, 3rd ed. Baltimore: Charles Saffell, 1894.

Scheer, George F., and Hugh F. Rankin. *Rebels & Redcoats: The American Revolution through the Eyes of Those Who Fought and Lived It.* New York: Da Capo Press, 1987.

Selby, John. *The Revolution in Virginia: 1775-1783.* Williamsburg, VA: The Colonial Williamsburg Foundation, 1988.

Showman, Richard K. *The Papers of General Nathanael Greene*, Vol. 7-11. Chapel Hill: University of North Carolina Press, 1997-2000.

Shy, John. ed. *Winding Down: The Revolutionary War Letters of Lieutenant Colonel Benjamin Gilbert of Massachusetts, 1780-83.* University of Michigan, Press: William L. Clements Library, 1989.

Simcoe, Lt. Col. John. *Simcoe's Military Journal: A History of the Operations of a Partisan Corps Called the Queen's Rangers, Commanded by Lieut. Col. J. G. Simcoe, During the War of Revolution.* New York: New York Times and Arno Press, 1968.

Smith, Paul H. ed., *Letters of Delegates to Congress: 1774-1789*, Vol. 1-4. Washington, D.C.: Library of Congress, 1976.

Smith, Samuel. *The Battle of Princeton.* Monmouth Beach, NJ: Philip Freneau Press, 1967.

Sparks, Jared. ed. *The Correspondence of the American Revolution being Letters of Eminent Men to George Washington, Vol. 2.* Boston : Little, Brown & Co., 1853.

Stedman, C. *The History of the Origin, Progress, and Termination of the American War,* Volume 1 & 2. London, 1794.

Stille, Charles. *Major-General Anthony Wayne and the Pennsylvania Line in the Continental Army.* Port Washington, NY: Kenniket Press, Inc., 1968. First published in 1893.

Stryker, William. *The Battles of Trenton and Princeton.* Republished by The Old Barracks Association, Trenton NJ: 2001. (Originally published in 1898).

Stryker, William. *The Battle of Monmouth*. Princeton: Princeton University Press, 1927.

Symonds, Craig L. *A Battlefield ATLAS of the American Revolution*. The Nautical & Aviation Publishing Co. of America Inc., 1986.

Tarleton, Banastre. *A History of the Campaigns of 1780 and 1781 in the Southern Provinces of North America*. North Stratford, NH: Ayer Co., Reprinted, 1999 Originally printed in 1787.

Thacher, James. *A Military Journal during the American Revolutionary War*. Hartford: CT, S. Andrus and Son, 1854. Reprint, New York: Arno Press, 1969.

Townsend, Joseph. "Some Account of the British Army under the Command of General Howe, and of the Battle of Brandywine," *Eyewitness Accounts of the American Revolution*. New York: Arno Press, 1969.

Uhlendorf, Bernhard A. ed. & trans. *The Siege of Charleston: With an Account of the Province of South Carolina: Diaries and Letters of Hessian Officers*. Ann Arbor, MI: University of Michigan Press, 1938.

Van Schreeven, William and Robert L. Scribner., et al., eds. *Revolutionary Virginia: The Road to Independence,* Vol. 1-7. Charlottesville: University Press of Virginia, 1973-1983.

Waller, George M. *The American Revolution in the West*. Chicago: Nelson-Hall, 1976.

Ward, Christopher. *The War of the Revolution*, Vol.1- 2. New York: The Macmillan Co., 1952.

Ward, Harry M. *Duty, Honor, or Country : General George Weedon and the American Revolution.* Philadelphia : American Philosophical Society, 1979.

Wilkinson, James. *Memoirs of My Own Times, Vol. 1* Philadelphia: Abraham Small, 1816. Reprinted by AMS Press Inc., : NY, 1973.

Willard, Margaret. ed., *Letters of the American Revolution: 1774-1776*. Boston & New York: Houghton Mifflin Co., 1925.

Williams, Glenn F. *Year of the Hangman: George Washington's Campaign Against the Iroquis.* Westholme, 2005.

Williams, John. *The Battle of Hubbardton: The American Rebels Stem the Tide*. Vermont Division of Historic Preservation, 1988.

Willis, Williams, *Journals of the Reverend Thomas Smith and the Reverend Samuel Deane*. Portland: Joseph S. Bailey, 1849.

Wirt, William. *The Life of Patrick Henry*. New York: M'Elrath & Bangs, 1832.

Wright, Robert K. *The Continental Army.* Washington, D.C. Center of Military History: United States Army, 1989.

Wroth, L. Kinvin ed. *Province in Rebellion: A Documentary History of the Founding of the Commonwealth of Massachusetts, 1774-75.* Cambridge, MA: Harvard University Press, 1975.

Zobel, Hiller B. *The Boston Massacre.* New York: W.W. Norton, 1970.

---------- *Journals of the Continental Congress.* Library of Congress Online at www.loc.gov.

---------- *Massachusetts Provincial Laws*, 2nd Session – 1774, Livermore & Knight Co., 1931.

---------- *Massachusetts Soldiers and Sailors in the War of the Revolution*, 17 vols. Secretary of the Commonwealth of Massachusetts, 1896-1908.

---------- *Public Papers of George Clinton, First Governor of New York.* Albany, State Printer, 1900.

Periodicals

Boyle, Joseph Lee. "From Saratoga to Valley Forge: The Diary of Lt. Samuel Armstrong," *The Pennsylvania Magazine of History and Biography*, Vol. 121, No. 3 July 1997.

Dawson, Henry B. "General Daniel Morgan: An Autobiography," *The Historical Magazine and Notes and Queries Concerning the Antiquities, History and Biography of America.* 2nd Series, Vol. 9. Morrisania, NY, 1871.

Dearborn, Henry. "A Narrative of the Saratoga Campaign Major General Henry Dearborn, 1815," *The Bulletin of the Fort Ticonderoga Museum*, Vol. 1 no. 5. January, 1929.

Elmer, Ebenezer. "The Journal of Ebenezer Elmer," *The Pennsylvania Magazine of History and Biography*. Vol. 35. Philadelphia: Historical Society of Pennsylvania, 1911.

Flickinger, B. Floyd. "Captain Morgan and His Riflemen," *Winchester-Frederick County Historical Society Journal*, Vol. 14, 2002.

Fraser, Simon. Gen. Fraser's Account of Burgoyne's Campaign on Lake Champlain and the Battle of Hubbardton, "Letter to John Robinson, 13 July, 1777," *Proceedings of the Vermont Historical Society*, 1898.

Gates, Horatio. "Horatio Gates, Major General, Commanding Southern Army. Letters and Orders from June 21 to August 31, 1780," *Magazine of American History*, Vol. 5, No. 4, October, 1880.

Goold, Nathan. "Capt. Johnson Moulton's Company: The First to Leave the District of Maine in the Revolution," *Collections and Proceedings of the Maine Historical Society*, 2nd ser. 10, 1899.

Goold, Nathan. "Col. Edmund Phinney's 18th Continental Regiment: One Year's Service Commencing January 1, 1776," *Collections and Proceedings of the Maine Historical Society*, 2nd Ser. 9, 1898.

Goold, Nathan. "Col. James Scamman's 30th Regiment of Foot, 1775," *Collections and Proceedings of the Maine Historical Society*, 2nd ser. 10, 1899.

Goold, Nathan. "Colonel Jonathan Mitchell's Cumberland County Regiment, Bagaduce Expedition, 1779," *Collections of the Maine Historical Society*, ser. 2, 10, 1899.

Goold, Nathan. "History of Col. Edmund Phinney's 31st Regiment of Foot: The First Regiment Raised in the County of Cumberland in the Revolutionary War," *Collections and Proceedings of the Maine Historical Society*, 2nd Ser. 7, 1895.

Goold, Nathan. "Peleg Wadsworth to William D. Williamson, January 1, 1828" Colonel Jonathan Mitchell's Cumberland County Regiment: Bagaduce Expedition," 1779, *Collections of the Maine Historical Society*, Vol. 10, 1899.

Heth, William. "Orderly Book of Major William Heth of the Third (sic) Virginia regiment, May 15 – July 1, 1777," *Virginia Historical Society Collections*, New Series, 11, 1892.

Katcher, Philip. "They Behaved Like Soldiers: The Third Virginia Regiment at Harlem Heights," *Virginia Cavalcade*, Vol. 26, No. 2, Autumn 1976.

McKendry, William. "Journal of William McKendry," *Collections of the Massachusetts Historical Society*, May 1880.

McMichael, James. "The Diary of Lt. James McMichael of the Pennsylvania Line, 1776-1778," *The Pennsylvania Magazine of History and Biography*. Vol. 16, no. 2, 1892.

Montresor, John. "Journal of Captain John Montresor," *The Pennsylvania Magazine of History and Biography*. Vol. 5. Philadelphia: The Historical Society of Pennsylvania, 1881.

Pell, Jr., Joshua. "Diary of Joshua Pell Jr., An Officer of the British Army in America: 1776-1777," *Bulletin of the Fort Ticonderoga Museum*, Vol. 1, No. 6, July 1929

Porterfield, Charles. "Diary of Colonel Charles Porterfield," *Magazine of American History*, Vol. 21. April 1889.

Rees, John. "The proportion of Women which ought to be allowed....: An Overview of Continental Army Female Camp Followers," *The Continental Soldier*, Vol. 8 no. 3, Spring 1995.

Rees, John. *"What is this you have been about to day?" : The New Jersey Brigade at the Battle of Monmouth*. 2003.

Schnitzer, Eric. "Battling for the Saratoga Landscape," *Cultural Landscape Report: Saratoga Battle, Saratoga National Park*, Vol. 1, Boston, MA: Olmsted Center for Landscape Preservation.

Selig, Robert. "The Revolution's Black Soldiers. They fought for both Sides in their Quest for Freedom," *The Journal of the Colonial Williamsburg Foundation* Vol. 19, No. 4, Summer 1997.

Sergeant R. "The Battle of Princeton," *The Pennsylvania Magazine of History and Biography,* Vol. 20, No. 1. 1896.

Seymour, William. "Journal of the Southern Expedition, 1780-1783," *The Pennsylvania Magazine of History And* Biography, Vol. 7. 1883.

Stirling, Major General William Alexander. "Lord Stirling, to William H. Drayton, 15 August, 1778," Letters of William Alexander, Lord Stirling," *Proceedings of the New Jersey Historical Society,* Vol. 60, no. 3. July 1942.

Stone, Enos "Capt. Enos Stone's Journal," *New England Historical and Genealogical Register*, Vol. 15, October, 1861, Vermont Historical Society, John Williams Papers, MS.

Sullivan, Thomas. "Before and After the Battle of Brandywine: Extracts from the Journal of Sergeant Thomas Sullivan of H.M. Forty-Ninth Regiment of Foot," *The Pennsylvania Magazine of History and Biography.* Vol. 31, Philadelphia: Historical Society of Pennsylvania, 1907.

Tyler, Lyon. "The Old Virginia Line in the Middle States During the American Revolution," *Tyler's Quarterly Historical and Genealogical Magazine:* Vol.12. Richmond, VA: Richmond Press Inc., 1931.

Waddell, J.A. " Diary of a Prisoner of War at Quebec, 1776," *Virginia Magazine of History and Biography, Vol. 9.* Richmond, VA: The Virginia Historical Society, July, 1901.

Wickman, Donald ed. "Breakfast on Chocolate: The Diary of Moses Greenleaf, 1777," *The Bulletin of the Fort Ticonderoga Museum.*

Williamson, Joseph. "Lieutenant Moore to his father, Sir John Moore at Castine During the Revolution," *Collections of the Maine Historical Society,* series 2, Vol. 2, 1891.

Yerxa, Donald A. "The Burning of Falmouth, 1775: A Case Study in British Imperial Pacification," *Maine Historical Society Quarterly,* Vol. 14,

------- "Diary of Colonel Charles Porterfield," *Magazine of American History,* Vol. 21, April 1889.

------- "General Peleg Wadsworth to William D. Williamson," *Collections of the Maine Historical Society,* Series 2, Vol. 2, 1891.

-------*Maine at Valley Forge: Proceedings at the Unveiling of the Maine Marker*, October 17, 1907, Augusta: Burleigh & Flynt, 1910

------- "Personal Recollections of Captain Enoch Anderson, an Officer of the Delaware Regiment in the Revolutionary War," *Papers of the Historical Society of Delaware, Vol. 16.* Wilmington: The Historical Society of Delaware, 1896.

Newspapers

"Extract of a letter from a Rev. Divine in London dated March 3, 1766," Purdie & Dixon, *Virginia Gazette*, 23 May, 1766

"Extract of a letter from a Gentleman in London to his friend in New York, February 27," Purdie & Dixon, *Virginia Gazette*, 23 May, 1766

Massachusetts Gazette & Boston News-Letter, 31 May, 1764

Unpublished Works and Primary Sources

Adams, John, Diary 11, entry for 18 December 1765 Adams Family Papers, Massachusetts Historical Society.

Boston Merchants Broadside, 31 October, 1767, Massachusetts Historical Society.

Butler, Lieutenant Colonel Richard to Col. James Wilson, 22 January, 1778 Gratz Collection, Case 4, Box 11, Historical Society of Pennsylvania.

Circular Letter from the Freeholders of Boston, 20 November, 1772, Massachusetts Historical Society.

Friar, Robert. *The Militia are Coming in from all Quarters: The Revolution in Virginia's Lower Counties.* .(unpublished)

Letter from Lt. J. Waller to a Friend, 21 June, 1775 Massachusetts Historical Society.

Letter from Peter Brown to his Mother, 25 June, 1775 Massachusetts Historical Society.

Letter from William Prescott to John Adams, 25 August, 1775 Massachusetts Historical Society.

Massachusetts Convention, 22 September, 1768, Massachusetts Historical Society.

Posey, Thomas. "*A Short Biography of the Life of Governor Thomas Posey,*" Thomas Posey Papers. Indiana Historical Society Library, Indianapolis, IN. (Unpublished)

Posey, Thomas, *Revolutionary War Journal*, Thomas Posey Papers, Indiana Historical Society Library, Indianapolis, IN.

Richardson, Mark Bradford. *The Virtues of Continental Soldiers With a History of Colonel Ichabod Alden's Regiment and the Seventh Massachusetts Regiment During the American Revolution*, 1993. (Unpublished)

Index

1st Continental Regiment, 148
1st Maryland Regiment, 126
2nd New Hampshire Regiment, 171, 174, 176, 177
3rd Virginia Regiment, 140, 151
4th Pennsylvania Regiment, 247, 249
9th British Regiment, 190
14th British Regiment, 17
20th British Regiment, 190
21st British Regiment, 190
24th British Regiment, 172, 175
29th British Regiment, 17
47th British Regiment, 189
62nd British Regiment, 190, 195, 197

Abercrombie, Lt. Col. Robert, 309
Adams, John, 10, 28-29, 58, 114, 118
Adams, Samuel, 39, 115, 117
Alden, Colonel Ichabod, 163, 250-251, 253
Allan, Colonel John, 252
Allen, Ethan, 102
Anburey, Lieutenant Thomas, 172, 198-200, 212-213,
Anderson, Captain Enoch, 142
Armstrong, Samuel, 190, 192
Arnold, Benedict,
   Colonel, 79, 81-82, 87, 91-94, 95, 98, 102,
   General, 107-108, 132-133, 135, 137-138, 181, 183, 188, 193, 205, 208-209, 282-283, 286, 294
Arundel, ME, 41
Bagaduce, (Castine, ME), 257, 259-260, 262, 265, 266-267, 282, 312
Bailey, Colonel John, 164
Bailey, Reverend Jacob, 64-69
Balcarress, Colonel Alexander, 202
Bangor, ME, 269
Barber, Lt. Col. Francis, 284
Bartlett, Josiah, 115
Bath, ME, 80
Baum, Lt. Col. Friedich, 184-185, 187
Beatty, Erkuries, 255-256
Bedel, Colonel Timothy, 106
Bemis Heights, NY, 188-189, 190, 201, 206

Bennet, William, 9
Bennington, Battle of, 185-187
Bernard, Governor Francis, 14
Berry, Samuel, 81
Berwick, ME, 41, 100
Biddeford, ME, 41
Bird, Joseph, 176
Boston Committee of Correspondence, 18-19
Boston Massacre, 17, 22,
Boston Tea Party, 20- 21
Bradford, Colonel, Gamaliel, 164
Brant, Joseph, 183, 249, 254-256
Brewer, Colonel Samuel, 162, 164
Breymann, Colonel Heinrich, 185, 187, 202, 207-211
Brooks, Colonel John, 223
Bruin, Peter, 97
Brunswick, ME, 25, 42, 101
Bucksport, ME, 267
Bunker Hill, Battle of, 53, 54-59, 61,114, 122
Burgoyne, General John, 166, 172, 179, 181, 183-185, 187-190,196-197, 199, 201- 205, 207, 211-213
Butler, Lt. Col. Richard, 232, 274, 276, 278, 301-302
Butler, Captain Walter, 249
Butler, Lt. Col. William, 247, 249

Butterfield, Major Isaac, 106
Buxton, ME, 22-23, 41
Cadwalader, General John, 147, 155, 158-159
Camden, SC, Battle of, 282
Cape Elizabeth, ME, 42
Carleton, General Guy, 77, 92, 133-134, 137-138
Carr, Captain James, 171, 174
Castleton, VT, 171, 175-177
Cedars, Battle of, 106-108
Charleston, SC, 20, 311- 312
  Fall of in 1780, 282
Cherry Valley, NY, 249-251
Chilton, Captain John, 140
Cilley, Colonel Joseph, 235
Clark, Colonel George Rogers, 281
Clinton, George,
  Governor, 226
  General, 249, 254
Clinton, General Henry, 123, 201, 228, 238-239, 295-296
Cobleskill, NY, 250
Colburn, Reuben, 79, 81-82, 88
Collier, Captain Sir George, 120, 214-215, 217, 252
Common Sense, 115-116
Conojoharie, NY, 253
Continental Congress, 25, 27-29, 39, 53, 77, 117- 118, 161, 221, 228, 247, 278

Cornwallis, General Charles, 123, 153-154, 230, 232, 288-292, 294-298, 307, 309-311
Coulson, Thomas, 42-43
Cowpens, SC, Battle of, 283
Cresswell, Nicholas, 115-116
Crown Point, NY, 113, 137-138
Cumberland County, ME 1, 9, 22, 25-26, 41, 52, 61, 73-74, 101, 259, 266
Cumberland County Convention of 1774, 26-27
Cushing, Charles, 101
Darby, Captain Samuel, 100, 121
Davis, Simon, 275
Dawes, William, 39
De Grasse, Admiral, 297
Deane, Reverend Samuel, 73
Dearborn, Henry,
 Captain, 88, 97,
 Major, 188, 190, 200, 204-205, 207, 209, 211-212
Declaratory Act, 12-13, 20
d'Estaing, Admiral Count, 239, 244-245
Digby, Lieutenant William, 192, 195, 198, 212
Dorchester Heights, MA 102
Dufais, Lieutenant, 135
Dunmore, Governor (of Virginia), 114
Easton, PA, 254

East India Company, 19
Eddy, Colonel Jonathan, 118-120, 214-215, 217-218
Enos, Lt. Col. Roger, 82, 87-88
Ewald, Captain Johann, 303-304, 310
Falmouth, (Portland, ME), 9, 11, 23-25, 41, 42-44, 63-69, 71-74, 77, 101, 114
Falmouth, burning of, 63-71
Falmouth Committle of Safety, 71
Febiger, Lt. Col. Christian, 274, 277
Feltman, Lieutenant William, 293-294, 304-305, 309
Ferguson, Major Patrick, 283
Fermoy, General, 170
Fletcher, Ebenezer, 172, 174-175
Fleury, Colonel, 278
Forster, Captain George, 106-108
Fort Anne, NY, 179-180, 184
Fort Cumberland, Nova Scotia, 118
Fort Defiance, NY, 249
Fort Edward, NY, 164, 170, 179-180, 183-184
Fort George, ME, 257, 264-265, 282
Fort George, NY, 134, 164, 179, 183
Fort Halifax, ME, 83
Fort Lee, NY, 140

Fort Miller, NY, 179, 184, 189
Fort Montgomery, NY, 272
Fort Pownal, ME, 101
Fort Stanwix, NY, 181, 183, 187-189, 250
Fort Ticonderoga, NY, 77, 102, 113, 132-134, 13-138, 144, 161-167, 169, 176-177-179, 189, 204
Fort Washington, NY 139
Fort Western, ME, 81
Fort William and Mary, NH, Gunpowder Incident, 32
Foster, Colonel Benjamin, 47, 50
Francis, Colonel Ebenezer, 162, 164, 170-171, 176-177
Fraser, General Simon, 171-172, 175-177, 189-190, 193, 197
Freeman's Farm, Battle of, 190-201
French and Indian War, 1, 3, 13
Frost, John, 101
Gage, General Thomas, 15-16, 21, 27, 31-33, 37, 40, 45, 52, 56, 102
Galvan, Major, 292-293
Gansevoort, Colonel Peter, 181,
Gardiner, ME, 79
Gates, General Horatio, 133, 135, 144, 165, 187-188, 190, 201, 203- 205, 211, 213, 282
Germain, Lord, 199
Getchell, Dennis, 81
Getchell, John, 81
Getchell, Nehemiah, 81
Gimat, Lt. Col. Jean-Joseph de, 284
Gloucester Point, Battle of, 300-301
Glover, John, Colonel, 132, 146, General, 161, 163, 165, 181, 219, 225, 239, 241
Godfrey, Nathaniel, 47, 49, 51
Gorham, Colonel Joseph, 119
Gorham, ME, 25, 41, 101
Governor's Island, NY, 103, 121, 126
Grant, General James, 123
Graves, Admiral Samuel, 63
Grayson, Colonel William, 232
Great Carrying Place, 84
Green Mountain Boys, 171, 175
Green Spring, Battle of, 291-294
Greene, General Nathanael, 147, 155, 239, 241-242, 245-246, 285-286, 288
Greene, Lt. Col. Christopher, 82, 97
Greenleaf, Captain Moses, 177

Greenwood, John, 106-107, 112-113, 133, 144, 146-149
Griffith, David, 142
Guilford Courthouse, Battle of, 288
H.M.S. Canceaux, 32, 42
H.M.S. Cerberus, 72
H.M.S. Diligent, 52
H.M.S Hope, 214
H.M.S. Margaretta, 46
H.M.S. Scarborough, 32
Hadden, James, 192-195
Hale, Colonel Nathan, 171
Halifax, Nova Scotia, 15, 102
Hamilton, Lt. Col. Alexander, 307
Hamilton, General James, 190, 194
Hancock, John, 39, 62
Hand, Edward, Colonel, 130, 148, General, 254-255
Haskell, Caleb, 81-82
Hazen, Colonel Moses, 284
Head of Elk, MD, 284
Heath, General William, 41, 61, 129-130, 139, 162-163
Height of Land, ME, 89
Heister, General, 123
Henry, Joseph, 86-87, 89, 93
Henry, Patrick, 12, 28
Herkimer, General Nicholas, 181, 183
Hews, Joseph, 117
Hill, Colonel John, 179

Horndon, Lieutenant William, 275
Horne, Jeremiah, 81
Howard, James, 81
Howe, General William, 57-58, 102, 121-123, 126, 129-130, 132, 139-140, 142, 145, 151-153, 160, 166, 213-214, 219, 228
Hubbardton, Battle of, 172-179
Hubbardton, VT, 170-171, 175-176
Hull, Major William, 193-194, 217, 274-275
Hutchinson, Lt. Governor Thomas, 9
Independent Continental Rifle Companies, 53
Intolerable Acts, 21-23, 25-29
Jackson, Colonel Henry, 230, 232
Jackson, Colonel Michael, 164
Jamaica Pass, NY, 123
Jamestown, VA, 291
Jefferson, Thomas, 118
Jones, Ichabod, 45-47
King George III, 20, 115
Kip's Bay, Battle of, 127-129
Kittery, ME, 41, 101
Knowlton, Captain Thomas, 56
Knox, Colonel Henry, 102, 148

Knox, Lieutenant George, 274
LaFayette, General Marquis de, 230, 232, 241, 284-286, 288-291, 294-296
Lamb, Roger, 195, 208
Laurens, Lt. Col. John, 234-235, 246
Learned, General Ebenezer Ebenezer, 161, 164, 181, 183, 188, 193, 197, 200, 204-205, 207-209, 219, 225
Lee, General Charles, 132, 139, 230, 232- 234
Lee, Richard Henry, 117
Leslie, Colonel Alexander, 33-34
Lewis, Fielding, 116
Lewis, Lieutenant Archelaus, 224
Lexington and Concord, Battle of, 37-45
Lincoln County, ME, 1, 22, 25, 52, 61, 101, 257, 259, 281
Lincoln, General Benjamin, 295
Littlefield, Major Daniel, 259, 261
Long Island, Battle of, 123-126
Long, Colonel, 170, 179
Lovell, General Solomon, 259-261, 263, 265- 267, 269

Luzerne, Chevalier de La, 285, 289
Lyons, Reverend James, 46-47, 49-51
Machias, ME, 44- 47, 49, 50-52, 63, 114, 118, 120, 213-217, 252, 257
Madison, ME, 84
Malecites Indians, 252
Marblehead, MA, 33- 35, 63
Margaretta Affair, 44-52
Marshall, Lieutenant John, 220, 227
Marshall, Colonel Thomas, 164
Martin, Joseph Plum, 127, 235-236, 302, 308
Mason, George, 11-12, 15- 16
Massachusetts Committee of Safety, 29, 41

Massachusetts Continental Regiments of 1775
30th Massachusetts Regiment, 41, 100
31st Massachusetts Regiment, 42-43

Massachusetts Contiental Regiments of 1776
7th Continental Regiment, 100, 103, 121, 126, 128-129, 139

15th Continental Regiment, 100, 103-104, 106-107, 111-112, 133, 144, 146, 148, 152
18th Continental Regiment, 100-101, 103, 133-134

Massachusetts Continental Regiments of 1777-1780
1st Massachusetts Regiment, 162-163, 224
2nd Massachusett Regiment, 162, 164
3rd Massachusetts Regiment, 163
4th Massachusetts Regiment, 163
5th Massachusetts Regiment, 163, 208
6th Massachusetts Regiment, 163, 176, 208
7th Massachusetts Regiment, 162-163, 180, 250-251, 253
8th Massachusetts Regiment, 162, 164, 193, 223
9th Massachusetts Regiment, 164, 232
10th Massachusetts Regiment, 164, 197
11th Massachusetts Regiment, 162, 164 170, 177
12th Massachusetts Regiment, 162, 164, 176
13th Massachusetts Regiment, 162-163,
14th Massachusetts Regiment, 164
15th Massachusetts Regiment, 163

Massachusetts Convention of 1768, 14-15
Massachusetts House of Representatives, 7-8, 14
Massachusetts General Court, 4
Massachusetts Provincial Congress, 27, 29, 31, 37, 41, 44-45, 52- 53, 59
Massachusetts Provincial Powder House Raid, 31
Mawhood, Lt. Col. Charles, 156, 159
Maxwell, General William, 110, 232, 255
McCobb, Samuel, Captain, 19, 80, 82, 87, Colonel, 259, 266
McLean, General Francis, 257, 263-265
McMichael, Lieutenant James, 124, 140, 156

Meigs, Major Return, 82,
Mercer, General Hugh, 145, 155, 156, 158-160
Mercer, Lt. Col. James, 292, 300
Micmac Indians, 252
Miles, Colonel Samuel, 122-124
Mitchell, Colonel Jonathan, 73, 259
Monckton, Colonel Henry, 234
Monmouth, Battle of, 230-238
Monroe, Lieutenant James, 151
Montgomery, General Richard, 91-92, 95, 98
Montreal, Canada, 91, 104, 106-108, 111-112
Moore, Lieutenant John, 264
Moore, Midshipman James, 47
Morgan, Daniel,
   Captain 84, 89, 94, 95-96, 98
   Colonel, 188, 190, 192-193, 203-205, 207, 208, 211
   General, 283
Morison, George, 80, 83-85, 89-91, 96-97
Morris, Robert, 116-117
Morristown, NJ, 160-161
Moulder, Captain William, 158-159

Mount Independence, NY, 133-134, 164, 166-167, 169, 189
Mount Vernon, VA, 296
Mowat, Henry,
   Lieutenant, 42-43, 64-69
   Captain, 257, 260, 265-266
Murfree, Major Hardy, 273, 276
Natanis, 81
Nautilus Island, ME, 260
New Gloucester, ME, 42
New Ireland, ME, 257
New Town, Battle of, 253-256
Newport, RI, 239, 241-245, 247
Nixon, General John, 161, 163, 180, 208
Non-Importation Association of 1769, 15-16
Norridgewock Falls, (Madison, ME), 84
North Yarmouth, ME, 22, 41
Nowell, Captain Jonathan, 100, 121
O'Brien, Jeremiah, 50
Old Georgetown, ME, 19
Oliver, Andrew, 8
Onoquaga, NY 249, 251
Otis, James, 7-8,
Paine, Thomas, 115-116
Parker, Captain John, 39
Passamaqquoddy Indians, 252

Paterson, John,
  Colonel, 100, 103-104, 106, 111, 133, 144, 146, 152
  General, 161, 164-165, 170, 219, 223-225
Patrick, Captain William, 250
Pausch, Captain George, 134-135, 197,
Peekskill, NY, 162-163, 165, 180-181
Pell, Joshua, 176
Pell's Point, Battle of, 132
Pendleton, Edmund, 21
Penobscot Expedition, 257-269
Penobscot Indians, 252
Percy, General Hugh, 40
Phillips, General William, 286, 288
Phinney, Colonel Edmund, 23, 41-43, 60-61, 74, 100-101, 103, 133-134,
Pigot, General Robert, 57, 239, 244
Pitcairn, Major John, 35- 36, 39
Poor, General Enoch, 164-165, 170, 193, 201, 204-205, 209, 255-256
Popp, Stephan, 304
Porterfield, Charles, 92-97
Portsmouth, VA, 291, 294
Posey, Captain Thomas, 205, 213,
Pownalborough (Dresden) ME, 80, 101

Prescott, Colonel William, 54, 56, 58, 100, 103, 121, 126, 128-130, 139
Princeton, Battle of, 154-160
Quebec, Canada, 77-80, 91-98, 103-104
Queens Rangers, 230
Rall, Colonel Johann, 151
Randolph, Peyton, 27
Reed, Lt. Col. Joseph, 75, 100
Revere, Paul, 37, 39,
  Lt. Col., 259- 260, 269,
Rhode Island, Battle of, 239-249
Riedesel, General Friedrich Von, 172, 177, 189, 197
Roberts, Lieutenant John, 276
Rochembeau, General Count de, 296-297
Rodney, Captain Thomas, 158-159,
Ross, Lieutenant John, 274
Rutland, VT, 177
Rutledge, Edward, 114-115, 301
Saco, ME, 41, 63
Salem, MA Gunpowder Incident, 33-35
Saltonstall, Commodore Dudley, 257, 260, 265-267, 269
Sanford, ME, 41
Saratoga, Battles of, 189-213
Sayer, Captain Samuel, 100

Scamman, Colonel James, 41, 60,-61, 100-101, 122
Scammell, Alexander,
   Major, 225
   Colonel, 295, 298
Scarborough, ME, 25, 42
Scholarie, NY, 249
Schuyler, General Philip, 77, 91-92, 138, 165- 167, 170, 179-181, 183, 184, 187
Scott, General Charles, 229, 232
Senter, Isaac, 85, 87-90, 104
Sergeant R, 152-153, 155, 159,
Sherburne, Major Henry, 106-107
Skenesborough, (Whitehall) NY, 113, 132, 170, 179
Skowhegan, ME, 83-84
Smith, Colonel Francis, 37, 39-40
Smith, Reverend Thomas, 9, 11
Sorel, Canada, 104, 108, 111
St. Clair, Arthur,
   Colonel, 26, 108-110, 148,
   General, 165-167, 169-171, 179
St. Johns, Canada, 113
St. Leger, Lt. Col. Barry, 181, 183
Stamp Act, 6-13, 22, 36
   Repealed, 11
Stamp Act Congress, 8
Stark, John,
   Colonel, 56-57, 59
   General, 185
Steele, Lieutenant Archibald, 81- 82, 86,
Stephens, General Adam, 146, 148
Steuben, General Baron von, 226-227,
Stirling, General William, 123, 126
Stocking, Abner, 83
Stone, Captain Enos, 176
Stony Point, Battle of, 270-279
Sugar Act, 4-5, 8, 13
Sullivan, Captain Ebenezer, 100, 106, 108
Sullivan, General John, 100, 108-109, 111-113, 115, 124, 144, 147-148, 155-156, 159-160, 239, 241-246, 252-254, 256, 257, 269
Swashan Chief, 79
Symons, Captain John, 72
Tarleton, Lt. Col. Banastre, 290, 294, 298, 300-301, 309
Tea Act, 19
Thacher, James, 169-170, 302-303, 305-306, 309-310
Thayer, Simon, 84
Thomas, General John, 104
Thompson, Benjamin, 74- 75
Thompson, General William, 108-109, 111

Thompson, Samuel, 25, 42, 65, 101
Thompson's War, 42- 43
Three Rivers, Battle of, 108-111
Throg's Neck, Battle of, 129-130
Throop, Josiah, 118-119
Ticonic Falls, Waterville, ME, 83
Tioga, NY, 254
Townshend Duties, 13-18, 20, 22
   Repealed, 17
Treaty of Paris 1763, 1, 3,
   Treaty of Paris 1783, 312
Trenton, Battle of, 145-152
Trois Riviers, Canada, 108
Tyng, William, 43
Unadilla, NY, 249
Valcour Island, Battle of, 134-139
Valley Forge Encampment, 220-228
Varnum, General James, 221
Vassalboro, ME, 81
Verplanks, NY, 270
Virginia House of Burgesses, 21, 27
Vose, Colonel Joseph, 163, 284
Wadsworth, General Peleg, 259, 261, 263, 266, 281-282,
Waller, Lieutenant John, 59

Warner, Colonel Seth, 171, 175, 187
Washington, Captain William, 151
Washington, General George, 15- 16, 53, 60-63, 71- 72, 74-75, 77, 79- 80, 99- 100, 102, 111, 116, 118, 121-123, 126-129, 132, 139-140, 142, 144-148, 151-156, 159-163, 165-167, 181, 188, 219-221, 223, 226-230, 232-235, 237-239, 241, 247, 252- 253, 270, 272-274, 276-278, 282-284, 295-298, 301-304, 311
Wayne, Anthony,
   Colonel, 109-111, 164, 165
   General, 229, 233, 237, 269-270, 272-274, 276, 277-278, 288, 290-294
Weeks, William, 225
Wells, ME, 41, 100
Welsh, Captain John, 263
Wentworth, Governor John, 32
Wesson, Colonel James, 164, 232
West Point, NY, 270, 282
Weston, Hannah, 52
Weston, Rebecca, 52
White Plains, NY, 132
Wigglesworth, Colonel Edward, 163

Wilkinson, Major James, 154-155, 190, 195-196, 201, 203, 205, 207-209
Windham, ME, 41
Wyoming Valley, PA, 247, 254

York County, ME, 1, 22, 25-27, 41, 52, 100, 101, 259
York County (ME) Convention of 1774, 26-27
Yorktown, Siege of, 297-311
Yorktown, VA, 295-96

www.ingramcontent.com/pod-product-compliance
Lightning Source LLC
Chambersburg PA
CBHW071313150426
43191CB00007B/613